THE UNSEEN FACE OF ISLAM

The Unseen Face of Islam

Sharing the Gospel with Ordinary Muslims

BILL A MUSK

MARC
Evangelical Missionary Alliance

First published 1989

Unless otherwise indicated all
biblical quotations are from the
New International Version © International Bible Society
1973, 1978, 1984

All Qur'ânic references, except where indicated, are taken
from Richard Bell, *The Qur'ān translated with a critical re-
arrangement of the Surahs,* (T & T Clark:
Edinburgh, 2 vols, 1937).

Cover design by W James Hammond
Front cover photo by Christine Osborne / Middle East Pictures

British Library Cataloguing in Publication Data

Musk, Bill
    The unseen face of Islam.
    1.   Islam. Folk religion, orthodox faith.
        Understanding Muslims.
    I.   Title
    297

ISBN 1-85424-018-8 (MARC)
     0-7324-0409-6 (Albatross)

Co-published in Australia by
Albatross Books Ltd, PO Box 320,
Sutherland, NSW 2232

The Evangelical Missionary Alliance is a fellowship of evangelical
missionary societies, agencies and training colleges that are committed
to world mission. Its aims are to encourage cooperation and provide
coordination between member societies and colleges, and to assist local
churches to fulfil their role in world mission. The EMA offices are at
Whitefield House, 186 Kennington Park Road, London SE11 4BT

Printed in Great Britain for
MARC, an imprint of Monarch Publications Ltd
1 St Anne's Road, Eastbourne, E Sussex BN21 3UN by
Courier International Ltd, Tiptree, Essex
Typeset by Nuprint Ltd, Harpenden, Herts AL5 4SE.

CONTENTS

APPENDICES

FOREWORD

A mosque is becoming a familiar sight in many British cities. The presence of Muslims in large numbers is a reality resented by some, tolerated by others, welcomed by others yet again. But how much are these men, women and children understood or their culture and background appreciated? With how many of them do we have an intelligent relationship? The answers to these questions, if honestly given, might be disquieting.

Dr Musk has spent fruitful years in a Muslim country, has thought deeply about the Christian approach to Muslims, and has now given us the first fruits of his experiences and study in this interesting book.

In writing it, he has had in mind people like himself whose life's work is that of missionaries to Muslims. The book will be of considerable value to such people, and to those who are preparing for similar work. But I hope that its readership will extend far beyond the 'specialists'. Thousands of Christians in these islands alone live cheek by jowl with Muslims—they are their neighbours. This book will help the Christian to understand them, the background of their culture, the basics of their beliefs, the subtle differences between their outlooks and assumptions and ours. Upon such understanding depends the success or failure of our approach. 'In Christian mission the aim must constantly be to get beneath the surface and discover the assumptions of ordinary Muslims in their complex, unpredictable and largely hostile world.'

'We have not even recognised the "world" in which many Muslims are living,' writes Dr Musk. This book will help us to do so, and in the light of that recognition to begin to see how best the Christ can be presented to them in all his love and power.

Donald Coggan

ACKNOWLEDGEMENTS

It is with gratitude to God that this writing marks a coming to grips with lessons slowly learned over many years, for the Lord's grace and strength have sustained and enlightened us in several terms of service in the Middle East. Middle Eastern friends, too, have been patient with 'those English' who have wanted to get to know them more deeply. We have enjoyed being part of the Episcopal Church in Egypt, a church founded on a solid base of men and women who came to Christ, at the beginning of the century, from a Muslim background.

In terms of learning to understand and evaluate a different culture and a different faith, I have benefited much from work with the Faculty of Arts at the University of South Africa in Pretoria. Much of the material which forms the core of this book was researched under the guidance of that faculty; the specific approach adopted derived from studies in the phenomenology of religion.[1] In the reflections made out of a theological and missiological concern, I owe much to the School of World Mission at Fuller Theological Seminary, California, USA. The harnessing of insights from the social sciences to missiological ends has been learned under that school's mentorship.[2]

My thanks are due also to Banstead Baptist Church for its support of our family during the summer months of 1987, while I wrote the major part of this book. My thanks are also due to Jane Syrett for her assistance with the translations from Arabic, and to Julie Overland for her help with the Arabic transliteration and her reflections on the first draft of the manuscript. I am thankful to various friends, including Sheila Hobson, Vivienne Stacey, Peter Tyson, Richard Smith, Barbara Parsons and Georges Houssney for their comments on the text. As a result of their involvement, I hope, the book is both truer to reality, and more readable!

My wife, Hilary, deserves most thanks for her enthusiastic commitment (along with that of our children) to living in the Middle East for the greater part of our married life. I am grateful for her careful review of the whole text and her encouragement in this project.

LIST OF FIGURES

TRANSLITERATION

A considerable number of non-English terms appear throughout this book. Italics have been used to indicate that a word is a transliteration, and does not appear as an English word in standard dictionaries. Some proper nouns have not been transliterated strictly, in order to ease reading. A glossary of all italicised transliterations is given in Appendix 4.

Many of the terms employed occur in Arabic. A standard form of transliteration, set out in Figure 1, has been used to express all Arabic expressions in English. A few words, such as 'Qur'ân' and '*hadîth*', which do feature in some English dictionaries, are transliterated in this text.

Figure 1

Transliteration and Pronunciation of Arabic Alphabet[3]

NAME IN ARABIC	SYMBOL	ENGLISH PRONUNCIATION WHERE NOT CLEAR
hamza	'	glottal stop, as 'a' in 'act'
âlif	a	
bâ'	b	
tâ'	t	
thâ'	th	as in 'thick'
jîm	j	
hâ'	h	(aspirated)
khâ'	kh	as in German *'nicht'*
dâl	d	

dhâl	dh	as in 'then'
râ'	r	
zâ'	z	
sîn	s	
shîn	sh	as in 'show'
ṣâd	ṣ	(velarised)
ḍâd	ḍ	(velarised
ṭâ'	ṭ	(velarised)
ẓâ'	ẓ	(velarised)
ʿayn	ʿ	equivalent of *ḥâ'*
ghayn	gh	similar to French '*r*'
fâ'	f	
qâf	q	(uvular) as '*k*', not '*kw*'
kâf	k	(palatal)
lâm	l	
mîm	m	
nûm	n	
hâ'	h	
wâw	w	
yâ'	y	
âlif yâ	ay	(diphthong)
âlif wâw	aw	(diphthong)
tâ' marbûṭa	a	
unmarked (short) vowels are:	a	as in 'bat'
	i	as in 'bit'
	u	as in 'boot'
vowels with a circumflex above are long:	â	as in 'aah'
	î	as in 'eee'
	û	as in 'ooo'

A short list explaining some of the more significant historical Muslim names and movements is also given at the end of the glossary in Appendix 4.

PREFACE

'Come to me, all you who are weary and burdened...' (Mt 11:28).

This book is about weary and burdened human beings. They constitute the 'ordinary people' of the Muslim world. As with the Jewish 'crowds' of Jesus' time, to whom his familiar words of invitation were initially addressed, so the masses of Muslims today live at two levels. Beneath a veneer of conformity to a major world faith, ordinary Muslims express deep needs in their daily living. In these chapters, the concerns of their lives become ours.

It is not the aim of this book to compare the 'best' in the Christian faith with the 'worst' in Islam. An exposition of popular Christianity could easily be explored along parallel lines to that pursued here with regard to popular Islam. Although evaluations are made, the mentality which dismisses the considered views of others as mere 'superstitions' is scrupulously avoided.

Neither is it the purpose of this book to promote some kind of theological mutual recognition of Islam and Christianity by comparing, for example, the Qur'ân and the Bible. We are not primarily interested in theology, although theological inferences, for both Muslims and Christians, will arise from our journey of discovery.

It is instead the aim of these chapters to explore and explain the beliefs and practices of ordinary Muslims. The objective, in such a search beneath the surface of religious behaviour, is to understand the particular weariness and burdens of contemporary Muslims. Out of a deeper empathy might spring an interceding which is more incisive, and a witnessing which is more compassionate.

The world of popular Islam is, at first sight, a strange one for Western onlookers. It is a world constantly in flux, full of all kinds of 'beings' and 'powers'. It is a world which knows processes of change from one state to another. As we shall see, it is in fact a world in many respects far closer to the biblical picture than the one seen as 'real' by most Western Christians.

In our strong separation of the sacred from the secular, in our materialism, humanism and scientism, Westerners, compared with many of our contemporaries, live in a dull, one-dimensional universe. We are satisfied with superficial explanations of important questions about the 'why' of things, since our detailed focus is consistently on questions concerning the 'how' of things.

We seek, for example, to discover how warm and cold fronts produce certain types of weather. We then plan our activities around the interpretations given by weathermen of information obtained by satellite pictures of cloud formations. We do not ask ourselves 'why' it should be that our harvest failed this year. We are not concerned with 'why' we should have a specific sickness in the family just at this moment. Seemingly inexplicable phenomena such as UFOs do not worry us unduly. We are confident that we shall one day unravel the riddles and understand, 'scientifically', what puzzles us today. We certainly do not countenance the possibility of concepts of 'being' outside the visible and touchable. Who, in the Western world at large, believes any longer in a personal Devil?

Faith in God 'fits' the Western worldview, if one is convinced enough, because God is spirit. His dwelling place is in another world, in unapproachable light. We can believe in a God who is spiritual in essence and who lives in a totally other realm. We can accept that that God might live on earth in an incarnated form, precisely because, while here on earth, the Word becomes 'flesh'. What Westerners find difficult to conceive of is spiritual beings which might operate, as spirits, in the earthly realm. For many of our brothers and sisters, who have come to Christ from within different views of the world, that difficulty is hard to understand. How Western Christians can make the Old and New Testaments their own, while effectively excising such main characters as Gabriel, Satan, or the demons from such Scripture, seems an incomprehensible contradiction to people from other cultures.

Ordinary Muslims, among others, see their lives as finding context in a far more complex, active environment. Perhaps for some Western Christians this look at popular Islam may awaken a deeper appreciation of the worlds and realities of the Old and New Testaments.

In the first part of the book, ten major subjects are introduced by short stories illustrating the item in view. Those anecdotes are nearly all based on documented experiences. After the stories, some analysis of the meaning of the subject under consideration is attempted. The analysis is followed by comment from a biblical and missiological perspective. Such comment is sometimes provocative but is not intended to be unfaithful. It is rather made in an attempt to enrich our perception of biblical truth.

In the second part of the book, the world of popular Islam is investigated in greater depth, in both an anthropological and a theological sense. The aim of such exploration is to find some conclusions for missions. Various suggestions are offered towards a more fruitful sharing of Christ with ordinary Muslims. Illustrations in this part of the book are also based on fact; details in all stories are altered in order to preserve anonymity.

The appendices provide an explanation of the important *ḥadîth* literature (the prophetic tradition) and a summary of the major sects of Islam. They conclude with an introductory bibliography concerning popular Islam and a glossary of all transliterated terms.

It is my prayer that this book may help Western Christians to empathise better with their Muslim neighbours and fellow-travellers. In our growing sensitivity towards such ordinary people, may new doors open for powerful, compassionate witness, and for encouraging them to come to the Jesus who will give them rest.

Bill A Musk

divided. A narrow track set off diagonally from the canal towards the outskirts of the village. From the fields where Ahmad had been working, the quickest way home would have been to take that path. His father's brick and mortar house sat solidly in the centre of the village, on the main street. At the bottom of the street, near the well, was the bicycle repair shop where big Fikry seemed to spend all day sleeping and all night welding and hammering. The shortest route lay down the diagonal path, round the well at the end of the village, on to the main street and home past Fikry's bicycle shop. Ahmad was tired, too. He had had a long day, irrigating the fast-drying earth, hoeing it and coaxing the rich soil to yield its third crop of the year. He would be glad to get home.

Almost without his realising it, Ahmad's mind leaped from the bargaining encounter to the choice of path before him. Hardly any villager ever used the diagonal passage and Ahmad was not about to touch it now. It led, en route to the well, past Widow Aziza's house. Widow Aziza was renowned for her evil eye. Ahmad had been warned from childhood that his family did not use that walk to and from their fields. The story of why had been repeatedly told at family get-togethers, and their tale was confirmed by others circulating among many neighbours. Ahmad's thoughts shifted to the anecdote about his grandfather and father as he carefully steered the donkey past the turn-off and along the longer canal route to the village centre.

Towards the end of his life, Ahmad's grandfather pawned a basketful of gold earrings and anklets. With the money he bought a female buffalo. The cow proved to be pregnant and quickly became the pride of his old age, especially when it calved and began producing milk. Ahmad's grandfather used to bring a pot of freshly drawn milk into the house, and the children would fight to swallow the most. Sometimes milk was sent across the street to uncles who lived nearby. Arrangements were even made for milk to be given to some neighbours in return for part ownership of some sheep. A new lease of life seemed to have come to Ahmad's grandfather and also to the rest of the family—until the day when Ahmad's father mistakenly steered the graceful, hairy beauty home from the fields past Widow Aziza's house. That was when the family learned the power of that woman's eye.

Widow Aziza's husband had died about three years before, and relationships between her and the rest of his family were not happy. Widow Aziza had been brought to her husband's home as wife from a distant village. Her husband had been a sick man when he became engaged to her. Widow Aziza's family had fought for a contract which would leave the property to Widow Aziza should her husband die first. They had won the unusual concession, but the marriage suffered as a result; Widow Aziza and her husband fought over everything. The battles continued after his death, as Widow Aziza claimed her contracted rights to the property. It was said by some that she used more than human powers to help her in her conflict. A rumour circulated that she had command over a certain *jinnî* who helped her accomplish her aims. She was certainly a tenacious fighter even though she came from far away and had no relatives at hand to support her.

Ahmad's grandfather had once scolded Widow Aziza in the village square for evil words she had spoken loudly concerning her husband's family. It would seem that Widow Aziza never forgot or forgave that scolding. Her anger burst out on the day she discovered Ahmad's father leading the prized buffalo cow past her house on the shortcut home. Widow Aziza slipped into the pathway, bent over and stared at the udders of the cow as it passed. Then with a chuckle she disappeared into the dark interior of her home. Ahmad's father was badly frightened and squealed the *Fâtiḥa*, the opening sura of the Qur'ân, all the way home. He told the family what had occurred. When grandfather next went to bring in some milk for the children, they knew that the thing

PART 1

CHAPTER ONE

WIDOW AZIZA'S EYE

Which pathway home?

DUST SPIRALLED AROUND each hoof like a miniature tornado, unwound in the hot air and drifted to earth again. The donkey trotted along the canal path. Torn ears twitched at the inquisitive flies. A searching nose savoured the poppy scent rising amid the cotton fields of the Nile's delta. A protective turquoise bead jiggled on its string around the animal's muddied neck. The donkey could find its own way.

Ahmad, astride its hind haunches with his flowing blue robe tucked up round his waist, certainly believed it could. He was enjoying his game of pretend. Really he was balanced on a camel, silhouetted high above the desert. He was a nomad, like the Bedouin who passed through his home village on their occasional forays into the brick world of settled Egypt. Ahmad admired those rough, noble men, lacking in this world's wealth, but proud and free lords of their families and herds.

During the Bedouin's visit of the last summer, Ahmad had also grown to admire the middle daughter of their leader, Abu Suleiman. Amina, as he had eventually discovered her

name to be after bribing her youngest brother with a cata-
pult, was just blossoming from girl to woman. Ahmad was
aware of changes taking place in his own fourteen-year-old
body, and it struck him as unfair. Just when he was proving
his adulthood by keeping the fast of Ramaḍân, the nubile
daughter of Abu Suleiman had to mark her growing maturity
by taking the veil and staying carefully with the womenfolk
of her clan.

Still, he had caught some glimpses of Amina at the canal
where she had gone with a gaggle of black-robed chatterers,
gossiping all the way, to give the cooking trays their daily
wash. The eyes that peeped out from the mystery of that
dark covering seemed too bright to be so imprisoned, too
bright and rather mischievous, taunting. He longed to study
the slender neck that vanished in a swathe of black cotton. It
was doubtless adorned with gold and silver chains and little
silver 'hands of Fâṭima' to protect Amina from the evil eye.
Yes, and to make her pretty! Staring casually from the small
wooden bridge a little upstream, Ahmad had willed her to
turn in his direction. In one flash of a glance he was sure that
fire had met fire. If it hadn't been that the older women were
beginning to notice this adolescent infatuation, he would
have settled on the bridge lazily, hungrily to keep watch. But
widows and aunts have sharp tongues and big vocabularies!

Now high on his camel, leader of a Saharan Bedouin
family, Ahmad the Tall reckoned out the bargaining procedure which would procure for himself a necklaced, bright-
eyed bride.

'Three buffaloes is the least to be dreamed of, and by the
Prophet they had better be strong!'

'By God, the girl is lame! One weak buffalo is too much!'

'She is the only daughter of my second wife, Selima the
beautiful. In God's name I would rather die than accept less
than two female buffaloes!'

The imaginary argument was well under way when
Ahmad's donkey-camel came to the point where the path

Envy (*ḥasad*) is seen almost as a tangible force. In many Muslims' minds it assumes the negative opposite of the positive force known as *baraka*. (See glossary, Appendix 4.) *Baraka* comprises the blessing or boon deriving, ultimately, from God. It is found in intense form in the Qur'ân, which is a 'blessed' book, in prophets, saints, shrines, and a multitude of other forms. But whereas *baraka* is nearly always obtained or conveyed by some kind of touch, the evil eye transfers its effect by non-tactile communication. It would seem that while the spread of blessing requires contact, a mere 'look' will suffice to bring harm upon someone.

The kinds of eye counted as evil vary, as the following illustrations from Iran exemplify. The rarest and most powerful genus of evil eye known in Iran is called 'the salty eye'. This eye has a permanent effect. It may be acquired by a child during gestation if, for example, its mother happens to view the face of a corpse. Whatever the resultant infant looks at, whether intentionally or inadvertently, is likely to come to harm. A person with this kind of eye could stop tractors or topple buildings with a glance. Such a condition is incurable, and a person diagnosed as possessing a 'salty eye' is carefully guarded.

The commonest Iranian expression of the evil eye is known as 'the bad eye'. This comes as a transitory condition. When a person grows jealous, envious or puffed up with undue pride, the glance his eye then gives is likely to be evil. Usually this kind of eye is cast unintentionally, so its effects need be only minor or temporary. They can be combatted, 'untied', by appropriate and often occult activity. Most Muslims take precautions against this kind of eye, and a vast world of prophylaxis (or protective measures) is geared to prevent the 'bad eye' from harming an individual or a possession.

A third kind of evil eye in Iran is that labelled 'the unclean eye'. Like the 'bad eye', this is also a passing condition. It occurs when the look is cast by someone in a state of ceremonial uncleanness, especially that caused by failure to take the purifying bath after sexual intercourse. Often the 'unclean eye' can be countered by preventative or curative means, but it can sometimes be lethal. Death is most likely if the victim of this eye is already suffering from injury or sickness.

Further varieties of evil eye, identified in other cultures, include 'the eye that wounds', 'the narrow eye' and 'the hot eye'.

Consideration of the concept of the evil eye projects us directly into the ordinary Muslim's ideas about causality. The world of popular Islam is complex and all-embracing. Often the Muslim sees himself as the victim of hostile activity by external beings and forces. He seeks explanations for what happens in his everyday life in terms of such activity. Equally, he identifies actions which will bring desired objectives into reality. How can success in the future be guaranteed? What will make sure that a proposed marriage is happy and fruitful? Which business venture will bring the greatest benefit to the family? Frequently the ordinary Muslim finds himself swallowed up in crises, and then it is especially important to have quick and accurate diagnosis of causes.

Among many contributing factors, the evil eye is seen as a major cause of crises in Muslims' lives. Diagnosis is often made by a mixture of case history and simple divination. One method used by practitioners—at this level often female—is the egg-breaking ceremony. Various magical figures are drawn on a fresh egg which is then placed inside a handkerchief. With interlocked fingers the woman holds the wrapped egg between her palms, elbows apart, so that her arms exert a gentle pressure on the egg. Names of persons who have recently seen the victim and who are therefore likely casters of the evil eye are recited aloud, usually beginning with the closest relatives. When the person who has cast the eye is named, the egg breaks. Cures are administered in different ways, although the most important part of any cure is the diagnosis itself, in identifying who is responsible. In extreme cases, no cure is feasible and the diagnosis of a person killed by the evil eye is purely for information. When the injury has not been fatal, the burning of incense, incantation, Qur'ân reading and visits to saints' tombs to obtain *baraka* may all be employed as part of the cure.

Muslims all over the world design and use a huge variety of protective measures as insurance against the evil eye. One of the most common kinds of charm is a glazed ceramic bead of bright turquoise colour. The 'hand of Fâṭima', sulphur, the *khamsa* (five fingers of the hand extended towards the potential inflicter of the glance), an eye transfixed with an arrow, rhymed inscriptions such as *al-ḥasûd lâ yasûd* ('the envier will not overcome'), cards containing Qur'ânic verses and dropped into the foundations of buildings—all are illustrative of the many forms which prophylaxis takes. (For illustrations of pronunciation and transliteration of the Arabic alphabet, see Figure 1, pp 13–14.)

A phrase of protection against the evil eye, frequent in everyday speech, is *mâ shâ'allah*, meaning 'what God has willed'. (Appendix 4 lists this and other non-English terms.) This phrase is used when congratulating a mother on a pretty child. It draws attention away from the child to God, who was responsible for the child's birth. Any unintentional envy in the beholder is thus prevented from touching the child. This protective formula is carefully employed in all situations of congratulation or admiration, and especially if the object or person subject to praise is seen as vulnerable to the influence of the evil eye.

The central place that the evil eye concept has in most Muslims' lives might suggest that it is an accepted component of the formal faith of Islam. Indeed, many Muslims believe that the evil eye is talked about in the Qur'ân. Surprisingly, the Qur'ân makes no direct mention of the evil eye. It makes implicit reference to human envy only twice, in suras 113:5 and 2:103. The *ḥadîth*, (strictly, *aḥadîth*, or Traditions), on the other hand, give strong licence for including the evil eye as a potent element in the Muslim's view of the world. (See Appendix 1.) According to the *ḥadîth*, Muhammad both acknowledged its reality and suggested that incantation be used in dealing with its effect. Inasmuch as the cosmology of the ordinary Muslim is upheld implicitly (in the Qur'ân) or explicitly (in the *ḥadîth*), the formal faith serves as much to reinforce the reality of the evil eye as to provide an adequate answer for its effects. Consequently, aspects of the formal religion are bent to serve in the folk-Islamic world. The Qur'ân, for example, is used as a defence mechanism, powerful in its intrinsic *baraka* to protect the wearer of it, as a miniature amulet, from the power of the evil eye. Or, if the eye strikes, verses from the Qur'ân may be said over the victim. He may be given water to drink in which paper containing verses from the Qur'ân has been soaked. From the perspective of the ordinary Muslim, the evil eye of envy is a proven, authorised and potent contributor to the disintegration of his life.

Envy answered

The Old Testament acknowledges the strength of envy. The most specific and visible example of an 'eye' of jealousy is discovered in King Saul's hatred towards David. The Hebrew original records that 'from that time on Saul kept a jealous eye on David' (1 Samuel 18:9). Envy, however, would seem to retain its ordinary human connection according to Scripture; it is not a force that passes from Saul to David. It is a feeling Saul has about David. In this sense, the eye of jealousy is closely related to the spiritual condition of the person involved.

The New Testament concern with envy reveals the same association with the human being behind the emotion. The two Greek words (*zêlos* and *phthonos*) are used as expressions of human feeling. Envy does not exist as a force in its own right. It is a quality which, sadly, Christians do express (Galatians 5:26). It is an emotion of which Christ's love does not approve (1 Corinthians 13:4). The Bible hardly permits a concept of the evil eye per se, though it does declare that human beings act in jealousy or envy. Nearly always such human expressions are sinful.

Refreshingly, the Bible also puts forward the possibility of a positive, upbuilding envy or jealousy. One of the names of the Lord is 'Jealous' (*qanna*). As one who lives in covenant relationship with the people of Israel, Yahweh is 'jealous' on their behalf (Exodus 34:14). He is in every sense the jealous God. He declares the same positive feeling after the break-up of the earthly kingdom of Israel and in promise of acts of renewal (Zechariah 1:14). Jealousy in this sense can be a positive expression of desiring, one which Paul in fact emulates in his *zêlos* for the immature Corinthian believers (2 Corinthians 11:2). He declares that he is moved with a 'godly jealousy' for them. The analogy is that of a Middle Eastern father preserving his daughter as a pure virgin for her husband on the wedding day. So Paul guards and protects the young Corinthian church which he would present spotless and mature to Christ. The picture of his jealousy could hardly be more positive.

Is there a biblical answer for the person who finds that he is a victim of the evil eye of envy? The Old Testament example of Saul and David is a case in point. Saul's 'eyeing' of David provokes David to a deeper dependence upon the Lord, rather than to fight off the effect of being 'eyed'. The psalms dating from this period reveal David's turning to Yahweh and calling on him as his strength, as his 'loving God' (eg Psalm 59). Fear is then reversed: 'Saul was afraid of David, because the Lord was with David but had left Saul.... In everything he [David] did he had great success, because the Lord was with him' (1 Samuel 18:12,14). The envious one was afraid of the one envied because of the latter's relationship with the truly Jealous.

The grip of the evil eye concept lies in its being based on human fear. Whether ontologically true as an independent force, or not, the evil eye is perceived as being responsible for calamity in the lives of many Muslims. One of the promises of Christ is that the divine Person residing in a member of his family is stronger than the evil abroad in the world. Christ protects us against all willed or unwitting malevolence. Indeed, there is nothing in all creation that can separate the believer from the love of God that is in Christ Jesus. In such answers to the problem of being 'eyed' lies a possibility for Christian witness to ordinary Muslims struggling within their daily round of attacks upon well-being. To know that the Lord is jealous for them against all envy and malice provides relief both from the immediate attack and also from the closed worldview which insists upon answering such malevolent force only with other non-absolute force. It is the eye of the Lord himself which provides comprehensive security: '...I will guide thee with mine eye' (Psalm 32:8, AV).

CHAPTER TWO

THE NIGHT BELONGS
TO THE JINN

Invitation to dance

IT TOOK HUSSEIN nearly a year to recover. For a long time the flies ran riot over his stubbled face. They shifted only when a young brother or sister swished a hand over his prostrate form. The family room was kept darkened. Incense burned day and night. The summer was swallowed up by winter, and the snows came and went. Somehow they kept him alive, massaging him, forcing tea and soup down him, praying and hoping.

Every now and then the breathing corpse stirred. He seemed to respond most to the gentle singing of his mother as she stroked his neck, kissed his sunken cheeks and whispered to his faraway mind memories of childhood days. Her storytelling was rewarded by an almost imperceptible squeeze of her hand and a willing, if still unconscious, agreement to accept some bread and olives, eased down with yoghurt.

The local midwife frequently looked in.

'Peace be upon you, *Mâddar-e* Hussein. How is our living dead today?'

'And peace be with you, deft Nabila. Our son sleeps on still. His strength remains, thanks be to God, but he has not yet returned to us. How long must his fate be thus?'

'By the Prophet, it is beyond me. This living death I have never seen, *Mâddar-e* Hussein. If God wills, he shall return to us.'

'If God wills.'

Quite candidly the able Nabila admitted that she was out of her depth. After several months, a wealthy uncle paid for Hussein to be taken by minibus to a renowned doctor in Tabriz, near the Caspian Sea. But in the end the heavy rains came earlier than the minibus, and the trip was abandoned. The only light on the illness came in early spring, just after the New Year celebration of *No Ruz*. In desperation, Hussein's grandmother betook herself to Mianeh and sought out Hafiz Muhammad, a reputed magician. With a professional eye he examined the unwashed headband which Hussein's grandmother had brought him. After some while he pronounced that the cause of the paralysis had been jinn. With much incantation and frequent mention of the Prophet's name, he wrote some magical signs and a certain verse of the Qur'ân on a scrap of paper. This he folded and refolded and sewed into a leather pouch. It was to be placed close to Hussein's heart. The *Fâtiha* should be recited every morning, noon and evening and a pair of new scissors, sharp ones, should be kept under Hussein's pillow to 'cut' the strong spell. Hussein's parents were happy to apply the suggested remedies, even if they weren't so happy to learn that the grandmother had taken six of the family's ten chickens to pay for the diagnosis and medicine. Imperceptibly at first, then more definitely, Hussein gradually improved.

After some six or seven months, as the spring flowers blossomed down in the valleys, Hussein spoke. At least, he made noises. His mother caressed his head in her hands and prayed—to God the All-Knowing, to the Prophet, to Fatima, to Hassan and Hussein, and to Ali especially: 'Let him come back to me! Pray for me, you angels near the throne. Let him come back to me!' She virtually willed her son back to consciousness. He was her eldest son, her favourite. She loved him so much.

Hussein had certainly been the family success. He had attended the school for young boys at the village mosque, and either natural talent or the mullah's swift stick had brought an ability to learn whole suras of the Qur'ân and various *hadîth* by heart. When he was fifteen, the family had fêted their neighbourhood in a wonderful celebration to mark Hussein's ability to recite the entire Qur'ân by heart. The occasion brought special joy to *Mâddar-e* Hussein, and she noticed that from that time the family's respect in the community seemed to be heightened. Her husband was frequently asked to mediate in arguments and clan disputes. When the big officials from the government in Tehran came to ask about the number of people and livestock in the large village, *Mâddar-e* Hussein's husband had been one of the elders chosen to entertain and guide the visitors in their important work. As the family's fortunes moved upward, it seemed only appropriate that Hussein should be selected for training to operate the electrical generator that Tehran decided to install in the village. The new power transformed the life of the people, and Hussein felt important to be such a significant part of the modern world. The villagers, even some of the old men, joked and teased him respectfully.

'Our womenfolk curse you, Hussein! They say that we sit in the coffee shop playing backgammon till after the stars shine, thanks to you!'

'Yes, Hussein! You and your fancy lights and wireless. Soon we shall have casinos and cinemas here, just like in Tabriz. Then our wives will truly curse you!'

'Hussein, you play at being God to alter how this village lives. Now, people sleep all day and play all night. Let's toast our friend with Pepsi from the new refrigerator!'

Soon, large water-pumps were being driven by electricity from Hussein's generator. With that help, virgin land was irrigated. More crops gradually became available for selling, and at last the villagers could consider doing what they had talked about for ages. They would erect a new mosque and a brick minaret. Perhaps they would even carpet it with cheap rugs from the bazaar at Tabriz. Hussein enjoyed his unique role in this waking, spirited, bantering community of work and play—until his sudden illness.

As Hussein's ability to speak recovered, he shared, first with his mother and then with the rest of his family, what had happened. Eventually, the story whispered its way around the village, and the elders nodded. It was the truth. The villagers had concentrated so much on this new electricity that they had forgotten the night belonged to other beings: jealous beings.

One Wednesday evening, Hussein had been walking home from Mianeh, the town ten kilometres down the valley. He had gone there to beg, borrow or steal more lights to string up in the village square outside the coffee shop. He had seen the kind of effect he wanted at a wedding festivity in Mianeh a few months before. As the demand on the generator from the pumps dropped in the evening, why not put the machine to use to brighten up the evening? As he toiled up the hill carrying a jumble of bulbs, cables, switches and fuse wire, the scented jasmine, queen of the evening, perfumed his brain. Just one more joy fired his imagination. Now that he'd mastered the generator, could he not learn the car mechanic's trade? He would move to Mianeh and start as an apprentice. Cars, he thought, are only complicated versions of generators. And if he could mend cars, maybe one day he could drive one, or a minibus, or even a truck. His vision sped to the large German articulated wheat carriers he had come across in the town. Monster vehicles and their drivers were sleeping out the day. The convoy would rumble through the town in the evening when the streets were empty, on their way south to the capital.

As he daydreamed up the valley, he gradually became aware of an evening celebration in an olive orchard ahead of him, on the right. Robed figures were clapping and dancing as an old man played a fiddle. Laughter filled the air. As he drew closer, Hussein could tell from the clothes, and then from the faces, that they were friends of his. He had not been aware of this party. Presumably someone had just become the father of a baby boy, or else an engagement had been announced. As he drew close to the orchard, someone hailed him.

'Hussein! We have been expecting you. Come and dance the "warrior round". It is time for a celebration. Drop your burden. Hear the tune? Now dance with us!'

The music was quite intoxicating, and the syncopated clapping of his friends quickly spun the spell that drew Hussein into the centre of the group. Soon he was clapping, then dancing, then sweeping in and out, up and down, round and back again. He was lost in the haunting melody that called forth his complete submission to the flame that danced within him. Eyes blurry with dizziness, he happened to glance down as he clapped hands with a friend and bent to tap his own knees.

Horror shot through him like lightning! In an instant he felt panicky, cold, feverish, sober, paralysed. As his body froze, his mind raced!

'My friends—their feet are on backwards! They have hollow eyes! It is Wednesday evening! These are jinn! Jinn! I've been tricked into joining a jinn celebration! Oh God, save me! Oh Ali, save me!...'

How Hussein had managed to call on God and Ali he had no idea, but as he recovered his speech and his sanity, he attributed his survival to that strangled plea. He had known nothing else until several months later, when he began to stir vaguely in his unconscious blackness. The smell of burning rue penetrated the dark mists and called him back to life. There was his mother, weeping and caressing and praying. There were his brothers and sisters, his grandfather, his grandmother, Aunt Nabila—all anxious-eyed, but with smiles forming.

'Praise to God! Welcome my son!'

'Oh Hussein, you are with us! Thanks be to God and his Prophet!'

As he gradually grew in strength, Hussein learned that at the elders' request the government people had come and removed the generator from their village. The elders had decided that the old ways were best. Human beings should be in bed before darkness falls; darkness belongs to other creatures.

The jinn

Although Iblîs or *al-Shayṭân* is once referred to in the Qur'ân as a *jinnî* (sura 18:48), for the most part the jinn seem to exist in the popular mind at least as a separate species of spirit. Created, reportedly, of fire (sura 55:14), they comprise a genus somewhere between angels and men. Like angels, they belong to the world of spirit. Like men, they are distinguished from angels in that their habitation is within the human domain, rather than in the heavens. Jinn might be believers or non-believers. Although theoretically neutral, most jinn are conceived of as being bad. They are intensely jealous of human men, women and children and seek constantly for opportunities to injure them. The fear of jinn, or the desire to subdue and use their services, are strong motivating forces in the practices of many ordinary Muslims.

Just as the names and functions of many of the angels are specified in the folk-Islamic world, so there is parallel identification of roles and titles for jinn. In Arabic, various labels for these spirits describe their typical activities. Jinn are referred to as *khâfi* from 'concealed', as *ghûl* from a root word meaning 'to destroy', or as *ʿafrît* from a root word meaning 'to roll in the dust'.

In order not to refer directly to jinn and thus incite their activity, people often speak of them by allusion. In the Arab world, a common term is *hâduk al-nâs* ('those people there'), while in Iran they are often designated as *az mâ bihtarân* ('those better than ourselves').

Named jinn are particularly feared. One of the outstanding features of such beings is their ability to change shape and form. A commonly known named *jinnîya* of Morocco is A'isha Qandisha. She presents herself to men as a beautiful woman, a seductress. If a man succumbs to her temptations and sleeps with her, he becomes her slave for ever. If he should recognise her (in the Moroccan instance she has camel's feet which she tries to keep hidden beneath a flowing gown) and should plunge a steel knife into the earth quickly enough, he can either reject her entirely, or make a 'marriage contract' with her to his own advantage. In Algeria, the equivalent personality is Betjallal, a contracted word in Arabic meaning 'lady of splendour'. Many Algerian men believe themselves to be 'married' to Betjallal, a relationship sealed in sexual intercourse.

A named *jinnîya* with a different trait is Al. Known among Iranian Muslims, Al attacks newborn children. If a baby becomes sick within the first six days of its life, the cause of sickness is often attributed to Al. In Egypt and the Sudan it is Umm al-Ṣubyân who plays this role. She is described as a lean and loathsome woman, travelling invisibly and destroying by her sheer presence. Miscarriages and stillbirths are her specialities, besides attacks upon mothers and newborn babies.

Umm al-Ṣubyân has the principal voice in the seal of the Seven Covenants of Suleiman. This popular charm is used throughout the contemporary Arabic-speaking world as a protective device, especially around the vulnerable months of childbirth. In the text of the seal, Umm al-Ṣubyân relates to the prophet Suleiman the covenant terms on which she will refrain from touching the sons of Adam and daughters of Eve. Before being forced by Suleiman to come to this agreement, she brags rather crudely both of her power to harm and her ability to appear as something other than what she is:

> I enter a house and crow like a cockerel; I bark like dogs, and drop manure like a bull or a cow; I cough like camels, and neigh like a horse; I bray like donkeys, and hiss like snakes; I mimic them perfectly. I close up wombs and destroy children without anyone suspecting me. I come to a woman and bind up her womb, preventing her from becoming pregnant. I make a woman barren. I come to a woman in pregnancy and destroy the foetus so that the woman miscarries. She is not able to keep the child. I come to the engaged girl or woman and tie the hems of her garments; then I announce the disaster to the matchmakers. I come to a man and render him impotent...

Among Turks the equivalent named *jinnîya* is al-Karisi; among Kabyles it is Taba.

Clearly, jinn form a strong component in the folk-Islamic concept of causality. Certain conditions of death, paralysis or illness may be attributable to named jinn. Among the Bosnian Turks, it is believed that if a child cries a great deal, Urok (a witch who appears in nightmares) is at work. If a Sudanese child has an epileptic fit, Umm al-Ṣubyân is blamed. Moreover, adults are hesitant to touch such an afflicted child for fear of possession. The most common signature of A'isha Qandisha is paralysis, especially of the lower limbs. With the kinds of affliction caused by this Moroccan *jinnîya*, there is often no recovery. Rather, the survival of the sufferer lies in developing a give-and-take relationship between him and the powerful *jinnîya*. One of the major roles of Moroccan Sufi-originated orders, such as the Ḥamadsha, becomes that of helping to initiate and maintain a peaceful relationship between the *jinnîya* and her human victims. The Ḥamadsha or the Gnawiyya thus provide the setting and the music in which devotees of A'isha Qandisha dance out their obedience to her in regular *ḥadrs*.

Jinn of the unnamed variety are also attributed with causing much sickness. Whooping cough could be the product of jinn tickling a child's lungs. Sudden death from an unknown cause is likely to be attributed to the work of an *cafrît*. Muslims often distinguish between being 'struck' by jinn and being totally possessed by them. Within each category a scale of intensity determines the impact made by the jinn on the human concerned. In Iran, a person struck by jinn is referred to as *ghashi* ('one who faints'). If a remedy is not quickly discovered, such a person is likely to grow more firmly controlled by jinn, a condition manifested in fainting spells and seizures. The *mârid* is the most powerful of Egyptian jinn and always strives to kill its victims. Strong magical help is needed to combat the evil force of a *mârid*.

In dealing with problems caused by jinn, diagnosis is often made by divination or medium trance. A practitioner of some power is required and his services tend to be expensive. He may sleep with part of the afflicted person's clothing and in the morning announce the solution that came to him in a dream. He may have in his personal control a powerful *jinnî* that aids him in diagnosis. Cures may not be possible. Where they are, they may require a variety of magical activities. Strong charms may assist in reducing or preventing the recurrence of attack. Sometimes, 'curing' may consist in establishing a symbiotic relationship between the afflicted person and afflicting spirit as in the case of A'isha Qandisha.

Concepts of space are important in the folk-Islamic worldview. (We shall examine them in depth in Chapter Ten.) They define for the Muslim safe and dangerous territory. Among the designated spaces appear those for the jinn. They vary for different communities, but they include brick kilns, rubbish pits (Iran), certain trees, sharks, crocodiles (Philippines), marshes, rivers, wells (Morocco), ruins, graveyards and toilets (Egypt). Dark rooms and the black of night are widely considered the haunts of jinn as in the case of Hussein from northern Iran, cited at the beginning of this chapter. On entering the vicinity of such areas, Muslims take the precaution of respecting the presence of other beings. For example, in going to a toilet, a person will cough, exclaim '*bismillâh*', '*yâ sâtir*', or some other protective formula, to warn the current occupant of his approach, or to claim God's defence as he enters enemy territory. Failure to do so could well result in an attack from a spirit of the toilet, a *rîh*.

The careful respect of such physical spaces is heightened by the connection made by many Muslims between activities of 'the flesh' (such as defecation, sexual arousal or haemorrhage) and the susceptibility of being invaded by evil spirit beings during such activities. The film *Rosemary's Baby* describes a situation in which a woman gives birth to a child after intercourse with the Devil. When this film was shown in Turkey, some Turks saw it as an illustration of an experience known in contemporary life rather than as a fantasy.

The value of prophylactic talismans is partly determined by their claimed ability to control the supernatural inhabitants of various places. The Muslim who carries a talisman wants one that allows him to move around and act with immunity in as many situations as possible. If a Muslim is aware that jinn commonly inhabit certain spots of the earth around him, he carefully avoids stepping into such dangerous space, however well protected with charms he may be.

For the ordinary Muslim, jinn are no mean force with which to reckon.

Evil spirits dispossessed

The Bible spares no words in identifying a real world of evil spirit beings. Satan himself is presented as intrinsically real, not a figment of the imagination. He is exposed as a fallen angel, ruler of the kingdom of the air, and prince of the devils. Although he opposes God, the sense of that opposition is far from dualistic. It is not a case of two equals, 'good' and 'evil', fighting things out. Rather, the Devil is ultimately only another created being, and his end in judgement is sure.

Strictly speaking, it would seem that the parallel concept within (folk) Islam is that of evil spirit rather than jinn. In some respects, however, the demons of the Bible have characteristics and produce effects similar to those of jinn in the folk-Islamic world.

The Old Testament discloses a class of evil spirit embodied in animals, a facet anticipatory of the folk-Islamic concept of metamorphosis. Such are the serpent (Genesis 3:14), satyrs (Leviticus 17:7), the nighthag (Isaiah 34:14) and others. Ascribed to them are 'unnatural' happenings, especially sickness, madness and death. This class of spirit is found especially in deserts, among tombs and in ruined houses (cf Isaiah 13:21).

The Old Testament also includes reference to heathen gods as demons (Deuteronomy 32:17). When other nations around Israel sacrifice to their idols, they are, in the biblical view, appeasing demons. The strongest condemnation is laid on the people of Yahweh for their spiritual prostitution in abandoning the Lord to worship such demons.

The New Testament acknowledges the reality of demons. The four Gospel writers carefully distinguish between demon possession and various forms of mere disease, including mental illness, although the conditions sometimes occur together (Mark 1:32,34). Jesus addresses demons directly and commands them, expecting their obedience (eg Matthew 8:29–32).

Paul presents a view similar to that of the Old Testament with regard to the deities of the gentile world. In his evangelising of Greece, his conclusions are sharpened. The gods of the gentiles are, in essence, a fiction (1 Corinthians 8:4–6); they do not exist. But behind the heathen idols lie demons, and it is to those demons that the Gentiles sacrifice (1 Corinthians 10:20). At the time of his later imprisonment Paul declares that evil spirits or demons are whisperers of false teaching among the community of the faithful (1 Timothy 4:1).

If the Bible acknowledges the reality of the world of evil spirits, even though it is not as detailed in its categorisation as folk Islam, it does so in order to declare that, in and through Christ, this world has been disarmed and judged. From the beginning of his public ministry, when Jesus is spurred into the desert by the Spirit, he takes the initiative against the occult world. There, in the space belonging in a special sense to the Evil One—in the wilderness—the leader of evil spirits is reproved. After that confrontation and until the cross, the picture given in the Gospels of the evil spirits which had possessed men is that they know there is nothing they can do to resist this Christ who had defeated their master. The first declaration in Mark's Gospel of the sonship of Christ is from a frightened evil spirit (Mark 1:24).

At the same time, evil spirits are provoked to violent activity among their charges before their exposure and expulsion. Often the Gospels record that a possessed man or child is especially tormented as the time approaches for Jesus to exorcise the spirit (eg Luke 4:35; Mark 9:20).

The cross provides the pivotal point of the conflict. In some special way the powers of darkness own this hour and act with authority in it. Yet, in their seeming triumph, they are judged. On the cross, Christ disarms all evil powers and authorities, triumphing over them (Colossians 2:15).

The biblical answer to the acknowledged reality of evil spirits, including jinn, is that cure from their oppressing and possessing of humans is available. Such cure comes, not by magical means, nor by formulas of exorcism, but by the word of power which Jesus speaks, and which he entrusts to his disciples. It is a power derived from the victory of his death on a cross.

CHAPTER THREE

SAINTS AND SONS

Reflections of an uncle

ENGINEER FARAJ DREW DEEPLY on the cigarette, recrossed his legs, and leant over to Azmy, shouting above the racket, 'Not bad, this Najwa?'

'Very professional, my brother! How much did you pay for her and the band?'

Faraj chose not to answer, but disguised his refusal to do so by jumping up and clapping his hands. The music paused. 'Let's have "The Qena Love Story"! Dr Yusuf, you shall dance the young farmer's boy from Sohag who falls in love with the daughter of the state governor. Miss Najwa, you must be the governor's flirtatious daughter, urging on the hopeless adoration. Dance Dr Yusuf off his feet and into your arms!'

A host of ribald remarks flew back and forth through the air, overtaken by the loud tapping of the tambourine. The pace was set. The violin began to weave its notes around the erotic beat. Najwa moved, from her hips. Voices hummed the well-loved story as the belly dancer, brought for the occasion from a club in Cairo, gyrated smoothly around the crowded room, calling the embarrassed doctor to play his part in the musical mime.

Faraj relaxed again. His hand reached for Selwa's. She smiled nervously at his touch, but the smile was warm, committed. They sat, garlanded with flowers, on the spotlit couch against the innermost wall of the room. It would be a long night, and the sweet drinks seemed to produce thirst as much as quench it. Many of their friends were with them, celebrating both their betrothal and Faraj's possession of the new flat that would become their future home.

Faraj looked round the spirited group. His quick eye searched for his two young nephews. They seemed to have gravitated to the kitchen. They were just like their uncle! Food was essential; other delights could wait! Their mother was chatting excitedly in the living-room with a group of female friends. They had all graduated from Helwan University about ten years before and now compared notes on married life and bringing up children. Doubtless his sister was relating how young Muhammad had done well at his first end-of-term exams, and how Ibrahim was just walking on his own. Faraj deeply loved his sister and her husband. The ups and downs of life had bonded them closely together.

For a long time, Faraj had lived with them in one of the new co-operative building complexes on the outskirts of Cairo, near the Pyramids. He had gradually worked his way through the engineering course at Cairo University. Eventually he had graduated and was now getting established, both in life and in work. In recent years, Faraj had become a second father to his fast-growing nephews. He had taken the elder to his first film in the open-air cinema near Giza Square. Only last year he had looked after both of the boys while his sister and her husband travelled to Assiut to attend the funeral of a relative. Through good and ill the small, extended family had offered strong, mutual support.

Faraj's mind drifted further back to the sad days at the beginning of his sister's marriage. Almost immediately,

Faraj had had to move in with them. His mother and father had suddenly been killed in a bus accident, and as each of the parents had been the youngest in quite small families, there was no one else to look after the teenaged Faraj. The closest adult relative was an uncle on the maternal side, but he had long been in Iraq. Every summer, rumours floated around the travelling community that he was on his way home, laden with gold, but every summer passed with no sign of either uncle or gold. The more accurate snippets of information seemed to suggest that he was actually in prison in Baghdad, and likely to remain there for some while. Faraj's sister and husband had meanwhile welcomed the young student into their small home, and Faraj worked hard to contribute to the household needs. During the day he studied engineering and after the evening call to prayer worked as a driver for one of the Giza minibus companies. Gradually, the three of them had improved the flat, and Faraj had even been able to put aside some money towards the day when he would graduate, find a job, and eventually marry.

One dark cloud hung constantly over the otherwise happy home, and Faraj could do little to help. His sister had become pregnant twice but each time had miscarried. Faraj's brother-in-law, Azmy, was a very gentle, patient man, one who wanted children for their own sake as well as for the sake of family honour. Faraj remembered the light fading from his eyes as a medical specialist advised them that it was highly unlikely that his wife would bring a baby to full term.

At last Faraj's sister had broken the silence on the subject, one Friday, after the men had returned from noon prayers. She had decided to ask for help from a saint. 'I must visit Sayyid Badawi.'

'You want to go to Tanta?'

She had confided in them, the thoughts tumbling out. 'Yes! I've thought about it for some time. I know that if I go and visit Sayyid Badawi, he will grant my request. He is the greatest of all the saints, and I am sure he will help me. I know several other women in the neighbourhood who now have sons, and a secure marriage, after visiting Sayyid Badawi.'

The two men had needed little persuading. 'Well, we will come with you. You will need to make a vow, and we will do the same.'

'No! I will make the vow to Sayyid Badawi. You men make your vows to Imam Shâfiᶜî. You can write well in Arabic. Then you can make your visit at his feast day, next month. I'm sure he would be the best saint to listen to you. But please accompany me, before then, to Tanta.'

The three of them had taken the train to Tanta a few weeks later. It had been the main *mawlid* of the great saint. The mosque and mausoleum were crowded. They could hardly get close enough to the screened tomb to touch it, but really one didn't need to touch. The whole place was alive with the saint's *baraka*. Many were there praying, crying, prostrating themselves and making requests of the saint. Others were there giving thanks for a child healed, a debt repaid, a son safely back from the war zone, a baby born.... There was holy water to drink, special relics to kiss, and a crowd of needy brothers and sisters to join with in prayer.

Quietly, secretly, Faraj's sister made her vow. 'O Shaykh Badawi! If you will give me a son, I will come and offer ten pounds every year. And when my son is born I will sacrifice a sheep in your honour!'

Not long afterwards, Faraj and his brother-in-law made their separate pilgrimage across Cairo to the Shâfiᶜî mausoleum. Having taken off their shoes and washed in the water outside the domed chamber, they moved quietly into the cool interior. As they walked around the tomb, each prayed the *Fâtiḥa* several times. They touched the wooden screen separating them from the actual sarcophagus and wiped their faces and clothes with their hands. They wanted to carry home some of the *baraka* of the holy place. Each prayed and made his vow to the great imam.

Had the saints helped? Two healthy boys had since been born to Faraj's sister. There had been no problems during pregnancy and no difficulties during birth. A sheep was slaughtered at the birth of Muhammad, and what a celebration that was! They were careful to give a fair portion of the meat to the poor.

Faithfully, Faraj's sister travels every year to Tanta to deliver the ten pounds. This year she was happy to take both boys with her. She joined the ranks of those wandering around the tomb murmuring their praises and thanks to the saint. Faithfully also, the two men make their annual visit to the shrine of Shâfiᶜî, on the edge of the City of the Dead. They each put their money secretly in the vow box. They also take along some rice and vegetables to give to the widows and children who sit outside the shrine asking alms of all. Inside the adjoining mosque, Faraj thanks the saint for his young nephews. While he is there he prays about his engineering work as well, and his fiancée, and his new flat, and his health, holidays and happiness.

Tonight, as Najwa led Dr Yusuf and the other self-styled 'lovers' in their dance drama, Faraj thanked God, the Prophet and the saints for those mischief-makers in the kitchen.

In a sweep to the end of the room, Najwa collected Engineer Faraj from his seat on the couch and tempted him to match her provocative movements. Responding to her lead and flicking his fingers rhythmically, the happy young uncle gave himself to the expressive dance.

The veneration of saints

All kinds of people in the Muslim world are involved in a give-and-take relationship with saints. This extensive cult of saint veneration most probably grew out of a concern for honouring the Prophet, Muhammad. It is certainly justified, in the popular mind at least, by the continuing celebration of the Prophet's birthday (*Mawlid al-Nabî*). A few strict sects, such as the Hanbalites and Wahhabites, deny any validity to such a cult. However, for most Muslims, saints (*awliyâ'* plural, *walî* singular) fulfil an important role in the world-view.

Saints may be variously designated. Some common references are *shâfiᶜ* (intercessor), *shaykh* (leader), *pîr* (elderly or wise person) or *murâbiṭ* ('one who has joined himself' to God). A major distinction occurs between living and dead saints. In the case of the former, the subcontinent of India, Pakistan and Bangladesh provides the most outstanding examples. In the historical heartlands of Islam, and on the continent of Africa, dead saints are more usually venerated. Here, the focus of pilgrimage and worship is as much centred on the shrine as upon the saint housed there.

The cult of *pîr* veneration in the subcontinent is highly developed. The most significant functions of the *pîr* are to make intercession and to bestow *baraka*. The position is often hereditary in a family that traces its lineage directly to the Prophet. The *pîr's* complex in Golra Sharif, near Islamabad, is a large establishment with a farm attached. The *pîr*, Sayyid Ghulâm Muḥyî al-Dîn Shâh, hosts all visitors and holds court for two hours every day. He is seen as a *murshid* ('guide') and gives guidance on all kinds of matters. Specifically religious instruction, however, he leaves in the hands of employed *mawlânâs*—theologians of the orthodox hierarchy.

Pîrs can be wealthy men, living off the gifts of money and food brought by their needy supplicants. A *pîr* may be sought out on a regular basis by the leaders of a community to give guidance concerning communal decisions. Equally, a family may bring a bag of rice for the *pîr* to blow upon. The transferred *baraka* is taken home and given with the rice to a sick relative. Some *pîrs* exercise a socio-political influence over their followers. Thus the power of the *pîr* of Pagara in Sind became apparent in 1977 during the political disturbances following the Pakistan election. When the then prime minister, Mr Bhutto, arrested all the opposition leaders, the *pîr* of Pagara was quickly released at the demand of his many followers.

Dead saints abound in the Muslim world. Morocco is the home of many Berber saints connected with local communities. In northern Nigeria, a well-known saint is Shehu Uthman dan Fodio, and in the west of that nation the female saint Bilikisu Sungbo is venerated. In many nations, historic saints of great holiness, such as Shaykh ᶜAbd al-Qâdir al-Jîlânî of Baghdad, are venerated. Al-Ḥusayn, brother of al-Ḥasan and son of ᶜAlî, is another well-known saint. There are also numerous local saints, usually holy men who expressed some form of supernatural power in their lives. In Turkey, patron saints watch over different crafts. Consequently a tailor, when beginning to cut a bolt of cloth, will commonly invoke the help of Idris Nebi, patron saint of tailoring.

Alive or dead, saints are believed to possess great power. The kind of miracles (*karâma*) attributed to them include raising the dead, walking on water, covering great distances in very short times, healing, having knowledge of the future, guarding people or tribes, and being in two places at one time. Shaykh Zuwayyid, one of several saints venerated today among the Bedouin of Sinai, is reputed to have filled a food bowl simply by looking at it.

Relics of the Prophet are carefully preserved and draw wonder and awe from pilgrims. Qandahar in Afghanistan hosts a cloak belonging to Muhammad. Topkapı Palace in Istanbul displays an encased hair from the Prophet's beard. At the shrine of Sayyid Jamâl al-Dîn, near Nazmakan in Iran, that saint's sword is carefully guarded at the saint's tomb and is venerated by pilgrims. The Qaitbey Mausoleum in Cairo's massive City of the Dead houses a stone block bearing the footprints of the Prophet.

An intrinsic part of the cult of saints is the concern for shrines and sacred places associated with them. Such holy sanctuaries are variously referred to as *mashhad* (strictly 'martyrium'), *mazâr* (place of pilgrimage), *qubba, turba* or *imâmzad* (strictly 'mausoleum'). Whitewashed, domed shrines dot the landscape of much of rural North Africa and the Middle East. Other city shrines, such as those of Sayyid al-Ḥusayn or al-Rifâᶜî in Cairo, or al-Mughrâbi in Latakia, Syria, attract pilgrims from across the Muslim world. Despite official prohibition, the visiting of shrines continues in Turkey, where the tomb of Eyüp is the most popular place of pilgrimage in the city of Istanbul. The most significant shrine among Shîᶜah Muslims is at Karbalâ' in Iraq. (See Appendix 2.) It commemorates the scene of the massacre of al-Ḥusayn, son of Imâm ᶜAlî. Mazâr-i-Sharîf, literally meaning Noble Tomb, is the most celebrated shrine in Afghanistan and has in fact given its name to the town in which it stands. Shrines patronised in Pakistan include that of Baba Farîd at Pakpattan, with its special feature of the Door to Heaven. During the annual pilgrimage, the educated and uneducated queue up in thousands to enter this door. On offer to all who pass through it during the festival season is a secure entrance to heaven on their deaths. The *darbar* (shrine) of the patron saint of Lahore, Data Ganj Bakhsh, is almost as popular. The annual festival of his death anniversary is celebrated in Safar month. Many Muslims in the southern Philippines visit *tampots* (shrines) to seek blessing, health and protection, and to make binding oaths.

Ordinary Muslims relate to saints in a few major ways. The processes are seen as being mutually beneficial. Saints possess *baraka* and are capable of performing miracles. They are expected to render certain services to believers. In return, adherents express their dependence and gratitude for services rendered in the form of vows, visits and celebrations of saints' days (*mawlids*).

Vow-making is done in two stages. The first stage is that of composing the vow. This may be done privately, although it is generally held to be more efficacious to compose the vow at a saint's tomb. One of the features of nearly every shrine is the *ṣandûq al-nudhûr* (vow box), or its equivalent. At the shrine of Shâfiⁿî in Cairo, the vow box is filled and the tomb is littered with vows written in classical, rather than colloquial, Arabic. Because Shâfiⁿî was a grand imam, a founder of one of the four schools of Islamic law (*madhrab*), it is assumed that he will respond especially to well-written letters. A vow could involve small or large commitments: to make various offerings at the shrine, to build a mausoleum for the saint, to give a donation for the upkeep of the shrine, to fulfil the *ḥajj* to Mecca, or to dedicate an animal to the saint. The second stage is that of fulfilling the vow. Fulfilment is of extreme importance, although often no fixed time is set. If a person who has not yet fulfilled a vow begins to have nightmares, he will consider them to be reminders by the saint to fulfil his vow.

Visits (*ziyârât*) to the shrine usually combine recognition of the saint and expression of the pilgrim's need. Money or valuables may be offered, candles may be lit, food may be left, or the *Fâtiḥa* may be recited—all this to benefit the saint. Then the pilgrim announces his own requests, often while walking around the grave. Frequently, pieces of cloth are fixed to the branches of trees near the shrine, with knots tied in them to represent the number of wishes. Sometimes, part of the clothing of a sick person is left at the shrine, or dust from the place is taken home.

The *mawlid* is an annual celebration of the saint's birth, or more usually his death. These festivities provide auspicious dates and sites for ceremonies such as circumcisions and weddings. They also provide opportunities for *baraka* collection by the common people. Feasting and merrymaking, with prayers and other more animistic rituals, feature significantly on such occasions. However, the overall objective is to honour the saint concerned.

Understanding of the dynamics involved in requesting a saint's help varies according to the education (in a formal, religious sense) of the person addressing the saint. Where there is a basic knowledge of official Islamic theology, it will be insisted that the request is actually asked of God. The saint is only involved as an intermediary in bringing the reward from God to the human concerned. Often, however, more immediate relationships are espoused between saints and individuals. Requests are made directly of the saints. Some saints are seen as specialising in certain activities: one is able to protect people from foreign invasion; another prevents crops from being stolen; a third is especially helpful for women who desire to bear children. According to the need of the hour, so an appropriate saint is approached.

The Qur'ân is careful in its defence of God as the sole arbiter of human affairs. Although it refers to vow fulfilment (sura 76:7), it does so in the context of such vows being made by individuals to God. The Qur'ân emphasises the importance of not appealing to intermediaries between man and God: 'Those whom they call upon apart from Him have no power of intercession...' (sura 43:85). The insistence upon direct submission of the individual to the all-powerful, all-knowing God leaves little room in the world of formal faith for saints and other intermediaries. All that might be allowed by the Qur'ân (sura 53:26) is the possibility of angels acting as intercessors by God's special permission. Such permission was obviously ruled out for Muhammad's Qurayshi contemporaries who mistakenly viewed the angels as divine.

The *hadîth*, although they deal quite extensively with the specific issues of vow-making and oaths, are equally careful about denying the possibility of help from any supernatural source apart from God. Vows are disallowed as a means of attempting to alter fate. Even where they are made legitimately, it is put in doubt as to whether they are efficacious.

Thus neither the *hadîth* nor the Qur'ân offers direct support for a cult of saint veneration. However, both *hadîth* and Qur'ân do admit a view of the world in which there is more to creation than meets the purely human eye. They both affirm a plethora of 'beings' and 'powers', thereby conceding the potential of appeal to a suprahuman domain.

The possibility of mediators, intercessors and repositories of *baraka* was quickly legitimised in the early veneration of Muhammad, Fatima, Ali and other historic figures of the faith. Devotion to them led easily to intercession to them, and answered prayers renewed their praises. Such devotion and intercession have been multiplied throughout families, tribes and communities, with local saints becoming the objects of veneration.

Among ordinary Muslims, many current myths declare that the *baraka*-endued power of saints is its own justifier. Such myths more than answer the demands of contemporary reformist movements for a laying aside of the veneration of saints. The cult of saints is validated, in the minds of needy Muslims, in terms of its known effectiveness.

Spectators only?

The term *hagîoi* (saints) is used sixty times in the New Testament. It has an Old Testament origin, meaning 'set apart to the service and praise of God'. It always occurs in the plural sense in the New Testament.

Gradually, the term came to apply to men and women of singular holiness; invariably they were martyrs. Pre-Nicene references to saints, as individuals of outstanding character, are found in the Odes of Solomon and the *Martyrium Polycarpi* (about AD 156). By the time of Origen, a definite cult of martyrs had developed, but it tended to be localised at first.

Prayer to such special witnesses was foreshadowed in some of the intertestamental Jewish aprocryphal writings.

Thus, for example, Judas Maccabeus saw Jeremiah in a vision, blessing the whole Jewish people with outstretched hands (2 Maccabees 15:12). The mediatorial powers of Christian saints was enhanced in people's minds during periods of intense persecution.

Gradually, a need was expressed in the Western church for formalisation of the process of defining 'saints'. The first official canonisation occurred in the tenth century, and from the twelfth century no canonisation occurred without the blessing of the Bishop of Rome. In the Eastern church, throughout its history, the process of recognition has, however, remained more informal and local. The cult of saints came under strong condemnation in Europe at the time of the Reformation. Nevertheless, most of the major Protestant denominations issuing from that period of European history have retained some saints' days as part of their liturgical calendar.

A high view of biblical inspiration is, clearly, non-negotiable. Yet it has to be admitted that the plural noun 'saints' embraces the idea of many individuals, each of whom is 'a saint'. It would seem that there are scriptural grounds for acknowledging that God has sovereignly used some of those men and women in unique ways. Such might be exemplified by the strange event which occurred at the tomb of the prophet Elisha. Once, when some Israelites were burying a man nearby, their funeral was interrupted by Moabite raiders. Hurriedly, they deposited the corpse in the nearby tomb of Elisha. When the dead Israelite's body touched the bones of Elisha, he came to life and stood up on his feet (2 Kings 13:21). One interpretation of the drama is that there was some kind of accumulation of power at the shrine. A residual holiness in the bones of the prophet contained the power to restore a corpse to life.

Equivalent New Testament incidents are found in the record of the Acts of the Apostles. The view of certain individuals as being uniquely powerful to bless others would seem to be permitted by such occurrences. It took only the shadow of the passing apostle Peter to bring hope and healing to Jerusalem's sick in post-Pentecost days (Acts 5:15). In Ephesus, some years later, God used the apostle Paul to touch others in an extraordinary way. Sweat bands and aprons which had touched the apostle were taken to the sick. By the use of those items of clothing, evil spirits were exorcised and illnesses were cured (Acts 19:12).

Thus there would seem to be biblical grounds for acknowledging that the word 'saints' includes some people of God with whom special manifestations of power have been associated. Such manifestations may occur during their lifetime or after their death. The recognition of those biblical grounds perhaps falls near the fringes of most Reformed theology while remaining more central—theologically—for the Roman Catholic and Orthodox Churches.

Certainly, in the experience of Orthodox and Catholic Christians living as minorities in Islamic nations, the fact that saints and martyrs play a role in their spiritual heritage makes their faith more accessible to their Muslim neighbours. Renewed Christian believers from these backgrounds know ministries of healing and exorcism which are often open to and experienced by Muslims as well as Christians. Saint George (Khidr to Muslims) is renowned in the Middle East for his frequent involvement in exorcising demons. In Cairo, a saint seen as approachable by Muslims as well as Christians is St Thérèse d'Avila. There are many from each religious community who feel that she has helped transform their lives.

Closely associated with the helpful work of powerful saints is the appreciation of appearances on a large scale of the Virgin Mary. In Cairo, in both 1968 and 1986, such apparitions were witnessed by hundreds of thousands of Egyptians. Various attested healings and deliverances were associated with both appearances. Muslims and Christians benefited from the extended 'light-visions', and each community made its own interpretation of the reasons for the visitations. (The purpose of these paragraphs is neither to promote nor to condemn such views by other Christian believers of ways in which the 'communion of saints' might affect the world of the senses. Nor is it to attempt any theory of identification as to whether the 'saints' involved might be other than what they seem to be.)

One can state categorically that the calling up of departed spirits by mediums is absolutely forbidden in the Bible. Equally, it needs to be borne in mind that 'communion of saints' implies communing, and a 'great cloud of witnesses' presupposes a living audience who listen to those giving witness from beyond this life. The faithful Stephen is exemplary of those for whom 'witness' included literal martyrdom. In his actual dying, Stephen's words and life point the earthly onlookers to the Son of Man standing at the right hand of God. The abiding witness from heaven of the great forerunners of faith (Hebrews 11) is designed to encourage the pilgrims on earth also to fix their eyes on Jesus. The witness might proceed in the other direction as well, from the living to the dead or 'sleeping'. The apostle Paul, in his defence of the resurrection, comments in passing on the Corinthian practice of baptising living believers on behalf of dead believers. He neither condemns nor even questions the practice in itself. He simply argues its futility if there is, after all, no resurrection of the dead (1 Corinthians 15:29).

The identification of 'being' seems to have been a constant problem for those limited by the human senses. The prophets of old could only describe as 'a man' what were obviously beings from the world beyond (for example Daniel and the angel in Daniel 10:5). Certainly Jesus knew the fellowship, in a special sense, of two transformed 'humans' (Moses and Elijah) on the Mount of Transfiguration (Matthew 17:3). How did the 'angel of the Lord' become in his dialogue with Gideon an appearance (theophany) of the Lord himself (Judges 6:11,14, etc)? In the discussion

between Yahweh and Abraham concerning Sodom's immin-
ent destruction, the patriarch is approached by 'three men'
(Genesis 18:2), one of whom turns out to be 'the Lord'
(verse 10). The other two are soon identified as 'angels'
(Genesis 19:1). How did the appearances in glory of Moses
and Elijah, who had not tasted death, differ from the manifestation to Saul's medium of the dead Samuel? What were
the qualities of Stephen's face which convinced the hostile
court that he looked just like an angel (Acts 6:15)? In the
biblical record, then, identification of being is not necessarily
as clearcut as Western, rationalistic minds would like to
make out.

Perhaps an awareness of the cult of saint veneration
among Muslims can provoke those of us who are Protestant
and Western to reconsider our understanding of the 'communion of the saints'. Maybe a sense of unity with the
enveloping 'cloud of witnesses' can help us retrieve our view
of 'sleeping' brothers and sisters from the fringes towards the
centre of our theologising. Is there room within a high view
of the Bible to re-evaluate the possibilities of such fellowship
to include a more tangible involvement of the 'saints' with
needy human beings of the Muslim world?

CHAPTER FOUR

UNRAVELLING THE FUTURE

A banker's question

B ENDING CAREFULLY TO AVOID cramping his troublesome back, Orhan gently drew off his house slippers and deposited them neatly in the shoe rack at the corner of the hall. Slipping on his brown Italian suedes (no laces so no bending), he checked the items he would need: loose change for the taxi fares, his banker's card for identification if he were asked, large notes for the casino later, and his umbrella. At this time of year you never knew if Istanbul's picturesque spring streets were going to be doused by a sudden downpour. He swung his light overcoat around his shoulders, picked the umbrella off the stand and slipped out of the door.

The day was just getting its second wind in the Beşiktaş suburb. At 10.00 pm most folk had eaten, and evening entertainment was the order of the hour. Blurred television flashes coloured the drawn curtains of neighbouring homes as Orhan set off down the hill to the main boulevard. Tonight's programme featured the long anticipated football final between Istanbul and Hamburg, being played in Germany. Istanbul would go to bed in a few hours either elated

or depressed; there was no halfway house with football. At
the bank tomorrow, Orhan would know who had won. No
one need say anything.

Orhan fingered the ebony prayer beads he had found in
his suit pocket. As he walked, he thought about the bank.
He had done well—very well. Starting as a clerk nearly
twenty-five years ago, he had moved from his job as a teller
into the service department. His selection for one of the first
computer courses run for the benefit of the merchant bank
had resulted in quick promotion.

What a day it had been when he had been called to a
board meeting at the head office in Taksim Square. He was
being recommended for the manager's position in a new
branch being established in one of the younger suburbs of
the sprawling metropolis. Orhan had hardly known whether
to congratulate himself or collapse in fright. Across the spit-
polished mahogany he had accepted the pomotion. Even as
the words left his lips, he felt that at last he was one of
'them'. Now, Bay Orhan Koyulmuş was also 'the bank'.
Cologne was passed round and then the inevitable tea in
delicate crystal glasses. Orhan had left shortly afterwards
with Mehmet, one of the older directors, and in fact the man
who had proposed Orhan for the new and strategic post.
Together they had gone across town to celebrate with something a little livelier than cologne and sweet tea.

Orhan smiled as he remembered facing his wife and
mother-in-law the following evening. They were of course
delighted over the new appointment. It meant a rise in their
social status. It meant that they could complete their summer
home up on the Black Sea coast earlier than they had ever
dreamed. It meant jewellery from the bazaar: in success,
Orhan always fêted his female partners with brooches and
rings. But did it really take this man until five in the morning
to return from a building in Taksim?

Orhan had stumbled into the house some while after the
dawn call to prayer and had gone straight to bed. It wasn't

until later in the day that he had shared the good news. The women had their suspicions about what hadn't been shared. Oh well, he had lived that down with some expensive and very nice bribes. With their new bank manager at the helm of his own branch, the small family quickly moved on to better things. The Black Sea villa was long since finished, and they loved the quiet, relaxed holidays there, sniffing the intoxicating perfume of the pine forests on the slopes behind, forgetting the summer smog and noise of sweltering Istanbul.

Orhan had enjoyed building an office team from scratch. True, he had stolen a few old friends from other branches around town, but, by and large, he had selected and trained people whom he sensed had an innate feel for what he wanted. Orhan's task was to capture a new clientele. With the growing stability that military rule had brought, international companies were beginning to show an interest in Turkey. Most of those companies were setting up headquarters in the newer suburbs of Istanbul where services, especially telecommunications, were at their best. Sleek hotels catered for overnight executives and entrepreneurs, and Orhan felt at ease in that world. Fluent in English, German and French, he capitalised on his growing understanding of Western efficiency-oriented business acumen, and his long-learned knowledge of how to get things done, Turkish style. It was a success story. It was success which had brought him to tonight.

Orhan hardly noticed the column of military vehicles parked in the bus station. They had become a familiar part of Istanbul traffic and no longer inspired the fear which had arisen in everyone's stomachs when the patrols first began. Rather, they gave a sense of security. The days of car bombs and mad machine-gun fights had long since passed. Thanks be to God!

Beyond the bus station was the taxi rank. Orhan climbed gingerly into the first cab. It was a Japanese runabout; they usually were these days. Orhan's reputation had grown through his involvement in making that international agreement work to Turkey's advantage.

'God be with you. The Konak Hotel, if it be his will.'

'With God helping, the Konak.'

Orhan offered the driver a cigarette and took one himself. From somewhere on the dashboard a lighter appeared, and both men drew on the calming nicotine.

Yes, Orhan was nervous. He'd fingered his prayer beads with more than normal rapidity as he'd walked along the bank of the Bosphorus to the taxi rank. Now he inhaled deeply. He was always nervous on these nights.

'I wonder what makes me agitated,' he mused, half aloud. 'Is it the actual decision itself, the pressure of the American client to know "yes" or "no" by tomorrow's deadline? Is it the risk involved? Exposure to the bank would be high, higher than ever before. Is it that I'm getting too old to carry these bargaining, waiting games as lightly as I could ten years ago? Or is it the anticipation of tonight: the dark room, the hushed, expectant, breathless atmosphere, the chilling realisation that another force is present, the hanging by a knife edge as the glass moves, and I know that the answer is coming?'

He lit another cigarette.

The taxi slid over the Galata bridge, its lights playing a winking game with the water as their reflection sparkled on and off through the passing railings. Other lights illuminated the Mosque of Sultan Ahmet up to the left on the skyline. Orhan picked out the six slender minarets. It certainly was one of the loveliest mosques in the world.

Orhan reflected on his life as a Muslim. He didn't say his prayers often—only during Ramaḍân, and then only the major noon prayers on a Friday. No one, not even the most irreligious 'leftist' in the office, would have understood if he hadn't at least prayed then. But Orhan's experience of prayer left him unmoved. It seemed a useless ritual. It certainly bore no relation to the rest of his life. Were his fellow

Turks so convinced that God was listening, as they lined up in their hundreds, bowed and prostrated themselves and recited wonderful lines in a language not their own? If God was listening to them then, did he go to sleep or turn a blind eye while those same Turks, himself included, upped and denied him for the rest of their waking hours? Where was God when those submitted to him drank their Bourbon, cheated on their almsgiving, invested for the highest yields, loved their wives during the day and their mistresses at night? Was God all-knowing, or wasn't he? Was he real, or wasn't he?

It was through his mother-in-law, oddly enough, that Orhan had been introduced to a power that had certainly proved itself very real. His wife's mother had been born to a high admiral and, as a young woman, had lived the protected life of a child of the élite. After the war with Russia, when social confusion was mounting in Turkey, she had married a professional man of whom her father disapproved. Her family had proudly disowned her, and she had been left to fight for a place among her husband's family and acquaintances. Fifteen years later, her husband was killed in an accident. Since her father had also died by then, some of the more forgiving of her relatives had accepted her, and her teenaged daughter, Gül, back into the family circle.

Orhan had met Gül at university. Their subsequent marriage had proved quite a splendid occasion. Some of mother-in-law's family had deigned to grace the festivities with their presence. Orhan seemed well able to indulge in quick repartee with the politicians, surgeons, lawyers and university people. The lofty family rapidly took a liking to the fast-moving, quick-talking petty banker.

Gradually, Orhan found himself more and more in the companionship of a clique that met infrequently in one of the private chambers of the Konak Hotel. After sweetmeats and cognac, cigars, and chitchat about the evils of the press, the bigotry of the fundamentalist movement, the audacity of

Greece, and general snippets of political and financial gossip, the select group turned to the real business of the evening.

The lights were dimmed, everyone assembled around a bare central table, and Madame Sinan took over. Words and letters were distributed randomly around the table surface, a glass was upturned and all put their hands on it. Slowly at first, and then more quickly, the glass moved in response to the questions asked by the group. All such questions were addressed through Madame Sinan, although Orhan had a feeling that strong psychic powers were his also. He always seemed to know in which direction the glass was going to move next. Invariably, he was correct. Sometimes the group asked after deceased relatives. At other times, parents would request information on the wisdom of a marriage proposal for their children. During the séances, the atmosphere was always tense, electric and strangely exhausting. After an hour or so, when Madame Sinan declared that she had had enough for an evening, the proceedings were closed. The power had been sufficiently tapped for one night.

It was to this power—this dynamic, real, answering power—that Orhan brought his own questions. This was the waking god that gave his life direction. He had proved it. His success underlined it. In fact, he wouldn't make a major decision any other way. Tonight, he wanted to ask about the American proposal. Should he go ahead or not? It would be in a darkened suite of the Konak Hotel that he would find his answer for the impatient executives sitting in Philadelphia.

Orhan eased himself from the taxi at the congested entrance to the rebuilt mansion. He paid his fare and a generous tip, stubbed out the remaining half of his fourth cigarette and entered the reception lounge. His eyes quickly found the notice. 'April fraternal: Saladin room.'

Nervous but confident, Orhan glided through the carpeted meeting area and made for the stairs.

Divination

The aim of divination is to understand the larger context of life. This search is often expressed in terms of finding out, or knowing, 'the future'. Divination is pursued so that present actions can be altered or regulated to best advantage. Practices of divination or fortune-telling are widespread and much sought after by ordinary Muslims.

Childbirth provides a common context for divination, especially among women. In a world in which a son is important, even necessary for securing a wife's continuing well-being, predictions by practitioners concerning the sex of an unborn child are much sought after. Often, in local communities, it will be the midwife who has the ability to discover the sex of the infant. A typical procedure in Morocco uses a simple pendulum and a sieve. The sieve is smeared white with flour over one half, and black with charcoal over the other half. When the pendulum is held by the midwife above the sieve, it begins to swing. If it swings to the dark side of the sieve, the baby concerned will be a girl, if to the light side, a boy. The midwife declares, with confidence, what kind of infant is to be expected.

Divination is also often used for discovering the cause of a sickness. Such diagnoses may be made in a trance state, either by the practitioner himself, or through a medium whom he uses. The aim is to get in touch with powers of the unseen world to find out what has brought about the problem in the patient. A similar process may be employed to determine cures for sicknesses. In Turkey, sick persons may be directed to appropriate 'hearths of healing' by divination. At such places, cures for specific problems may be applied, often magically. The important art is to discover which place is suitable for the patient concerned.

How are marriage partners to be selected? In Malaya, a divinatory activity is used to match potential husbands and wives. Known as *raksi*, it works by juxtaposing the numerical values of the persons' names in an Arabic alphabet. When they fit in an appropriate manner, that union will work. If a marriage relationship has turned sour, how can it be put right? In Palestine, a marriage was going wrong. Upon consultation, the sheikh advised that the wife's name did not fit her husband's 'house' or 'star'. Her 'house' (or constellation) was of fire, whereas her husband's was of earth, so her house was 'higher' than his. The woman's name was altered from Ṣabîḥa to Fâṭima, thus putting her in a different category. Because the new 'house' meshed suitably with that of her husband's name, the marriage improved rapidly.

A common method of divination is found in 'cutting' the Qur'ân (*estekhareh* in Farsi, *istikhâra* in Arabic). A Qur'ân is opened at random and words on that page are interpreted to give light to a person seeking to make some kind of decision. An alternative process is performed with prayer beads. After repeating the *Fâtiḥa*, the beads are breathed upon, in order to transfer the magic power of the sacred chapter into the beads. Then a bead from the chain is randomly selected, and the enquirer counts towards the 'pointer' bead, using the words 'God', 'Muhammad', 'Abu Jahl'. If the count terminates with the word 'God', it means that the matter under consideration will turn out favourably. If the count terminates with 'Abu Jahl', the prognosis is bad. If it ends with 'Muhammad', the issue is doubtful.

Divination and the associated practices of soothsaying, augury and fortune-telling rest upon a certain view of the world. That view gives the lie to the common generalisation that Muslims are strongly fatalistic in their attitudes. Far from everyone's fate being *maktûb* ('written'), it is believed that there may be means of altering the manner in which life treats a person. The world in which such a possibility exists is a highly complex one. It is a world implied in the Qur'ân, somewhat expounded in the *ḥadîth*, and given detailed exposition in local folklore.

Let us turn our attention to this popular view of the world. The universe of popular Islam comprises seven heavens, seven earths and seven seas, each inhabited and ruled over by different beings.

The heavens provide the abiding places for angels and archangels. They are also the invasion ground of other spirit beings. It is commonly thought that up to the time of Jesus, the jinn had freedom to enter any of the seven heavens. With Jesus' birth, they were excluded from three of those heavens. With Muhammad's birth, they were shut out of the remaining four. Yet, even after this, the jinn continued to ascend to the boundaries of the first heaven to listen to angels talking together about God's decrees. Meteors are said to be fiery darts, hurled after jinn who try to eavesdrop. Celestial bodies are sometimes seen as presiding over different days of the week. Other planets and stars have the ability to modify the states of animate and inanimate objects. The Milky Way shows the path to Mecca. Phases of the moon touch people, animals and crops. A waning moon could well mean that a sick person will lose strength, whereas a waxing moon promises health. A shooting star is the life of a human being extinguished.

The earth on which humans dwell was created on the surface of the water in two days and is made firm by mountains, the roots of which are joined to the roots of Mount Qâf, the mountain surrounding the earth. Legend declares that the earth was still too unstable, so God provided a huge angel to bear up the earth on its shoulders. However, there was no foothold for the angel, and so a square rock of emerald was created for the angel to stand firmly upon. The rock in its turn needed support, so a great bull, al-Rayyân, was created to carry it. Then a fish named Behemoth was created to uphold the bull. Natural phenomena on the earth take on a double meaning according to this well-known myth of creation. Earthquakes are the result of the bull (with some 70,000 heads) shifting the globe from one horn to another.

The earth itself is alive and breathes. Spring and the renewal of plant life comes with its reawakening after winter sleep. Little children are taught to walk lightly lest they hurt the ground. The relative fertility of the earth may be explained by events in the lives of human beings. Thus, for example, one area of Iran is today a prosperous region because the fourth imam, Ali, shook out his tablecloth there after eating. Another area is worthless because the leader of that region was involved in the murder of Hussein at Karbalâ'. A related concept is that of a certain place on earth drawing a person to itself before death, because that person was created, in the first instance, of dust from that spot. Rain is dropped by an angel with a thousand hands and with millions of fingers on each hand. The rainbow, Bride of the Rain, is a fortunate sign. Winds, on the contrary, are harmful, and certain physical disabilities are referred to in Iran by the term 'a wind'. Comets, thunder, lightning, day and night, sea, springs, lakes, flora and fauna are all personalised in popular Islamic folklore.

The physical world is merely a part of a continuum of 'living things', which leads onwards to animals, humans, spirits, demons, angels and finally to God. The universe is a living, vibrant, interacting reality. Thus the world is anything but mechanistic: it gives and takes, can be altered with a magic word, and can affect creatures within it. In the dry lands of the Middle East much attention has focused inevitably on water. Springs and streams are frequently regarded as the creations of saints. Contamination of water is strongly warned against in folk tales, and Muslims hold a deep belief in the magical qualities of water. It cleanses from all impurities and can wash away spells of every kind. Even demons may be driven away by washing. Man needs to live out his life in careful relationship with the elements. It is not his calling to subjugate nature, nor does he submit easily to the prospect of living in subjection to nature. Rather, a careful symbiotic relationship must be pursued and maintained. Bread is not to be worshipped, but neither is it to be treated as if it had no 'life' (the Egyptian, Arabic term for bread means 'life') of its own. If a person respects the bread, its intrinsic *baraka* will enrich him. Hence, a Muslim pauses on a busy city street to pick up a chunk of dropped bread, to kiss it and place it safely on a wall or ledge. The bread is honoured and the Muslim is blessed. The universe is a complex of such interrelationships.

Figure 2

Living Things in Balance in Popular Islam and their Effect on One Another

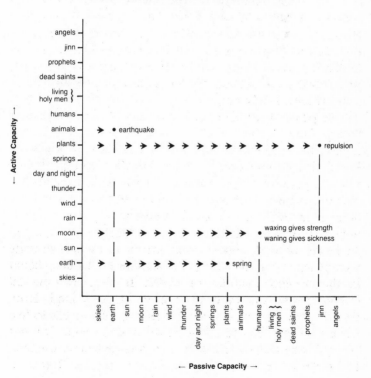

'Living things' in the folk-Islamic universe operate in an active and passive give and take, altering one another. Involved are the planets, the seasons, the plant, animal and human worlds, and the inhabitants of the supernatural world. Events, normal or abnormal, find their true interpretation in the context of this interaction of living things. Man's own existence finds meaning in the midst of such a universe replete with active and passive potentials.

A few examples of those interrelationships are given in Figure 2. Animals may be seen as affecting the earth. For example, it is the bull which causes earthquakes by tossing the earth from one horn to another. (In some parts of the Muslim world, the bull is replaced by a water buffalo.) Equally, the earth may be seen as having effect on trees and plants. For example, the earth wakes from its winter sleep and begins to breathe, thus bringing life to trees and plants growing on its surface. They live again because the earth lives. Plants, in their turn, may have an effect on malevolent jinn. The most significant example is probably that of rue, which is guaranteed to drive away such tormentors of human beings.

Divination provides a major key for finding which of many possibilities may have caused the current circumstances in a Muslim's life. Divination may also indicate remedies, and more generally direct a person's life, so that it is lived in as great as possible harmony with the larger world of the ordinary Muslim. The Turkish banker, Orhan, may view himself as only superficially Muslim in a formal, religious sense. But his commitment to this underlying, complex view of the world is expressed by his confidence in and dependence upon the appeal to divination for finding direction. In his business decisions, Orhan's questions concern which pathway will best 'fit' the universe of which he sees himself to be a part. Orhan's questions also concern which actions will bring him most peace of mind and financial security.

Biblical man and his world

Divination—in the sense of appealing to mediums, and through them to some supposed, causative world beyond—is strongly condemned in both Old and New Testaments. The Bible specifically warns against such appeal as being unalterably opposed by God.

However, this kind of universe in which the ordinary Muslim perceives himself to be living is not so foreign to Scripture. The biblical portrayal is clearly far removed from a closed, mechanistic view: the heavens declare the glory of God; if children didn't sing hosannas to the Son of David, the stones would; donkeys respond to angels; a fish can co-operate in disciplining a renegade prophet; people of faith and generosity host angels unawares; angels and archangels fight in the heavens with spirit beings who claim some authority over the nations of Persia and Greece; the prayers of the saints share in unleashing supernatural occurrences (Revelation 5:8); Jesus' death on a cross leads to a mass return to life of holy people who have died and been buried nearby, and many in Jerusalem are surprised to see them raised to life (Matthew 27:52–53); a curtain in the Temple is torn in two by the same event.

Furthermore, the involvement of the Creator with his creation argues against man's usurping of his authority behind his back. Man is given liberty to subdue, but not to subjugate, the world. He is only a tenant. He remains accountable to the Creator. Obedience or disobedience have huge repercussions for the whole of creation. Sin adversely affects man's relationship with everyone and everything, including God, fellow-man, angels (Genesis 6:1–4) and nature. Groaning and travail become the lot of nature and the human race until a new creation will replace the marred version. Blood cries out to God from the ground. For the people of Israel, their happy and fruitful dwelling in the land of promise is conditional upon their behaviour towards

Yahweh. To neglect fellowship with him will result in lions prowling the territory, blight eating the crops, war and defeat decimating the nation. King David sins against Uriah the Hittite, an alien. As a result, his baby by Bathsheba dies. Obedience to Yahweh, in contrast, will issue in fruitfulness in both personal and national life, in agricultural and military activities. Elijah's personal obedience sees ravens bringing him food, and rain ceasing or starting at his word. The people's repentance and intercession during the period of the judges leads to deliverance from perennial enemies.

The created world is living and vibrant. It participates in the ills of man's disobedience. It benefits from man's obedience towards God and longs with him for the final transformation of all things created. Within this world, the Creator provides various means for promoting and maintaining a healthy relationship with the people made in his own image.

In the Old Testament it was especially through the prophets that the people of Israel were to remain in touch with Yahweh. The prophetic voice spoke of how the people were to live in a way that pleased their God, best satisfied them as his people, and would produce the most beneficial circumstances in their lives. Similarly, within the New Testament, the Holy Spirit reveals himself as the Lord of the harvest, the one who brings forth fruitfulness from Jesus' death. He blows where he wills. He fills the children of God to overflowing, giving direction and security to their lives.

In both Old and New Testaments, individuals and groups outside the people of God reach towards the living God. The Bible reveals a consistency in the manner in which the Creator responds to such seeking of him. A person such as Naaman the Syrian comes to a healing experience at the hands of the prophet Elisha. In terms of Naaman's subsequent relating to Yahweh, a very inadequate state of affairs is accepted, at least for the time being:

...may the Lord forgive your servant for this one thing: When my master enters the temple of Rimmon to bow down and he is leaning on my arm and I bow there also—when I bow down in the temple of Rimmon, may the Lord forgive your servant for this (2 Kings 5:17–19).

Yahweh is willing for some accommodation in the beginnings of a relationship with a Syrian. The intention of the officer is accepted even if the expression of his worship is for the moment immature.

In the New Testament, magi who had seen a star in the East came to worship the new king of the Jews. Astrology was their initial introduction to the Lord of creation. In the grace of God, such motivation for the long journeying to Bethlehem is accepted and turned into a picture of the search for Christ by the gentile world. Elsewhere the fuller good news is preached to those who 'worship' a God not yet known to them. A godfearer's alms and prayers move the Creator to unveil to him the possibilities of complete relationship through Christ. It took several years of Paul's witness in Ephesus before the believers (not the unbelievers, Acts 19:18) learned, from the Holy Spirit, that occult attempts to direct their lives in the complex universe in which they participated were not acceptable. That realisation came about as a result of Paul's ministry, when an alternative dynamic at work within the Ephesians' experience took seriously the reality of possessing spirits.

What then of ordinary Muslims who try to unravel 'the future'? What of the varieties of search for stability and meaning in life that arise from ordinary Muslims' perceptions of their own needs? What of the intentions of those for whom life is played out on a vast stage with many actors?

Figure 3 illustrates ways in which such ordinary Muslims seek answers for their needs in the context of their universe and worldview. Divination features as one of the courses of action pursued in their quest for equilibrium. The diagram

Figure 3
Felt Needs in Popular Islam

Felt Needs in Popular Islam	Popular-level Answers to Felt Needs More Animistic ➤ ➤ Less Animistic			Spiritual Crisis	Felt Needs Met by Jesus Christ
fear of the unknown	idolatry, stone worship	fetishes, talismans, charms	superstition		security in Christ as keeper, guide
fear of evil spirits	witchcraft	amulets, knots	exorcism		exorcism by Christ; power over spirits
powerlessness before power of shaman	sorcery	prophylaxes	prophylaxes		protection from attack; offensive weapon for spiritual warfare
fear of the future	angel worship	divination, spells	fatalism, fanaticism		trust in Christ as Lord of the future
shame of not being in the in-group	curse	hair/nail trimmings		POWER ENCOUNTER WITH JESUS CHRIST	acceptance in the fellowship of believers
disequilibrium	magic	divination			restoration and answered prayer
sickness	tree/saint worship	healing magic			divine healing in Christ's power
helplessness in crisis	magic	vows	intercession of saint		Christ answering prayer directly
meaninglessness of life		turning to spirit world			purpose in life as God's child; using gifts, abilities
vulnerability of women	occult influence	*zâr*-type ceremony	practices at birth, etc		security in Christ; influence as prayer warriors

suggests that there are some elements in such seeking which may be more or less animistic. Perhaps there are some levels of answer to need that would not necessarily be the immediate focus of encounter in a turning to Christ; perhaps, by contrast, there are some other levels which would provide the very focus of such encounter. That there needs to occur some crisis of meeting with the living Christ is suggested as essential. (We shall return to this suggestion in Chapter Sixteen.) Briefly proposed also are some ways in which satisfying answers might address the needs of ordinary Muslims. Those answers are focused in a relationship with Christ as Lord of the universe in which they perceive themselves to be living. We do not deny the universe itself; rather, what we propose concerns the witness that best communicates the gospel to such people. In terms of the specific issue of divination, for example, the following question needs to be asked: Is there a biblical alternative to divination being demonstrated among ordinary Muslims which acknowledges the complexities of their world, but which operates in it in holy power?

CHAPTER FIVE

THE DRAMA OF DEVOTION

Music and magic

THE SISTERS WIJDAN AND HIND paused by the spice stall to listen more carefully to the anecdote bursting, in staccato phrases, from the overloaded public address system.

The midwife was called to Mullah Nasrudin's wife. She hurried into the house, went into the bedroom, and soon afterwards, as night was falling, put her head around the door to command the anxious Mullah to 'bring a candle at once.'

Nasrudin took her a lighted candle.

In a very few minutes the midwife called out: 'It's a boy!'

Nasrudin was delighted. Five minutes later, to his surprise came the cry: 'Mullah, another boy!'

'Excellent!' shouted the Mullah.

A few minutes afterwards, the voice of the midwife came again: 'Now a girl, Nasrudin!'

Mullah Nasrudin rushed into the room and blew out the candle.

'Why on earth are you doing that?'

'Midwife, surely the candle has done its duty—and now it doesn't know where to stop!'[4]

Wijdan and Hind laughed together at the outrageous tale and moved on in the press of people around the perimeter of the square. The next story, of Nasrudin and the rusty coin, was lost to them as other sights and sounds clamoured for their attention.

The sisters loved this festival. Hind had begged their father to let her go this year with Wijdan, in their eldest brother's taxi, instead of having to stay close to her parents. Her father had relented. Earlier that evening, Wijdan and Hind, and a carload of cousins from Jebel Ḥusayn, had crammed into the ageing Peugeot and freewheeled down towards the city centre. The hub of Amman during *Mawlid al-Nabî* was transformed. No vehicles were allowed—only the police and army, and the occasional Red Crescent ambulance. Abu Bakr al-Ṣadiq Street was a sea of happy Jordanians joking, singing, shouting quick commands to straying toddlers, all moving wavelike towards the Ḥusayn Mosque. The crush of people eddied around the courtyards of the mosque and overflowed into the Boukari market nearby. Brightly dressed families bustled through the gold bazaar behind King Faisal Street. Other human streams came and went along Ḥusayn, al-Hashimi and Zaid bin Horitha streets. Aromas of coffee, spices and roasting chicken wafted along on the warm air. Wijdan and Hind couldn't wait to join the lively crowd.

Holding hands tightly, the young ladies squirmed their way around the edge of the courtyard of the Ḥusayn Mosque. Makeshift stalls and overflowing shops decorated the edges of the square. The swift sweep of an arm caught their attention. A proprietor was perched on a high stool at the open entrance to his small restaurant. In the dim interior, beyond those eating beans and bread, a rather mediocre belly dancer entertained the diners as a fat, breathless clarinetist mimicked a popular folktune. The proprietor was wielding a switch with which he kept the crowd moving past his little treasure trove. No one was going to enjoy his entertainment without sitting down and ordering at least one cup of sweet tea.

The girls squeezed past between good-humoured strokes of the cane. Next door, vying with the belly dancer and the clarinetist, was a man selling potions. This clever Palestinian had constructed a little public address system of his own, through which he yelled at the passing throng. '...head-aches! Three times daily for one week, and you will never have another headache, by the Prophet!'

An old woman paused at the stall, eyes wandering to an assortment of bottles, all different sizes, with makeshift stoppers of coloured cloth.

'Zamzam water, mother. Healing unction from the holiest place on earth!'

Then the salesman's quick eye caught sight of Wijdan and Hind pushing past, pretending not to notice his wares. 'Love potion of the strongest kind! This will turn the heart of any wealthy young man! If God wills, in a year you will be married!'

The girls blushed beneath their protective veils and hurried on.

'Did you see his eyes, Wijdan? Big and blue, and you couldn't see to the end of them!'

'Yes! He must be a seer from out of town. Did you catch his accent? Oh! Look at those chickens! They're trying to escape!' Wijdan pushed her sister on, round the stalls, quickly changing the subject. She hoped that Hind hadn't noticed her involuntary start at the mention of a love potion.

Why did the stall owner mention that just then—just as they were passing? He must truly be a fortune-teller! Perhaps he even knew the secret thoughts that had been troubling her for the last year or so. She didn't want to marry her cousin, her father's brother's eldest boy. Instead she had fallen in love with a wealthy student from Zarqa, who studied in the law faculty at the university. A whole year had sped by, and the Zarqan hadn't noticed her. She had tried everything permissible, for a veiled young lady, to attract his attention. Now it looked as if he would go his way and she would be left for her cousin to marry...unless the strong love potion from the Palestinian could help?

She pushed the thoughts to the back of her mind as she scrambled after her sister, past trays of plastic sandals, combs and earrings. They slowed at a large display of beautifully inscribed Qur'âns, many presented in cleverly inlaid Damascus boxes. They continued round the circuit past a weight-lifting contest.

'Hind, don't stare!' Wijdan dragged her thirteen-year-old sister away from the sight of muscular army recruits, competing for the strong man prize. They almost fell into their parents' arms by the colourful stall of an old woman.

'Peace be with you, Father. Peace be with you, Mother.'

'Hello, daughters of mine. What a wonderful evening.'

A voice reached them across the collection of blue ceramic beads at their feet. It was the stall owner. 'Protect yourself against the eye!' she croaked through toothless gums. 'For your daughters, sir, buy this seal of the Seven Covenants of Suleiman. Protect them now against Umm al-Ṣubyân so that they may keep their husbands happy with children, and so keep their husbands!' A wise smile creased her chapped face. The girls' father thanked her, blessed her, and gave her a small note, but took nothing.

'Have you girls noticed,' he asked, turning from the seller of amulets, 'that the *Burda* is now being chanted?'

Through the noisy public address system, the tales of Nasrudin had given way to a more solemn story. The girls knew part of it by heart. Everyone loved al-Bûṣîrî's Mantle poem, especially tonight.

Wijdan thought to herself, 'Didn't that poem celebrate a miraculous change in a man's fortunes? Maybe there's hope for my heart's desire yet!'

The tradition ran that al-Bûṣîrî was partially paralysed and lived in much distress. One night, in a dream, the Prophet

Muhammad appeared to him and covered him with his striped mantle. When al-Bûṣîrî awoke in the morning, he found that his paralysis had completely disappeared. In gratitude for his miraculous cure, al-Bûṣîrî composed his poem, 'The Mantle', in honour of the Prophet.

'If a dream worked for al-Bûṣîrî, why not a love potion for me? Perhaps I could get Basma to slip it into his coffee. He wouldn't notice a thing....'

Her musings blanked out the sharp context of the poet's famous words. In her daydream, Wijdan applied to the long-desired Zarqan the song of praise to Muhammad.

> ...Cloaked is he in beauty marked by a joyful countenance.
> Like a flower in delicate freshness; like the full moon in
>   splendour,
>   Like the sea in bountifulness, and like time in aspiration.
> Even when he is alone in his majesty, it is as though
>   He were in the midst of soldiers, with attendants thrown
>   around him.
> It is as though a pearl hidden in an oyster were
>   In the two mines of his speech and his smile.
> No perfume can equal the dust that has gathered on his
>   limbs....[5]

As they listened to the chant, each thinking his own thoughts, Wijdan's father managed to steer his three charges closer to the raised platform in the centre of the square. Here took place that part of the *Mawlid* celebration which he most enjoyed. The green and gold costumes of the dancers shimmered and flashed in the hot spotlights as they whirled, accentuating the chant filling the air.

'...-*Ḥayy! Allah al-Ḥayy! Allah al-Ḥayy!*...'

Each chanted cry was followed by a rolling wave of deep breathing: monotonous, exciting, hypnotic. Wijdan's father soon felt himself gliding, losing control, at the edge of ecstasy, as he joined by proxy in the revolving, gentle merry-

go-round of the entranced Sufis. 'Oh God, this is too wonderful. O God, God, God!'

Wijdan noticed her father's trance. With a quick word to
her mother and sister, she excused herself. The woman's
room was on the other side of the square, behind the
females' entrance to the mosque. That was where she
headed at first. Then, as soon as she felt herself camouflaged
by the pressing crowd, Wijdan doubled back. She pushed
past the weight-lifters, the blue beads, the trinkets, to a stall
run by a Palestinian with big blue eyes. There was something
there she wanted to buy.

Muslim festivals

Festivals constitute public affirmations of commitment to
Islam. By and large, they are joyful and noisy. They come
round, year by year, like the Christians' Christmas and
Easter. In them, the story of the faith's life and meaning is
told and retold.

At the same time, the festivals provide other opportunities for satisfaction. During the festivals of Islam, alternative views of life and meaning come to the surface.
Muslims like Wijdan and her father are able to indulge in
less formal aspects of their religious inheritance during these
annual events. The celebrations provide opportunity for
commerce in more folk-Islamic interpretations of life.

The major festivals of the Muslim calendar are summarised in Figure 4. The months of the year are given and
represent a lunar year. Both Sunnî and Shîᶜah festivals are
listed, with their most common titles. As may be seen, many
festivals are common to both major sects. Significant festivals, especially during the month of Safar, belong only to
the Shîᶜah sect.

Three major festivals are celebrated by all Muslims,
although the strictly orthodox would claim that only two are
legitimate. In their view, *Mawlid al-Nabî* is really an optional

Figure 4[6]
Major Muslim Festivals

Month/Day	Name of Festival	Sunnî	Shî'ah
Muḥarram 1 1–10	*Muḥarram*	time for alms	commemoration of Hussein
10	*'Ashûrâ'*	voluntary fast for two days	Hussein's martyrdom at Karbalâ'
Safar 10 or 21	*Chihlam*		end of commemoration of Hussein's death
24	*'îd al-'Umar*		anniversary of 'Umar's death
27	*Char Shamba Suri*		feast to ward off misfortunes
29	*Qatli*		commemoration of Hassan's death
Rabî'al-Awwal 12	*Mawlid al-Nabî (Bâŕa Wafât)*	Muhammad's birthday	
17	*'Îd al-Mawlid*		Hussein's birthday
Rabî'al-Thânî			
Jumâdâ al-Ûlâ			
Jumâdâ al-Âkhira			
Rajab 13	*'Îd Milâd al-Hadrat 'Alî*		Ali's birthday
27	*Laylat al-Isrâ' wa 'l-Mi'âj*	Night journey/ascension	
Sha'bân 14	*Laylat al-Barâ'a*	Night of liberation	

Ramaḍân all	*Ramaḍân*	Month-long fast
21		Ali's martyrdom
27	*Laylat al-Qadr*	Night of destiny
Shawwâl 1	*ᶜÎd al-Fiṭr*	Feast of fast-breaking
2–7		voluntary fast
Dhû'l-Qaᶜda		
Dhû'l-Ḥijja 1-5	*Al-Ḥijja*	Pilgrimage to Mecca
10	*ᶜÎd al-Aḍha*	Feast of sacrifice
18	*Ghadîr Khumm*	Ali's investiture

extra. The prescribed festivals are those of *ᶜÎd al-Fiṭr* (the Feast of the Fast-breaking) and *al-ᶜÎd al-Kabîr* (the Great Feast).

The festival of the breaking of the fast, *ᶜîd al-Fiṭr*, known also as *ᶜîd al-Ṣadaqa* (the Feast of Alms) and *al-ᶜîd al-Ṣaghîr* (the Minor Feast), occurs at the end of the month-long fast of *Ramaḍân*. It is celebrated on the first of Shawwâl, the tenth month of the Islamic year. The festival is largely a family affair, and homes are brightly decorated and painted. Gifts are bought, and *ᶜîd* cards (equivalent to Christmas cards) are sent to relatives, neighbours and friends. The departed kin are kept as much in view as the living. While the men go to the mosque on the first morning for *ᶜîd* prayers, the women often go to the cemeteries with sweets, fruit, water and flowers. Many men join their families at the cemeteries, and special Qur'ân recitations are made over the graves of deceased relatives. Later there is feasting while story-tellers, jugglers, dancers and singers entertain. In some homes, people burn incense as a precaution at *ᶜîd* time against the intervention of malevolent spirits.

The Great Feast, *al-ᶜîd al-Kabîr*, known also as *ᶜîd al-Ḥajj* (the Feast of the Pilgrimage) and *ᶜîd al-Aḍha* (the Feast of the Sacrifice), is celebrated two months and nine days after ᶜîd al-Fiṭr, on the ninth and tenth of Dhû'l-Ḥijja, the last month of the year. The festival takes place on the day following the Meccan pilgrims' visit to the Plain of Arafat. The sacrificing of animals around the Muslim world thus coincides with the sacrifices being made in the Valley of Minâ. Muslims believe that great merit goes to those who keep this feast. A well-known *ḥadîth* from ᶜÂ'isha states that Muhammad declared:

> Man hath not done anything, on the day of sacrifice, more pleasing to God than spilling blood: I mean sacrifice: for verily the animal sacrificed will come, on the day of resurrection, with its horns, its hair, its hoofs, and will make the scales of his [good] actions heavy....[7]

In many Muslim communities, the Great Feast also commences with congregational prayers for men at the local mosque, and visits to the cemetery to read the *Fâtiḥa* and pray in memory of deceased relatives and friends.

The Prophet's birthday, *Mawlid al-Nabî*, is celebrated on the twelfth of Rabîᶜ al-Awwal, the third month of the Islamic year. In the morning of that day in AD 570, Muhammad was born. By coincidence, it was also on that day that he died some sixty-three years later. For Muslims, the birth of the Prophet is one of the most important events in the history of the world. In many places, the whole of the month of Rabîᶜ al-Awwal is celebrated by groups of believers gathering together to remember him.

Believers chant various paeans of praise, extolling the virtues of the Prophet Muhammad. Those chants may be by individuals or by whole groups. On the actual evening of *Mawlid al-Nabî*—for the 'day' begins at dusk—such songs of praise are piped over public address systems to congregating crowds of celebrants. Al-Bûṣîrî's Mantle poem is one of the most popular recitations in the Arab world. In Turkey, a common recitation for the *Mawlid* is Süleyman Chelebi's

Mevlidi Sherif. The following lines illustrate its tone. Three angelic beings are greeting Muhammad's mother, Amina, as she is about to give birth to the Prophet. They extol the qualities of the coming babe in extravagant words:

> Sultan is he, all hidden truth possessing,
> Full knowledge of the Unity professing.
> For love of him, thy son [Amina], the skies are turning;
> Mankind and angels for his face are yearning.
> This is the night foretold in song and story,
> In which the worlds rejoice to see his glory.[8]

In India, al-Barzanji's *Iqd al-Jawâhir* is well loved. In Nigeria, the long poem, *Ishrîniya* by al-Fazzazi, is often recited. In all such recitations, the inspiring story of Muhammad's life, mission, character, sufferings and success are told.

Processions frequently take place, too, with singing through the streets. Sufi orders may lead public dances in honour of the Prophet. Everyone taking part in the *Mawlid* gatherings calls out praises and asks God's blessings on Muhammad. They buy and wear new clothes and eat special sweets. Villages and towns vie with one another to put on the most spectacular *Mawlid* entertainments.

Other festivals have joined *Mawlid al-Nabî* as extra members of the cyclical, reinforcing rites that give so much consistency and meaning to existence. They also provide occasions for the expression of other folk-Islamic views of life. Amulets are offered for sale; fortune-tellers do brisk business; magic potions may be purchased; trance dances authorise participation in Sufi-type worship; veneration of prophets and saints is encouraged. Thus the folklore which validates the folk-Islamic worldview is reiterated alongside Qur'ân readings.

Muḥarram, the New Year's festival at the beginning of the first month of the year, is widely celebrated with joy. The tenth of that month, *cÂshûrâ'*, is made famous by the *hadîth* literature. It marks the day when rain first fell, when Adam and Eve were created, and when the divine mission was given to the spirits of ten thousand prophets. It is a significant day in the unseen realm. All over the contemporary Muslim world, *cÂshûrâ'* is held in esteem as the 'day of the guarded tablet' when the decrees of God are written, or the 'day of the pen' when such decrees are transcribed in the books of fate. Many Muslims therefore stay awake in prayer all through the night in order to gain a favourable inscription.

cÂshûrâ' has a different complexion for Shî*c*ah Muslims. The first ten days of the month of Muḥarram are impregnated with a sense of mourning. The details of the last hours of Hussein—son of Ali and grandson of Muhammad, who was murdered at Karbalâ' on the tenth of the month—are recalled in detail. The *rawḍah-khânî*, celebrated on that tenth day, comprises a combination of sermon, poem recitation, Qur'ân reading and drama which together depict the tragic ending to Hussein's life. The *rawḍah* often culminates in a passion play portraying the actual martyrdom. In many situations, the celebration includes a procession, sometimes featuring the carrying of a *ta*c*zîya* or model of Hussein's tomb around the neighbourhood. The procession moves slowly while participants act out rites of mourning. They may wail '*Yâ* Hassan! *Yâ* Hussein!' Some may cut themselves with swords or razors, or indulge in other forms of real or mock self-flagellation.

In India and Pakistan, emphasis is placed on a saint's 'deathday', or day of union with God, rather than on his birthday. So the day celebrated elsewhere as *Mawlid al-Nabî* is remembered there as *Bâra Wafât* (literally 'death on the twelfth' of the month).

*Laylat al-Mi*c*râj*, the night of the Prophet's ascent into heavenly places, is celebrated on the twenty-seventh of Rajab. It is viewed as a time of special mercy. With it is associated the unveiling of the seven heavens with their occupants, and the potential for prophets and angels being accessible to help frail mortals.

The *Nisfu Sha^cbân* festival, celebrated by Malay Muslims in the middle of the month of Sha^cbân, marks the night when souls of the dead come and visit the houses of their living relatives. Known as *Laylat al-Barâ'a* in Arabic, it indicates the time when the Tree of Life in heaven is shaken. The names of those destined to die within the year are written on the leaves that fall to the ground. In some communities, the festival proclaims the night when God comes down to the lowest heaven to call out to men in order to forgive them their sins. Whichever interpretation is followed, those participating in this festival fervently offer prayer and petition.

Laylat al-Qadr falls on the twenty-seventh night of Ramaḍân. Alluded to in the Qur'ân as being the night of the 'descent' of that revelation, *Laylat al-Qadr* is thought to bring innumerable blessings in its wake. One common belief is that angels shower down from heaven the peace and blessings of God on all who remain awake during this night of power.

Many festivals take place around the *mawlids* of local saints. They provide opportunities for vow-making, *baraka* collection and other practices by participating Muslims. Various tribal or community festivals celebrate spring or harvest, or renewal of life, and seem to act more as fertility rites than as expressions of an Islamic conviction.

Witness in devotion?

The Old Testament people of God learned to express their relatedness to God, on a national level, in the context of festival devotion. The weekly 'Sabbath of rest, a day of sacred assembly' (Leviticus 23:3) was to reflect among human beings the pattern of activity and rest belonging to their Creator: six days of work succeeded by one day of rest.

The intention was not merely negative, however. It was to be a day 'to the Lord' in which Yahweh's centrality, as redeemer of the people from Egypt, was celebrated (Deuteronomy 5:15). The Old Testament Sabbath was far removed from the later Islamic concept of *yawm al jumᶜa* (Friday) when, once prayers have been said, business may resume. The Sabbath was primarily to be a feast day, focused on the Lord.

Apart from the recurring Sabbath, six major feasts were defined for the Israelites at which offerings were to be brought to the Lord and in which different aspects of Yahweh's relationship with them were to be remembered. On the Feast of Passover and Unleavened Bread, the people were to recall their deliverance from bondage and Yahweh's mercy towards them in bringing them out of Egypt. In the Feast of Firstfruits, the people acknowledged that the land of which they were currently tenants was the Lord's land. The Feast of Weeks expressed dependence on the Lord for the new grain on which the people were to thrive. The Feast of Trumpets, the Day of Atonement and Tabernacles in the seventh month revolved around the people's confession of sin; in them were enacted the people's need of expiation and forgiveness.

The Old Testament insists that such festival devotion only has validity if it expresses a continuing relationship with the living God. Going through the motions as part of a hypocritical religious tradition is unacceptable. Through some of the later prophets, Yahweh shouted his opposition to the very festivals he had inaugurated:

> I hate, I despise your religious feasts;
>   I cannot stand your assemblies.
> Even though you bring me burnt offerings and grain offerings,
>   I will not accept them.
> Though you bring choice fellowship offerings,
>   I will have no regard for them (Amos 5:21–22).

The festivals were to be part of a cycle of ritual, expressing relationship between Yahweh and his people. When those people lost their relatedness to God, the rituals became farcical, meaningless and even sinful.

The church emerging in the New Testament certainly knew some ritual festivals. At first modelled on synagogue worship, but increasingly establishing meaningful Christian ritual in pagan contexts, the New Testament celebration most evident was the Lord's Day worship.

The four Gospel writers recorded that Jesus was crucified on a Friday and rose again from the dead on the first day of the week. Consequently, the community of believers felt it important to gather for worship on the first day of every week (Acts 20:7). The aged John on Patmos distinguished the Lord's Day from other days in his imprisonment there. For a while, then, a dual situation existed. The Jewish Christian churches maintained an observance of the Torah and the Sabbath, while the gentile Christian churches ignored the Sabbath commandment, considering it to be no longer binding. Their case for dropping the Sabbath celebration was argued by Paul himself (Galatians 4:8–10), and eventually the Christian community parted—on a large scale—from the synagogue on this very question.

Worship on the Lord's Day focused in unity and joy on the resurrection of Jesus Christ. It sometimes involved a love feast, as well as a sharing of bread and cup in remembrance of Jesus' death (1 Corinthians 11:33–34).

Early on, the apostles invested some of the traditional Jewish feasts with new meaning. With the Lord's Day worship, those feasts became important markers in their round of devotions. The Feasts of Passover and Pentecost especially came to be given new significance as memorials of the death of Jesus and the giving of the Holy Spirit.

As the gospel message was carried with power among the pagans, Christian rites widely replaced pre-Christian rites. This process was enhanced with the fourth-century authorisation of Christianity as the religion of the empire. Unfortunately, that authorisation also opened the way for pagan meanings and functions to infiltrate faith and become part of the official devotional rituals of Christendom.

An equivalent adulteration has perhaps affected the development of the Islamic faith. Beliefs and practices coming to the surface of Muslim devotion at festival times betray a rift between the faith as it is ideally expressed and the everyday religious allegiances of its adherents. Naturally, it is with the immediate needs of their everyday lives that many Muslims are concerned, and festivals provide opportunities for seeking answers to those needs.

One comment concerning contemporary Orthodox Christian witness among Muslim neighbours may be pertinent here. The annual festival in which Middle-Eastern Christians invest the most significance is not the December or January Christmas rite, but Holy Week. For them, Palm Sunday, Maundy Thursday, Good Friday, Holy Saturday and Easter Sunday are the peak of the yearly cycle. In some situations, it is those days which command a holiday for Christians, even in majority Muslim societies. The concentration upon risen life, linked often to a church lectionary that proceeds through a martyrs' year, points to a relationship with God which looks at neither special birth nor special death as the last word, but at *resurrection*. In renewed festival devotion, centred on a living Christ, there exists a channel for exciting witness to those who affirm, in their own religious festivals, their need of powerful help in life.

By contrast, Western Christianity's concentration upon Christmas as the major religious festival of the year (significant though the actual Incarnation was) has tended to minimise the distinctiveness of that festival's witness to Muslims. The Western celebration of Christmas is so largely compromised by the incorporation of many irrelevant pagan elements that the wonder of the Incarnation is all but lost. Are Western missionaries to Muslims willing to forego many of the traditional embellishments of their Christmas celebration in an agreement with their Eastern brothers and sisters that 'resurrection' must become the last word?

Where Easter and Pentecost find dynamic expression in everyday community living, there is found a possibility of introducing ordinary, needy Muslims to the divine subject of Easter and Pentecost. Christ the risen King, giver of the Spirit, is the Lord who is present in his people. Festival devotion which celebrates such presence holds forth a message of hope in its own very rejoicing.

CHAPTER SIX

A HEALING TOUCH

Ismet finds his legs

A SHOUT CAME FROM the bedroom, 'Mummy, Mummy, come quickly!'

Hoda was used to sudden alarms, but something in the tone of her daughter's cry raised a whisper of hope in her sensitive spirit. She pushed the pan of heating oil on to the unlit burner at the back of the stove and hurried out of the kitchen. A confusion of thoughts raced through her mind as she ran down the corridor to the bedroom door.

She turned into the room. Her daughter was pointing to the floor beside the large, family bed.

'Mummy, look! Look at Ismet! He's been pulling himself up by the bedding!'

Hoda could hardly believe her eyes. A rather wobbly little individual, with a big grin on his face, was clinging tightly to the sheet-and-blanket combination of the room's double bed, swaying to and fro. He was obviously very pleased with his achievement, although completely exhausted by the effort.

'Oh, Ismet!' cried his mother, scooping the frail little boy into her arms, and collapsing on the edge of the bed. Tears streaked her cheeks. 'Oh, Ismet! At last! I don't believe it!'

Later that week, Hoda and her husband made the familiar journey down-town to the office blocks where the Cairo doctors hold their private clinics. The consultant in Ismet's complex case couldn't believe his eyes either. 'Praise to God! This is unbelievable!' He examined the young lad in detail.

Ismet's reflexes were normal although, of course, very weak from the long illness. The muscle atrophy was somehow quite significantly reversed; his two spindly legs, which had seemed matchlike in fragility, were learning to support his body, even to kick. The consultant arranged for a course of physiotherapy at a colleague's clinic. What had happened to bring about this remarkable change in a six-year-old paralytic he did not understand. Nor did the boy's father.

But Hoda did.

As they travelled home by taxi, Hoda reflected on her life as mother to young Ismet. She had married a wonderful man. The two families were related, and there was a tradition of close, mutual support and trust between them. Her husband had worked in the government's manpower commission during office hours, and then at different jobs in the evenings. He was the sort of man who would try anything and succeed at most things. They had settled happily into a little flat in one of Cairo's crowded but relatively new quarters, not far from her husband's daytime office. There, their lives had been blessed with two lovely babies, a girl and a boy.

When the boy was around one year old a few hesitant questions began to nag at Hoda's mind. While her friends talked of their children beginning to stand unaided, and even taking some hesitant steps, she noticed that Ismet preferred to stay horizontal. He managed very well and very quickly, with a combination of a sideways roll and a forwards jerk.

Maybe speed was favoured over the hazards of attempting movement in an upright position.

By the time Ismet was eighteen months old, Hoda was becoming frantic. She worried that his feet always seemed to fall away to the sides, and there was still no sign of the child wanting to stand or even sit up. She talked about it with her mother-in-law. It was eventually agreed that Ismet should be taken to a doctor.

That moment began a way of life that remained theirs for four years. They made visits to the doctor, then to consultants, then to this or that hospital for tests. The child had to be carried everywhere. Someone needed to look after his older sister and see her settled in school. When Ismet was ill with measles, mumps or one of the nastier viruses that always seemed to latch on to him rather than anyone else in the family, there were sleepless nights and more frequent visits to clinics with the distressed infant. Hoda's husband was very understanding, and the whole family rallied round to give help, but the emotional and physical strain took its toll on them all.

In her darker moments, Hoda wondered if this was somehow her fault. Was there something she had done she shouldn't have done? Was there something she should have done she hadn't done? Why her child? Why her son? She had always prayed the *ṣalât*, the required prayers of Islam, at home, at least the noon and night prayers if not the other three. She had kept the fast of Ramaḍân every year, apart from when she had been pregnant. She wore the veil when she left the flat. She knew that her husband trusted her. Was this awful life going to go on for ever? Was Ismet going to get weaker and weaker before their eyes? Was there no hope?

It was her friend Samia who awakened her to 'hope' right on her doorstep.

'Hoda, have you been to ask St Thérèse to do something for Ismet?'

'You mean, go to that Christian church, Samia? I couldn't do that!'

'Many people do, Hoda. I mean believers, good Muslims like you and me. I know that St Thérèse helped my brother's wife's sister. She could not conceive, and in the end she went to the church one Easter feast and made a vow. Now they have four children! Very healthy children, I might add!'

'Well, Samia, I have heard that St Thérèse especially loves children.'

'Yes, that's right, Hoda! Oh, Hoda, let's go and ask her to help poor Ismet! I'll come with you.'

One Friday, while their husbands were at the mosque, Hoda and Samia crossed Shoubra on foot and found the Church of St Thérèse d'Avila. There was a spacious garden between the large church and the road, with a few trees giving some shade. Small groups of people were sitting on the darker patches of ground, resting in the cool morning. At the entrance to the church the women were surprised to see writing all over the outside walls. They were actually small plaques, all saying 'thank you' to St Thérèse for her assistance. There must have been more than a thousand of them, many of them written by Muslims. As they read some of the inscriptions, Hoda and Samia gained confidence for taking the next big step in their quest for Ismet's healing.

Muttering the *bismillâh'* under their breath, the two women entered the dark building. They immediately noticed a few other people inside. Some were obviously Muslims. They stepped further in. They were shocked. They knew that Christians worshipped idols, but there was no image at all in this place. The air was heavily scented with incense, and that comforted them. The perfume would keep evil spirits at bay. Over on the right, near the sanctuary of the church, must be the chapel of St Thérèse, for the shrine was a colourful mêlée of flowers. They made their way round the aisles towards that spot.

'Oh look, Hoda!' whispered Samia. Hoda stopped and turned, staring where her friend pointed. At the rear of the church, above the entrance, was a huge inscription in gold lettering on a green background, right across the width of the church.

'All this is from the goodness of the Lord,' she read.

'That is from the Qur'ân, Samia,' she whispered back. She was feeling a lot more comfortable. 'I'm sure it's right that we came here,' she added.

Samia nodded, and with growing excitement they made their way to the side chapel dedicated to St Thérèse. They watched as a widow, a Christian with a little cross tattooed on her right wrist, lit a candle and set it in the sand-box already sparkling with many little lights burning as prayer reminders to the saint. Hoda silently recited the *Fâtiha* and then prayed for Ismet. Her lips quivered with the emotion of the moment. Samia moved a half-step back.

The prayer over, the two women quietly slipped out of the peaceful place and compared notes. Hoda felt somehow lighter, somehow less burdened, as they weaved their way in and out of the Friday morning traffic, buying some fruit from a stall on the edge of their neighbourhood.

Several months had passed. Now, here they were, riding home from the consultant's office with an increasingly healthy Ismet. Praise be to God, and thanks to St Thérèse!

During the night after the wonderful discovery in the bedroom, Hoda dreamed vividly. She knew that it was the saint herself, though if you asked her how she could be so sure, she couldn't tell you. She just knew. St Thérèse appeared to her, shining white, so pure, and with such kind eyes. She asked Hoda to come and pay a little money as a vow fulfilment.

'Oh yes, of course!' Hoda had responded. 'I will come at the Christmas and Easter feasts as well, to honour you, dear saint! Thank you for healing my son!'

The complex world of sickness and causality

Sickness produces sudden and often serious instability in the life of an individual, family or community; the problem of sickness affects ordinary Muslims on a day-by-day basis. Their resolution especially concentrates on diagnosis and remedy: crisis rites aim at defining, explaining, and meeting these sudden needs. As they deal with them, skilled practitioners and their patients frequently engage in various folk-Islamic activities.

As we have seen in several other chapters, the cause of sickness is frequently discovered by divinatory means. In Uzbekistan, for example, a shaman is called in when serious illness or other misfortunes occur. He contacts his familiar spirit via a séance and discovers the true cause of the problem.

Healing may come at the practised hands of a 'wise woman' in Turkey, or a *pangu-ngubat* (medicine man) in the Philippines. Herbal medicine is widely used to combat sickness. Thus the *saḥḥâra* ('sorceress') of Morocco mixes a tiny black seed *(ḥubb al-rashîd)* with other spices, throws it on to a charcoal fire, and waves the resultant healing fumes over the patient. Where sickness is perceived to be the result of an attack by malevolent jinn, other rites are employed. Exorcism (*ᶜazîma*, 'incantation') is most often used when a person is struck by an unnamed *jinnî*, but when the attacking *jinnîya* is of a named variety, the establishment of a symbiotic relationship between a person and a possessing spirit is attempted. Exorcism cures are relatively simple, involving for example the placing of tar on the victim's orifices, bathing him in *baraka*-endowed water, or burning incense over him. By contrast, symbiotic cures are more elaborate, involving the incorporation of the patient into a continuing cult. (Chapter Seven explains such cures more fully.) Vow-making and visits to saints may well be associated with healing.

Muslims believe they must take care when visiting the sick or those near death, because of the presence there of other beings whose actions are influenced by the words of the visitor. Death is not mentioned (for example) lest that invite its premature occurrence. Rather, focus is made upon positive words, even if the sick person is actually dying. A *hadîth*, related by Umm Salamah, justifies such an attitude: 'When you are present with a sick person, or one near death, then supplicate a blessing for yourself and the sick, because the angels say amen to what you repeat and supplicate.'[9]

Because of their focus on diagnosis and remedy, crisis rites throw into the limelight the issue of causality. Some aspects of causal connections made in the minds of ordinary Muslims have been mentioned in previous chapters. Here, a fuller exposition is given.

Many sicknesses are seen as the result of natural causes. Various natural phenomena are believed to have positive effects. As a result, many explanations of natural causes tend to emphasise mechanistic connections. Syphilis may be caused by menstrual fluid, and gonorrhea by semen backing up into the kidneys, if a man is not careful to urinate after making love. Poisoning by one's enemies is a frequent explanation for wasting diseases. Such diagnoses are usually made by a medicine man or woman, often a herbalist, based on an examination of physical symptoms.

Some folk-Islamic communities make an analysis of foods on a hot and cold system. Remedies may simply be arranged by balancing hot with cold or vice versa. For example, an Iranian child may suffer from earache, eye ailments, or swollen glands in the neck. Such conditions are thought to be 'hot'. The remedy, therefore, consists in providing something extra 'cold' to counterbalance the overheating. Temperamental problems can also be analysed on a hot/cold basis. Thus *pîrs* in Pakistan are generally conceived of as 'cool' and are sought out in times of indisposition or 'heat'.

For this reason also, they often act as mediators in secular conflicts when disputants become too 'heated'.

For a few naturally caused illnesses, magical cures may be prescribed, as for example in Morocco, for warts, arthritis, rheumatism, sciatica and other problems.

The breaking of taboo is recognised as a potential cause of sickness in folk-Islamic thought. In Nigeria, Yoruba women and dogs suffer from their having visited, either wittingly or unwittingly, the shrine of Bilikisu Sungbo. This female saint tabooed the presence of women and dogs at the site of her burial before her death, and that taboo has been strictly adhered to ever since. Among the Bedouin of Sinai, some activities such as felling certain trees, or associating with ceremonially impure people or with animals with human traits, are taboo. Failure to observe taboos will reap serious illness for the person concerned.

Diagnosis is by case history. Has the patient or have the patients' neighbours or friends broken any taboos? Has someone, for example, mocked a pregnant woman, thus causing the birth of a squint-eyed child? Remedies lie in securing repentance, and often penance, in a way recognisable by the community. In the complex *mushâhara* customs of Egypt, sickness in a person who is in a state of sacred vulnerability is nearly always seen as the result of taboo-breaking, since taboos are aimed at protecting people from dangerous spirit beings who threaten fertility and life during the temporary states of vulnerability, especially those associated with childbirth.

The evil eye is recognised as a frequent cause of sickness, despite the many precautions taken to prevent its effect. Diagnosis is usually made by a mixture of case history and simple divination. Normally a remedy can be carried out by a practitioner such as the herbalist, medicine man or midwife.

Sorcery and black magic are seen as strong causes of illness or misfortune. They are qualitatively different from the evil eye. The evil eye operates in the realm of the ordinary. Witchcraft (*suḥûr*), by contrast, is usually seen as extraordinary in its working. In Sudan, sudden death or paralysis, or even unemployment, may be blamed on black magic or witchcraft. Among the Philippine Tausug and the Turkish Yürük, a sick person's soul may have been stolen by a human sorcerer. Diagnosis of this kind of cause is usually performed by a special practitioner who uses some form of divination. Exposure of the source often breaks the spell 'binding' the sick person, and the appropriation of a counter-spell of stronger nature will ensure freedom from the illness.

Certain named jinn, such as Al, Umm al-Ṣubyân and al-Karisi, are thought to cause specific diseases, or death, as has been earlier described. Unnamed, but ubiquitous, jinn are probably renowned as the greatest single cause of illness among human beings. Again, diagnosis is often made by divination or medium trance, and again, a special practitioner is required to produce a cure.

The spirit double of the human being (*qarîna*) is also thought to be responsible for some sicknesses. Among Egyptians, it is reckoned that if a woman has given birth to several children who have died in childbirth or soon after, the *qarîna* has killed them. Such a mother resorts to a female practitioner who performs the *muta'awwaqa* or 'cutting of the flower'. The aim is to bring bad luck on the *qarîna*, to break its monopoly on the woman's womb. Both husband and wife take part in this ceremony. In Iran, the *hamzad* or twin *jinnî*, born or created at the same moment as the individual, may be a believer or an infidel. If a person is constantly ill, or constitutionally frail, it is suspected that the *hamzad* is an infidel. Remedy can be found in charms written by *duᶜâ'* writers. Similarly, in the Philippines, sickness may be seen as the result of offending the *inikadowa* or twin-spirit of a person.

Fate is often blamed for sickness, especially where it leads to permanent disability or death. Among the Bedouin of Sinai, different words distinguish the degree of harm brought upon a victim. If death is not involved, fate is referred to as *nasîb*—literally, that which is 'set up' for one. Where death is involved, fate is referred to by the plural word *manâyâ*. *Manâyâ* carries the connotation of women who snare the doomed with rope.

The ultimate appeal in the question of causality is to God. It may be because of God's anger with sin, or it may be the result of his arbitrary will. In sickness, God is usually seen to be the ultimate cause when death is the outcome. In the case of fatal road accidents, lawsuits by relatives of victims may gradually be dropped because it is recognised that God willed the victim to die at such a time and in such a way.

A verse in the Qur'ân on causality is arresting: 'Every man's bird (of omen) have We fastened on his neck, and We shall bring forth to him on the resurrection-day a book which he will meet spread open' (sura 17:14). Several interpretations of this verse are possible. It could be taken to mean that the future of each person is dependent upon his own good or evil deeds—'on his own head be it'. It could mean that fate itself (*tâ'ir*, literally 'bird'), attached to an individual, is the driving force in his life. So a man's future is intricately linked with birds or omens or stars. This understanding of the verse leans on the fact that the Arab tribes of the seventh century used to read the mysteries of human fate from the flight of birds. Or again, the verse could mean that God himself is absolutely in control of each man's destiny. He alone decides, and applies, the fate of each individual.

Just as different interpretations of this Qur'ânic verse are possible, so a range of views are justified in the diagnosis and treatment of sicknesses. Each specific human problem could well be due to a combination of causes. If that possibility is admitted, then accurate and complete diagnosis is all the more important.

Figure 5 summarises something of the folk-Islamic view of causality in relation to sickness. Increasing seriousness of the illness is implied in the progression down the diagram, and

Figure 5

Causality and Sickness in Popular Islam

Cause	Diagnosis	Practitioner	Remedy
natural causes	physical symptoms	medicine man, herbalist	natural, charms
breaking taboo	case history	old woman	repentance, penance
evil eye	case history, divination	midwife, medicine man	breaking the 'look'
sorcery	divination	powerful magician	find source and counter it
jinn	divination, medium trance	magician	charms, no remedy?
qarîna	divination	magician	charms, no remedy?
fate	hindsight		no remedy
God	hindsight		no remedy

the manner of diagnosis most often used, the kind of practitioner usually involved, and the sort of remedy applied are all suggested. For the more extreme illnesses, including those ending in death, no remedy is available.

Sickness, then, is one of any number of crises ordinary Muslims have to face. Formal theology might emphasise the sovereignty of God, even in a sense which suggests determinism or fatalism. In practice, however, Muslims spend their days and nights—and hard-earned wages—trying to find ways and means of rewriting what is supposedly *maktûb* ('written').

Ordinary Muslims have a complex view of reality in which 'living things' interrelate in active and passive capacities. (See Figure 2, page 71.) A rigorous causal system tends to develop out of such a view of reality—one that is pragmatic and retroactive in its application. It makes sense of the varying kinds and extents of force affecting the ordinary Muslim in crisis. For example, if a sickness is diagnosed as being caused by jinn, a case history can usually be established in which, at some point, the victim put himself in the vicinity of such jinn. Muslim society is integrated by its beliefs about causal concepts; as we understand them, they enable us to glance beneath the surface and discover the assumptions by which Muslims are actually living.

Healed, restored and forgiven

The Bible is familiar with human crisis, sickness included. Moreover, the Bible also attributes sickness to a variety of causes. Among the people of Israel, disobedience towards Yahweh precipitated nationwide plagues on several occasions. Similarly, among early Christian believers, a failure to discern the Lord's body in the Communion celebrations brought mortal sickness. An apostle might hand someone over to Satan so that his body might somehow be broken (1 Corinthians 5:5). Or the Lord himself might put someone in Satan's hands to be smitten, hurt and stripped of family and health, not because of sinfulness, but because of his righteousness (Job 2:3,6). Daniel the prophet lay paralysed because of an encounter with an angel (Daniel 10:8). Ezekiel the prophet sat overwhelmed in soul and body because of an experience of the glory of the Lord (Ezekiel 3:15). The Gadarene demoniac exhibited suicidal tendencies, cutting himself with stones, because of his possession by evil spirits (Mark 5:2,5). A man who had been an invalid for nearly forty years was instantly healed at Jesus' word and was told to stop sinning, lest something worse happen to him (John 5:14). Congenital abnormalities leading to 'giants' may be the result of a wrong relationship between the human and angelic worlds (Genesis 6:2). King Saul was sick in mind because an evil spirit touched him, at the Lord's direction. Many Egyptian children and animals died because of a Pharaoh's commitment to gods other than Yahweh. A famous king of Israel contracted leprosy because he grew proud of his own importance.

According to the Bible, sickness, disease and tragedy may be caused by many different agents. They may result from a network of dynamics within and crossing the boundaries of the seen and unseen realms. The biblical picture of causality in sickness is in fact far removed from the typical Western view. For the Westerner, germs, bacteria, and other strictly empirical phenomena are responsible. Even where psychosomatic processes are admitted, treatment still proceeds on the assumption that the reasons for illness lie within the patient himself. It is his reaction to stress; it is a virus in his body. The Western emphasis subordinates the question 'why' to that of 'how', whereas the Bible all along majors on the question 'why', rather than on the physical or psychological details of 'how'.

In contrast to the folk-Islamic view, the emphasis of Scripture is also strongly ethical. The Creator, the Lord, is he to whom all creation is accountable either immediately or ultimately. Whoever or whatever is responsible for disease does not act independently or without prospect of judgement.

Our discussion of sickness has serious repercussions for medical missions, where those missions operate among ordinary Muslims. As far as such Muslims are concerned, the causes of sickness in a person's life are varied and interwoven. Within their view of the world, diagnosis is therefore of paramount importance. Do Western missionary doctors only conduct their diagnostic sessions in a rationalistic, 'scientific' manner, questioning the patient to establish a case history? Or do Western missionary doctors declare, in an overt manner, their dependence upon God for help in diagnosis? In the cultures of ordinary Muslims, the attraction of a seer, or *pîr*, or medicine man, lies in that person's ability to discover the cause of the problem intuitively. It is only lesser practitioners, the equivalents of 'quacks', who actually ask the patient for information. Are Christ's representatives communicating that they are truly in touch with the Lord of creation, as they claim with their lips, or do their medical practices unwittingly announce that they are only 'quacks'?

Similarly, what role do prayer, the laying on of hands, and public thanksgiving play in treatment? Is it acknowledged that Christ has been at work in and through the surgeon or pharmacist? And what of prayer for direct, divine healing in Jesus' powerful name? Just as I write these paragraphs, a report has come of a miraculous healing in answer to public prayer in Christ's name in a strongly Muslim country of the Middle East. Because a company director's daughter was healed in such a manner, many have believed in Jesus Christ.

Of course ordinary Muslims are happy to make use of antibiotics and cough mixtures, surgery and hospital care. But their doing so does not mean that they believe any less fervently in the power of the evil eye, jinn, or sorcery to cause sickness. Their goal is to apply whatever works to relieve the immediate problem. Consequently, an inability to include in medical missionary work an addressing of the whole problem—as ordinary Muslims see it—will lead to a credibility gap between the medical practices of the missionaries and the words they speak about the healing power of Jesus.

When Jesus Christ is presented as the powerful Lord over human sickness, an opposite pitfall to be avoided is that Jesus may be seen simply as a worker of stronger magic, as a greater saint. In the Islamic world, ordinary Muslims already make appeal to Jesus. Although Jesus is definitely seen as non-divine, certain characteristics cause him to stand out above other prophets. His remarkable birth, his role at judgement time, his special relation to Muhammad, his power over disease, death and nature, his angelic and spirit-like qualities, his ability to mediate with God, his superior relationship to Satan—all speak of a special person.

Without a full presentation of the truth of who Jesus Christ is, in moments of power encounter, Muslims will probably see Jesus only as being like other saints or healers. That Jesus of Nazareth accepted such a view as a *starting-point* in a relationship with himself is demonstrated in the Gospels. His intention, however, was consistently to draw the devotee into an encounter with himself as Son of Man, as Lord; out of a view of life that allowed no direct relationship with the Creator.

Thus, in the case of the woman with an issue of blood (Matthew 9:20–22), Jesus accepted the superstitious approach the woman made to him. The twelve-years'-sick woman had come to Jesus seeking 'virtue' (Authorised Version) or—in the terminology of folk Islam—*baraka*. She was looking for a force stronger than the evil in her body. As he healed the woman, Jesus transformed her cosmology, as well as changing her bodily symptoms:

> Then the woman, seeing that she could not go unnoticed, came trembling and fell at his feet. In the presence of all the people, she told why she had touched him and how she had been instantly healed. Then he said to her, 'Daughter, your faith has healed you. Go in peace' (Luke 8:47–48).

The woman was faced with a Lord before whom she had to bow. He was not one to be manipulated or used. As Lord, Jesus had seen deeply into her needy life, the life of someone 'unclean' in a spiritual as well as a physical sense. He freely granted her wholesome peace. 'Daughter' included her in a new family; the means of relationship becomes one of faith, of trust; it is two persons communicating on a father/daughter, divine/human basis. The woman's closed cosmology is broken open, and now she can truly go in peace, in wholeness.

Many motivations among ordinary Muslims may be acceptable as starting-points in their seeking of Jesus' help in their lives. Jesus' ambassadors must faithfully represent their

Master in responding freely to the cries for help of desperate
human beings. However, the Master's ambassadors also
need in this power encounter truly to introduce Muslims to
the risen, holy, divine Lord Jesus. The encounter must
become a personal one. Jesus Christ must speak for himself
with those who, healed and restored, need to fall on their
knees before him in worship, knowing that they have also
been forgiven.

CHAPTER SEVEN

THE LEADERSHIP IN QUESTION

Zeinab's girls

THE AIR WAS ELECTRIC in the small, hot chamber.

'Always! Let it be always!' muttered several of the women under their breath as they watched intently.

Umm Mahfuz was slipping into a trance. Her last conscious thought had been a hope that today's celebration would sort out her domestic and personal problems. Now, if she had any thoughts at all, they were stimulated by the realities of another world. Gently, two or three of those watching lowered her on to a pillow.

The other women who had still been sitting chatting in the outer salon, crowded into what was normally a bedroom. Children ran backwards and forwards. Babies nursed or climbed and crawled among the women's legs. Warm female bodies congregated around Zeinab. The carpeted floor had been cleared of furniture except for a few pillows around the walls of the room. Underneath the one open window sat the musicians, who provided the percussive bass with a combination of drum and tambourine, while they sang and coaxed the melody out of a keyless flute. This was the musicians' hour, and they meandered from tune to tune, partly in response to Zeinab's instructions, partly because they knew by now which tune belonged to which woman. A few of the participants had already had their tunes played before that of Umm Mahfuz. They were now swooning gently, exhausted on the floor. The last woman entered the bedroom as Zeinab dropped a scarf over Umm Mahfuz's face to keep off the flies, and for another reason.

The ladies had been meeting under Zeinab's direction for a long while, and how they enjoyed these celebrations. No one could say that Zeinab was not a good *zâr* leader. She knew the spirits, and in an uncanny way she knew her clientele also. Today they were gathering in Umm Mahfuz's home because she had finally decided to sponsor a *zâr* ceremony. They didn't know all the details of Umm Mahfuz's life; they would ease them out of her in future chitchat, but they did know that it had something to do with her paralysis. She was lame in one foot, and could only shuffle around, dragging the offending foot behind her. There was talk in the neighbourhood that her husband was considering taking a second wife. It wasn't that Umm Mahfuz had failed to bear him sons and daughters, so it must be that she was ageing and didn't please him as much as before. If that was the case, it was easy to understand. The world was a man's world after all. Perhaps, however, something could be done for Umm Mahfuz, especially if the paralysis could be lessened through a spirit's help. They had known worse problems solved in their *zâr* ceremonies. The women wondered at the reasons as Umm Mahfuz lay before them, children stepping lightly around her, finding nothing abnormal in her resting there so quietly.

What they did know was that Umm Mahfuz had decided to sponsor a *zâr* ceremony. It had been whispered around the quarter.

'At last the rich Umm Mahfuz will be one of us!'

The women loved these get-togethers. Zeinab had identified the spirit possessing each one. Underneath their black *jallâbîyas* they now wore lovely, brightly coloured clothing and plenty of jewellery of the kind directed by the possessing spirits. What the spirit willed was their delight to wear, and wasn't it amazing how the spirit's desires so often fitted with the personal preferences of the woman concerned? Zeinab was a gifted practitioner—as proved by the case of whiney old Selma, who was unpopular in the neighbourhood for her meanness. Her *zâr* spirit had revealed through Zeinab that he loved the colour black. He demanded that she go and kiss crosses and icons in the Amir Tadros churches in the Christian quarter. Yes, Zeinab certainly was an uncanny *shaykha*.

Now, it seemed that Umm Mahfuz's possessing spirit had revealed himself to be the infamous Red Sultan. The musicians had sung his song:

> Red king of kings, you king of jinn, recall your
> spirits so that all of them will be present.... Oh
> you little bride holding a lighted candle in your
> hand, you are the bride of the Sultan, and your
> groom is like a lighted candle.[10]

Umm Mahfuz had slowly responded as the insistent chant repeated itself. It was the answer to her paralysis and threatened marriage. Her *zâr* spirit was the famous Red Sultan. Both tune and words had called to her, and she unfolded her will to them. She began to beat her chest, to breathe heavily. Every now and then she let out a shout that seemed to well up from deep within her. Then, in an instant, it happened. She found herself upon her feet—both feet—swaying from side to side as the song moved deeper into her soul. She lost herself to it, bending double to the floor from her waist in great sweeping circles. Finally she danced, wildly, from one foot to another, back and forth. Eventually she fell into a trance and gently swooned on to the pillows. Her spirit was certainly the Red Sultan!

Zeinab smiled. This would be a profitable day for her. Umm Mahfuz's problems were big ones, and she was not a poor woman. Zeinab checked the incense burner. The smell of rue filled the house and was intoxicating. Brightly dressed women caught her eye, trying to persuade her to order the musicians to play their tunes next. Although today's meeting was really in benefit of Umm Mahfuz, Zeinab had persuaded her to sponsor a *zâr* for all the regulars as well. There would be food later, and a chance to pass around the latest neighbourhood gossip. Now the important focus of each female, and the key to Zeinab's control of those ladies, was each one's tune. Zeinab began to chant a new melody, and the instruments followed her.

As the music shifted, and different women moved to their feet and finally to their backs, the dancing was distinguished in the actions they made just prior to sinking to the ground in a trance. Some of their dancing was wild, like Umm Mahfuz's, as if the women had pent-up energy that simply had to be released. One spinster had a possessing spirit called the Prophet. The others liked her to dance early because she entertained them so well. Though unmarried, she writhed in an obviously sexual way, gliding slowly, head back, round the room, as if pressed against by the spirit. Another younger woman danced very intensely, though with hardly any movement at all. Her spirit was Yarwa Bey, and she slowly gyrated, shaking with heavy sobs, tears streaming down both cheeks, until she collapsed, crying, on a cushion. That afternoon, nearly everyone danced.

When the music finally subsided and most of the women had revived, Zeinab announced that Umm Mahfuz's spirit was definitely the Red Sultan. The other women congratulated Umm Mahfuz in a mixture of awe and jealousy, for the Red Sultan was one of the strongest spirits. Umm Mahfuz would have to wear red clothes underneath her covering

jallâbîya. She would have to dedicate red candles for future *zâr* celebrations. Today she would have to sacrifice a chicken.

Women and children moved outside. A hen appeared from a dusty corner of the family courtyard, was seized and firmly held. Zeinab pronounced the *bismillâh'* and severed the chicken's head from its body. As the blood spurted, she deftly sprinkled a little over Umm Mahfuz's head. Then she dropped the decapitated bird to run its death flutter around the yard. Umm Mahfuz was today's special 'bride'. She must be properly marked with sacrificial blood.

Now that the Red Sultan was appeased, more mundane needs could be satisfied. The musicians and then the guests were offered tea, soft drinks, cigarettes and, later, rice and chicken.

Zeinab returned to the bed chamber to revive one or two of the women who still lay in trances. The woman possessed by the Prophet was deep in sleep, and it took Zeinab some time to massage her and sprinkle water on her face, before she returned to life. A few of those lying on the floor had veils over their faces. Zeinab had developed that practice because she knew what ugly expressions some of the women wore as they went into a trance. She didn't want anyone to be put off by their horrible contortions.

When all the women had come round, Zeinab returned to take her place outside in the midst of the banter. She accepted tea and a cigarette and stored away a few titbits of gossip. Later, the 'bride' of today's ceremony would slip her a few large notes. Zeinab smiled knowingly to herself. With the Red Sultan, there was always promise of more.

The practitioners of popular Islam

Islam knows both a formal religious hierarchy and a host of informal practitioners. Such non-theological leaders (male and female) oversee the crisis rites, and certain aspects of the cyclical rites, of ordinary Muslims. Their major qualification is their proven power, and their many functions vary, depending on their abilities. Some of them are held in considerable awe because of their control of powerful human and non-human forces.

At a simple level of ability are the prayer-writers. Such practitioners are common throughout the Muslim world. The *faqîr* ('poor' wanderer) of Sri Lanka, or the wise woman of Iraq, selects special verses from the Qur'ân and makes them up into charms and talismans. Some more specialised prayer-writers, like the *jadoogar*, or village magician, of Iran, may also practise fortune-telling by the reading of omens.

The medicine man or his equivalent performs a variety of functions. In Morocco, the *ᶜajûza*, an 'old woman' who has understanding of herbal and magical brews, is often called on to help in times of sickness. Morocco also acknowledges the *matîyalûn* or 'curers', who have the reputation of being able to ease pain and disease by supernatural means. For many years medicine men, like the *bororo* of West Africa or the *bôkâ* of Nigeria, carried the expansion of Islam, via their herbal medicines, charms, amulets, exorcism and healing, into local African communities. In Afghanistan the *ḥakîm*, or 'wise person', is much respected as a traditional healer. The *bomor* of Malaya specialises in healing, both by application of herbal lore and by the use of trance cures. The *mangubat* plays an equivalent role among the Filipino Tausug, where his knowledge is attributed to his intimacy with the offending spirits.

Diviners operate in two major realms. They discover the causes of, and cures for, sickness; and they predict future events. In Morocco, the *shawwâfa* performs the office of fortune-teller, using a variety of paraphernalia to assist her in her art. In Iran, the common practice of divination by *estekhareh* is carried out for more crucial decisions by old women or specialists in the occult world. In Afghan Tur-

kestan, the *talajabîn* predict the future by observing the ripples in a basin of water, whereas the *ramal* uses dice and a book of interpretation for the combinations of numbers, in order to predict the future. In the Sudan, a *faqîh* may use a child as a medium in a form of divination in which the entranced boy makes signs in the dust. Those signs are then interpreted by the *faqîh*. In the Philippines, a *pamumutika* divines the best medicines for diseases.

Exorcists play an important role in societies which see many human problems as the result of spirits' interference. The *ṭalla* of Morocco attempts to identify possessing jinn by various divinatory practices. The male *bakhshi* of Afghanistan exorcises by entering a trance in which he transfers the evil spirit from its victim to himself, and then expels it.

In the world of magic and sorcery, practitioners of real power vie with one another for authority. The *jadoogar* of Iran, if he has stronger charisma than the village *du^câ'*-writer, will enter trance states in order to communicate with the spirit world. His goal is to harm a person's enemy, or to break the power of offensive magic against his own client. Among the Bedouin of Kuwait, a *saḥḥâra* is a woman with the power of sorcery who can control men by casting spells over them. The *jâdu* of Afghan Turkestan is a black magician who creates 'talismans for evil'; he cuts a figurine of the intended victim out of sheep's fat, earth and wax, pierces it and burns it, thus causing the death of the person identified in the proxy ritual. Sometimes a magician will use another person, often a child, as a medium, in which case the child concerned may well exhibit strange characteristics like a stutter or a non-human voice. And in Malaya ordinary Muslims appeal to the *pawang* in every kind of dealing with the hostile spirit world; often, the *pawang* have familiar spirits in their own employ.

Pîrs and marabouts, the holy men of Eastern and Western Islam respectively, have the role of practitioners among ordi-

nary Muslims. They may tell fortunes, compose charms, or divine sicknesses and cures. In such activities, as well as in their giving guidance and emanating *baraka*, they provide an unorthodox approach to religious living different from that of the clerics of orthodox Islam. In some of their various practices, and certainly in their devotees' use of their *baraka*, many of the functions of popular religion are realised.

The common stereotype of an Islamic community relegates women to purdah (seclusion), childbearing and menial tasks. In reality, though often from within the walls of their husbands' homes, women extend a strong influence over their families' lives. Such influence frequently derives from an association with the occult world. Besides a general power in activities involving the supernatural world, individual women also hold specific positions in Muslim communities which give them authority in matters pertaining to folk religion. That authority rises to the surface at times of crisis, or in perpetuating some aspects of the various rites of passage. (We shall look more closely at rites of passage in Chapter Eight.)

The midwife is a major practitioner of the folk-Islamic world. Known as the *qâbila* in Morocco, she is the sorceress of the proletariat. Her specialities include herbal remedies and sympathetic magic. She is called to help make the barren fertile and the overly fertile less productive. The equivalent figure in the Sudan, the *dâyat al-habîl* ('robe midwife') also practises fortune-telling. In Uzbekistan, the *momo* handles all magical aspects of the delicate processes of pregnancy and birth. For the Sulu Samals, the *pandai* does the same; she is also consulted in her capacity as a healer of common ailments.

A sorceress who specialises in love magic is known as *sahhâra* in Algeria. She can weaken or intensify sexual desire. She can make a woman desire a particular man, can make a man impotent with any woman other than his wife, or can make a woman leave her husband for another man.

The *shawwâfa* of North Africa specialises in the matching of potential marriage partners.

The female *shaykha* (such as Zeinab), who officiates at the *zâr* ceremonies of the Arab world, and the female *bakhshi*, who performs a similar function in Afghan Turkestan, hold considerable authority among women in their local communities. The identification of a possessing spirit, without the intention of exorcism, guarantees a continuation both of the ceremony and of the practitioner's role in the community. Such women have a predominantly female clientele, but their activities and instructions have indirect implications for the families and homes of those who seek their help.

Female washers of the dead are also seen as people of power. In Morocco, they are generally feared as sorceresses.

The major criterion for recognition of practitioners in the folk-Islamic world is that of proven power. Female Muslims may be given a somewhat secondary place in the practices of formal Islam: Islamic theology would appear to blame their sexuality, and inconsistency, for producing a situation in which men's innate weaknesses are easily exploited; menstruation places the category of ceremonial uncleanness regularly upon women. Within the home, however, and in certain aspects of both crisis and cyclical rites, women shine as power possessors. Men and women alike seek their help.

Who is seen to have power in Islam raises many issues. While the official hierarchy places authority in the hands of identified leaders within the structure of the status quo, popular Islam places authority in the hands of individuals with proven abilities. Alternative kinds of power appear to be more strongly differentiated in some situations, more strongly combined in others.

As one moves away from the intellectual centres of the faith, towards the villages, the more one sees greater involvement in the folk-Islamic world by all kinds of Muslims. The same pattern is generally true in respect of language use. As one moves away from Arabic usage towards indigenous ways of expression, there is less likelihood of orthodox Islam having such a strong hold over people.

Moreover, as one travels from the centre towards the boundaries of ideal belief and practice, the very practitioners of that belief and practice tend to compromise their allegiance to formal Islam. More and more they indulge in the beliefs and acts of popular Islam. For many of such village officials, existence is probably only made viable for the extra income derived from their practices of magic and charm-writing, healing and so on.

In Turkey, the village *hoca* (religious leader) may well be the village sorcerer. Certainly, the practitioners of therapy for mental diseases seen to be the result of jinn activity or the evil eye include such local *hocas*. The Kurds turn to the local mullah for prayers, charms and exorcism in cases of sickness. The many unofficial mullahs in the Muslim regions of the USSR are usually itinerants who know a little Arabic and are thus able to perform the essential religious rites of Islam. They are, however, more in demand for other functions, especially sorcery and healing. In the villages of Bangladesh, the people come to the mullah for amulets and charms to deal with all kinds of crisis situations, and for general protection. Among the Siasi Tao Sug, illness is sometimes remedied by the use of offering boats (*ambal*), which are paddled to the open sea after being laden with food, to appease the unknown cause of the sickness. The local imam is involved in the launching ceremony for the *ambal*. He addresses the evil spirits, exhorting them to take away the attack from the person concerned.

Figure 6 demonstrates the relative positions held and functions performed by some of the practitioners of both ideal and popular Islam. As one moves from the centre to the boundaries of orthodoxy, the clerics of ideal Islam become more deeply committed to folk-Islamic belief and

ship with Yahweh, are likely to share in the detailed out-working of that relationship. The nation as a whole reflects Yahweh's life and knows his blessing in its midst.

But when the hierarchy moved out of touch with Yahweh, alternative centres of power usually developed. God invested these non-official centres with authority and used them to humble the abusers of official religion and to provide the common masses with a true witness. Here the tensions between many of the Israelite kings, or leaders, and the prophets of Yahweh, who speak out of internal conviction, illustrate such a process. Amos' call to the prophetic ministry and his clash with the official leadership at Bethel, is a case in point, for Yahweh invests his authority in the shepherd and uses Amos to confound the religious and political hierarchy of the Northern Kingdom of Israel.

When both the official hierarchy and the local centres of power moved out of touch with God, Yahweh withdrew his Spirit from the people of Israel at a national and local level. The people themselves ran after other gods. They expressed their prostitution in an alternative cult, as for example that set up by Jeroboam I as a deliberate substitute for the worship of Yahweh in Jerusalem. Jeroboam provided alternative gods, at alternative sites, to consolidate his separation from the kingdom of Judah after the death of Solomon. Equally, they manifested such prostitution by setting up small local shrines, places established for the performance of fertility rites, and centres of power organised under the aegis of mediums.

Yahweh's longing is for a hierarchy that obeys him and that also allows for expressions of divine life in local communities or families. Yahweh abandons the status quo if it abandons its own calling to remain faithful to him. Instead he invests authority in individual persons he raises up. When both the centralised institutions and the local clans of his people abandon his ways, Yahweh lays them all aside. His vision focuses on a tiny, post-exilic remnant, and supremely on his own obedient Servant, the Messiah.

It is not the purpose of this book to debate the function that the formal religion of Islam has in developing people's relationship with the living God. Instead it is to recognise that, in the experience of the masses, the official faith by and large fails to address everyday needs. Such a sense of failure may not be expressed aloud so much as by commitment to alternative meanings and functions of the formal religion. The God of Islamic theology would appear to be so far removed from humans' lives that substitute focuses of power are sought in the accessible practitioners of popular Islam.

In the way they function, however, such practitioners, know little accountability to an ethical revelation. They are not leaders of protest movements, calling people back to the God of the original, ideal revelation—as were the Old Testament prophets, or Jesus in his controversy with the Pharisees and lawyers. They are proponents of a radically different view of life, and they operate in a context of pragmatism and immediate goals. In fact they give allegiance to a spiritual force which seems far removed from that of Moses or Christ.

The Bible concerns itself with a King, and with the transfer of people from the kingdom of darkness to his kingdom of light. The issue is not just about power, but about the source of power. By contrast folk religion represents a belonging to the kingdom of darkness. It is motivated by selfishness, and its end is manipulation. Control is sought over oneself, others, spirit beings, even God—if that were possible. It is non-ethical and non-accountable. In essence it is a manifestation of mankind's subservience to the Evil One.

The resources of Christ are specifically given to enable the church to break such false allegiance and transfer it to the Father. A significant factor in the biblical view of authority is that holy power belongs to God, or Christ. It is not the property or attribute of the agent. So our concern is not to set Christianity against the religions, or one worldview against another, but to set the power of God against the powers of evil.

The New Testament intention is that a body of believers, from every tribe and tongue, should live vitally in touch with God. The authority of Christ is invested in such a 'people'. Christian witness is consequently to be existentially powerful, for believers are power-holders in Christ. At the same time, Christian witness is to remain faithful to a New Testament ethic, the whole body's ministry under its divine head. Practitioners are to acknowledge one another in their different gifts and functions, and are to work together to win their fellow-creatures to the Lord. The ultimate practitioner in witness to ordinary Muslims is one divine Holy Spirit.

CHAPTER EIGHT

FROM CRADLE TO GRAVE

Angels at twilight

OLD MUHAMMAD TURNED in the half-light ready for their coming.

It was his daughter-in-law, not the expected angels, who had slipped to the bedside. She wiped his face with a cool cloth. 'Are you comfortable, Father dear?'

'They will soon be here,' whispered the old man, white stubble glistening with droplets of water. He took shallow, panting breaths, trying to prevent the gasps from ending in those aching convulsions. His body tensed with the effort to stay in control. Yet his mind was relaxed. As each seizure subsided, Muhammad allowed himself to feed on those wise words of Imam Musa.

Muhammad had first invited the imam to his apartment a few months before. He had felt deep inside that somehow this enveloping sickness of his chest was going to be his last. He wished he could face death peacefully; yet he knew that he couldn't. He had lived his life as a fairly good believer, but were the good deeds enough to tip the balance that would determine his eternal destiny? Was it true anyway?

Were there heaven and hell? If only one could be as sure about those matters as about the affairs of this earth!

Muhammad was proud of his achievements in business and commerce. He had spent his life working in that busy world. He had laboured hard and, God knows, he had achieved success without cheating too much. He had made his family a name in the city. Some of the lesser government ministers would ask his opinion on trade matters, especially in recent days, with the new ideas of limiting some imports. Muhammad had always advised impartially—well, with only a little self-interest. That was expected, anyway.

The last attack had been acute. Muhammad only vaguely remembered the journey to the private clinic. During the parts of the ride where he had remained conscious, his whole body seemed to burn and freeze all at once. Then came the move in an ambulance to a more specialised hospital for blood tests and initial treatment. Everyone tried hard not to tell him, but he was sure the second place was the cancer hospital. The treatment was certainly sickening and seemed to last for ever. They said he had pneumonia and needed to go every month for antibiotic treatment. He knew better than that. The problem was undoubtedly with his lungs. It felt as if a series of breathing tubes was shutting down one by one. Was it pneumonia or something far worse? Gradually, he had rallied in the months of lying in the small room at the back of his son's apartment. As he strengthened in body, so the questions forced themselves to the top of his mind. 'After death, what?'

He decided to put the issue to Imam Musa. Over several leisurely visits, the seventy-year-old theologian convinced Muhammad. Cleverly, he appealed to al-Ghazâlî. Muhammad had early on admitted respect for the renowned writer of *The Revival of Religious Sciences*. Perhaps this was because he knew that al-Ghazâlî had himself started as a sceptic but had become convinced that the mystic route to God was the best. Muhammad didn't agree with al-Ghazâlî's conclusions, but he respected his approach to matters of religion. Imam Musa concluded that al-Ghazâlî's argument from probability would be the way to Muhammad's heart.

'Muhammad, my friend, you question whether there is a future life. You ask whether there is really a questioning awaiting each Muslim in the grave. You wonder whether angels really can help, and whether hell is really hot. You feel that the doctrine of a future life is so involved in doubt and mystery that it is impossible to decide if it is true or not. Others down through the years have called the same doctrine into question. Listen to al-Ghazâlî's reply. He says that the sceptic, to be an honest realist himself, should give the doctrine of a future life the benefit of the doubt. Al-Ghazâlî asks what a sick person will do if an astrologer says, "When the moon has entered a certain constellation, drink such and such a medicine, and you will recover." Though he may have very little faith in astrology, won't he try the experiment in case the astrologer is right? Or, if a charm-writer says to a sick person, "Give me a shilling and I will write a charm which you can tie round your neck, and it will cure you," won't the sick person pay the shilling and take the charm, on the chance of benefiting from it? After asking these questions, Al-Ghazâlî makes his own suggestion. It would be wise to put some trust in the words of the prophets, saints, and holy men, who were convinced about the details of death and judgement and future life. For those people are far more trustworthy than any astrologer or charm-writer.'[11]

The imam's weekly monologues contained much wisdom. As he listened, Muhammad knew that he couldn't for ever fight the Qur'ân, tradition, and the views of the theologians.

Imam Musa suspected that he was near victory and, one evening, concluded with a personal thrust. 'Muhammad *Bey*, you have taken considerable risks for the sake of merely probable profit in the business world. Don't you think that a little trust in the more strongly probable fulfilment of prophets' words is reasonable?' He refrained from adding

'...in the closing months of your life'. The silence said that anyway.

Muhammad was finally convinced. Life around him in the last days of his earthly pilgrimage changed. Everything was arranged to make his passing easy. Money was lavishly spent to hire a blind *ḥâfiẓ*, well known in the city, to come every evening and recite the Qur'ân by Muhammad's bed. After his death, Qur'ân recitals would be made in a tent in the street outside the home for the first week. On the fortieth day, and then after a year, further recitals would be made in order to help Muhammad in his journey beyond the grave. Incense was burned in the bedroom; not too much because it congested Muhammad's weakened lungs, but enough to give notice to any evil jinn seeking to attack him in this vulnerable period of his life. Care was taken to keep away from the old man any person in a state of pollution. Indeed, very few visitors were allowed to see him: only those of whom the family was sure. A small Qur'ân rested underneath Muhammad's pillow, and every evening a little Zamzam water was sprinkled on his head before the family retired for the night.

Each evening, Muhammad turned towards Mecca before he went to sleep, in case that night was to be the night. It was essential to be facing Mecca when he died. Muhammad called on the prophets and the saints when he was awakened by pain, especially praying that it would be a Friday when he died. In that way, he would be spared the dreaded squeeze of the grave.

If any of his son's children came to visit him, the old man would make only one request of them. He loved them to read the sura *Yâ Sîn* to him. Muhammad had discovered that that sura was truly the great door for the dead. He wanted to get familiar with it now, so that after his death, when he was lying in the tomb and heard it read by his relatives, he would know that he was indeed dead. There was one part of that sura which sent shivers down Muhammad's spine. He knew it described him:

Does not man know that We have created him from a mere
sperm-drop? Then he becomes a persistent disputer; he forgets
the process of his own creation but has a lot to say concerning
Us. He asks: Who will quicken the bones when they are
decayed? Tell them: He Who created them the first time will
quicken them. He knows well every type of creation; the One
Who produces fire for you out of the green tree, which you
kindle. Has not He Who created the heavens and the earth the
power to create the like of them? Yea, and He is indeed the
supreme Creator, the All-Knowing. His power is such that when
He intends a thing He says concerning it Be; and it is. Thus Holy
is He, in Whose hand is the kingdom over all things. To Him will
you all be brought back.[12]

There was comfort and terror in the ending of sura *Yâ Sîn*.
Muhammad prayed to the archangels bearing up the throne
of God, that they would intercede for him. Sadly, he had
been a persistent disputer with God.

That night, Muhammad's daughter-in-law couldn't sleep.
She went to the kitchen to fetch some water. On the way
back, she passed the open door of her father-in-law's room.
Not hearing his quick pants, she peeped in. Old Muhammad
was curled up under the sheet like a baby, facing away from
her; towards Mecca. She tiptoed closer. There was no sound,
no movement. The stiff fingers of his right hand gripped a
string of prayer beads. His eyes were open, glazed, but at
peace, as if they had recognised someone. She drew the
sheet up over his body and hurried from the room.

The angels had come.

Rites of passage in Islam

In the rites of passage of any community the beliefs, ideas
and attitudes of the people concerned become visible. Birth,
naming, circumcision, marriage and death constitute the
major rites of passage in Islamic societies. With religious
festivals, these constitute the cyclical recurring rites which

give cohesion and meaning to Muslim peoples. They comple-
ment the crisis rites which arise haphazardly and suddenly,
demanding immediate response from professional practitioners. The cyclical rites are more planned, to some degree
even institutionalised, and in them the folk-Islamic beliefs
and practices of Muslims are to be discovered as clearly as in
the crisis rites. Their rituals express the focal points of existence as Muslims move from one recognised state to another.

Pregnancy and birth are viewed as far more than mere
biological activities. A common *ḥadîth* relates how, early on
in a mother's womb, an angel comes to the forming infant
and breathes the spirit of life into him. That angel carries
four words of command to pass on concerning the child's
fortune, life span, works and destiny. A pregnant woman is
therefore to be dealt with carefully. She should not be
wakened from sleep, for example, lest the angel who is busy
forming the child be frightened away.

The first cry of a newborn baby is considered as a sign that
Satan has just touched it; only Mary and Jesus escaped this
touch of Satan at birth. It is important, therefore, that a child
be born into this world with the sound of the *adhân* (call to
prayer) breathed into its right ear. Sometimes the *Fâtiḥa* is
whispered in its left ear.

Both mother and newborn baby are supposedly exposed
to the attacks of malevolent forces, and much is done to
protect them. Among some Algerians, a baby is rubbed
lightly with olive or peanut oil, rather than water, which
would expose it to attack by jinn; and the placenta may be
buried by the midwife in a cemetery. Amulets to protect the
infant against the evil eye are pinned on its clothing from
birth. In Malaya, the *langsuyar*, or ghost of a woman who
has died in childbirth, is feared at such a time. It is held that
this ghost seeks to suck the blood of women at childbirth.
Various precautions are taken to defend against the attacks
of the *langsuyar*, such as hanging thorny branches in the
windows of the house where a woman is giving birth. Many

taboos are established concerning who may or may not see mother or child during the initial period of vulnerability. Such a period usually lasts at least forty days.

All kinds of magical activities are associated with various diseases of infancy. A common remedy for infant sickness in Turkey is found in the practice of *tütsü*. Salt and garlic may, for example, be thrown into a fireplace in the child's presence. The room subsequently fills with smoke which is said to drive the offending demons away. Another practice, called *kurşun dökmek* ('to cast lead'), consists of heating a piece of lead and plunging it into a bowl of water. Qur'ânic verses are repeated; then the sick child is made to drink the water. Visits to a *şeyh*, a professional healer, may also be undertaken should a sickness prove too strong for the parents to dispel. Infancy as a whole is seen as a transitional period in which there is considerable vulnerability.

Naming ceremonies (*tasmîya*) occur as a distinguishing rite in many parts of the Muslim world. In the details of the rite, folk-Islamic belief and practice make a considerable contribution. Often, the name to be adopted is selected after astrological consideration. Sometimes the child is called by a derogatory name, such as Dog or Ugly, to discourage the attention of the jinn. Similarly, boys may be dressed as girls and called by female names for a while, to mislead the jinn. Alternatively, a name such as Mashallah (*mâ shâ'allah*, what God wills) may be selected in order to protect the infant from the evil eye. No one can admire, or address, a child named Mashallah without invoking the protection of God upon it.

Ceremonies of naming are traditionally accompanied by the ʿ*aqîqa* sacrifice, a practice still continuing in some communities. The ʿ*aqîqa* ceremony takes place on the seventh day after birth. The child is named, its hair is shaved, and an animal is slaughtered. The idea behind the sacrifice seems to be that of substitution, so that malevolent forces will be satisfied with an animal victim in place of the child concerned.

The folk-Islamic worldview enters into the realm of the formal ritual of circumcision (*khitân*) mainly in the questions of the time and site of circumcision. The day for the rite may be fixed by an astrologer. The place of operation is located at a saint's tomb, if that is feasible; the *baraka* of the saint and shrine will bring blessing to the boy and family. Often, however, part of the family visits a shrine before a circumcision at home. Boys in Istanbul are taken to the shrine of Eyüp to ward off the influence of the evil eye, and to obtain protective *baraka* against any dangers in the forthcoming operation.

At an earlier time, the wedding ceremony possibly provided the female equivalent of the male circumcision ceremony. As a child-wife, the girl gained the new status of a woman in the community. Whether or not the result of the raising of the marriage age, contemporary circumcision of infant females is still a common practice, especially in rural areas of the Muslim world. In towns and cities, circumcision of females occurs with varying frequency throughout society. More complex types of female circumcision are rarer, though in some countries major operations are still conducted, such as the 'Pharaonic circumcision', or infibulation, of northern Sudan. With such operations, protective activity and the accumulation of *baraka* are important aspects of the rite.

Apart from actual circumcision, perhaps another contemporary female counterpart to the male circumcision rite is found in the taking of the veil. In Turkey, this special day is known as *yaşmak günü*, on which a girl has her fingernails dyed with henna and is given a party. From then on, she wears a veil in public.

Marriage in itself is viewed as a means of fulfilling religious duty. Half of the religion of Islam is completed through marriage, according to one common *ḥadîth*. The bridegroom and bride are seen as possessors of *baraka*, and part of the ritual of the wedding ceremony is designed to protect that *baraka* from theft or contamination. Often potential marriage partners are evaluated from an astrological perspective, to see if their 'stars' are compatible. The covering of the bride's head is widely seen as a form of protection against the evil eye, and the religious rite which validates the marriage, the *nikâḥ*, is performed by an imam. In many situations, this rite is done in secret, in order to prevent enemies of the couple from tying magic knots—which might render the groom impotent, or the bride infertile—at that delicate moment.

As with circumcision, the performance of weddings at saints' shrines and the timing of such events on *mawlids*, are designed to bring as much *baraka* as possible into the new union. In Turkey, a common pilgrimage centre for newlyweds is the grave of the saint Telebaba. The party arrives in a motorcade with the bride's car bedecked with ribbons, carnations and a large doll (an image of the hoped-for baby), which squats on the bonnet. Some tinsel from the bride's headdress is left at the shrine as a prayer for fertility.

Divorce is permitted in Islam, although it is considered to be the worst of all actions allowed by law. In many Muslim societies it is nevertheless extremely common and tragic in its effects, especially upon women and children. As far as popular Islam is concerned, the main intrusion of such belief and practice into this rite is the activity (mostly of women) to prevent divorce from taking place. They make vows to saints, appeals to angelic mediators, and try all kinds of magic to repair a threatened marriage.

Beliefs and activities involved in death rites lean heavily on the folk-Islamic view of the world. The dying person is turned towards Mecca in the last moments of life to enable an easier passing. Often the dying person or surrounding family members call upon a saint to sustain him during the coming transition. Meanwhile, taboos prevent a person in a state of pollution from coming near a dying person.

After preparation of the body, the corpse is buried, again facing Mecca. Sometimes messages addressed to the archangels on behalf of the deceased are buried with him. Death is viewed as the permanent withdrawal of the soul from the body, although that withdrawal may be quite prolonged. It is often considered, for example, that the souls of the dead are detained for forty days in the neighbourhood of the grave. The Qur'ân is read at the grave during that period to assist the archangel Gabriel in defending the soul of a deceased relative against the Devil. Qur'ân readings focus on the recitation of the sura *Yâ Sîn* and assist the deceased during the dreaded 'squeeze of the grave'. At the time of the 'squeeze', the corpse sneezes and repeats a verse from the sura *Yâ Sîn*. In preparation for this event, pious exclamations after sneezing are practised throughout life on earth by many Muslims. Nakîr and Munkar, the famous angels of the grave, then appear and carry out their interrogation of the deceased. During the period of questioning, family and friends read the Qur'ân above the grave, and good deeds are done so that merit accrues to the deceased. On the seventh and fortieth nights, the dead person returns in spirit to his own home to see what is being done for the peace of his soul.

After the death period is over, disembodied souls may visit their human relatives, often incognito. At the same time, mourners make special prayers and supplications (*aᶜmâl*) by which they may see deceased loved ones in dreams. In some parts of the Muslim world, the soul of a dead person is believed to return to the graveyard every Thursday afternoon and sit by its grave. Often, therefore, living relatives visit graves on Thursday afternoons. They read the Qur'ân there and leave certain foods on the tombstone.

Figure 7 expresses some of the intentions of Muslims in their major rites of passage. The overall goal is the mainten-

Figure 7

Positive and Negative Activities to Preserve Equilibrium during Rites of Passage

Positive Activities	Negative Activities
Presence of practitioners with inherent or acquired power	Protection against those who would bring danger
Performance of activities on auspicious days (shown by divination)	Inauspicious times avoided
Location at site of holy grave; orientation towards Mecca	Locations avoided where possible contact with jinn
Use of prophylaxes against evil eye, jinn	Exclusion of those with a history of evil eye
Sacrifice or vow to bind a saint to the needed task	Taboos maintained in order to prevent cancellation of the bond
Observance of ritual purity	Exclusion of those ritually unclean
Attempts to deceive potential harmers (by dressing boy as girl; dummy bride)	Observance of *mâ shâ ' allah* syndrome

ance of equilibrium at such precarious moments of living. Equilibrium is preserved by both positive and negative actions. On the positive side, various powers for good are appropriated. Appeal is also made to a variety of trans-empirical beings, such as angels and saints. On the negative side, taboos are strictly observed to gain protection against harmful influences.

Other life cycle events may also be occasions for the expression of movement from one status to another. The cutting of a first tooth, the starting of school, the completion of reading or memorising the Qur'ân, the end of an apprenticeship, or the acceptance into a craft guild, the entry into, or return from, military service, and other such transitional activities—all provide occasions for ritual in which folk-Islamic beliefs and practices find expression.

Jesus in transition

In the New Testament account of the birth, life and death of Jesus of Nazareth, the rites of passage find considerable prominence. Since he comes as a firstborn child of Jewish parents, certain ceremonies follow customary local procedures. At the same time, Jesus is given as a Son from above, so various heavenly comments are made about the divine dimension in Jesus' life—comments that interpret the rites of passage for Jesus of Nazareth in a special manner.

Jesus' birth fulfils the carefully prepared prophecies given hundreds of years before. More immediately, a barren, older relative of the young Mary is miraculously enabled to bear a son, to be called John, who will make ready a way for his soon-coming Lord. Mary's own pregnancy is announced by an angel, Gabriel. The Holy Spirit brings substance to that annunciation in the virgin's womb. The Palestinian girl is protected from the understandable misgivings of her upright fiancé, Joseph, through a dream. The pregnancy is brought to full term in Bethlehem, the place of great David's own birth, where angels gather shepherds to the manger to worship the special child. At some stage, magi from the East are led by a star to the boy-king. The evil of the man-king, Herod, is then unleashed, and parents and baby are forced to be refugees. Thus the events surrounding pregnancy and childbirth are accompanied by inspired declarations of the greater context in which Jesus' rite of passage is taking place: 'He will be great and will be called the Son of the Most High. The Lord God will give him the throne of his father David, and he will reign over the house of Jacob for ever; his kingdom will never end' (Luke 1:32–33). Here is much for the young mother to treasure up and ponder in her heart.

The rites of circumcision and naming are combined on the eighth day after birth. The name given is that proposed by an angel before the child was even conceived: 'Jesus'.

Soon after these initial rites, the child, as a firstborn male, is taken to the Temple at Jerusalem by his parents to be presented to the Lord. The ceremony is interrupted by prophetic declarations. An old man, Simeon, is moved by the Spirit to go into the Temple courts at the same moment as Joseph and Mary enter. He sees the child, takes him into his arms, and declares Yahweh's commitment to this special, living 'sign'. He will be a light, for revelation to the Gentiles, as well as for the glory of the people of Israel. An old prophetess, Anna, also arrives in the courtyard at that instant. She declares publicly her knowledge that in this child is invested the redemption of Jerusalem. In their miraculously timed appearances, and in their words from a world above, Simeon and Anna bring divine perspective into this common rite of passage. Again, Jesus' parents marvel at what is being said about the baby. Again, there are ominous hints of piercing swords and opposition.

When he is twelve, another change of status takes place for Jesus. After the Passover Feast in Jerusalem, the family party sets out to return to Nazareth, unaware that they are missing one child. Jesus is at last found in the most unlikely place for a boy of his age: sitting among the teachers in the Temple courts, listening, asking questions and giving answers. Although his human parents hardly understand his words, Jesus declares to them a change in status. His mother rebukes him for shaming his earthly father. Jesus speaks to her of his primary allegiance to his heavenly Father. Yes, Jesus will go down to Nazareth with his parents, three days delayed. He will be obedient to them there. At the same time, they need to know that another Father has first call on Jesus' life. Again, Mary has more thoughts to treasure in her heart. In the conflict of allegiances, even within the Galilean family, hints emerge of greater anguish to come.

Baptism marks the next great rite of passage. Once more, the act is interrupted from above. At the moment of Jesus' immersion, the skies open and the Holy Spirit descends on him in bodily form like a dove. The Father speaks audibly from heaven. John, the earthly baptiser, declares that he is unworthy to baptise Jesus, that Jesus is the Lamb of God who in reality takes away the sins of the world, and that Jesus must increase while he decreases. The baptist's testimony is that Jesus is not simply son of Joseph, or son of Mary, but truly Son of God.

The public ministry of Jesus begins after his baptism in the River Jordan. Immediately, battle is engaged. The Spirit of God thrusts Jesus out into the desert, the home ground of evil spirits, to meet—and undo—the prince of demons. Jesus fasts; he fights with Satan; he is fed by angels.

Jesus does not know human marriage. Perhaps, in one sense, it is baptism that constitutes for him a life-consuming commitment to his heavenly Father. From that moment, in a public ministry, Jesus is wholly given to obeying his Father's will. The relationship between them is certainly one of greater unity than that between man and woman, for Son and Father are essentially one. The final agony will be that of unbelievable separation, in which the relationship is severed. The Father forsakes the Son, because of the shame, evil and sin that the Son has taken on himself.

Jesus' death is the rite of passage most prominent in the four Gospels. In the event itself, natural and supernatural worlds combine to underline the significance of this rite. Darkness comes over the whole land; the Temple curtain tears in two from top to bottom, frightening the priests by exposing the Holy of Holies; the earth shakes and rocks split; selected tombs open, and the bodies of many holy people who have died are revived; a Roman centurion who has seen hundreds of deaths can only exclaim that this criminal is the Son of God. Somehow, in this rite, Jesus disarms the spiritual powers and authorities, even making a public spectacle of them, triumphing over them by the cross. In the agony, Jesus scorns the shame, looking beyond it to the joy ahead.

In the resurrection, Jesus passes through death to a new kind of living. He has a recognisable body, but it is not subject to the constraints of this world; it is fitted for life in a larger context.

The ascension of Jesus is the final rite of passage described in the Gospels. He is taken up into heaven with scarred hands extended, blessing his disciples. As he departs, they worship him, his promise of the Holy Spirit ringing in their ears. They gaze intently as Jesus ascends, exalted at last to the right hand of God, reunited in fullest communion with the Father. This rite underlines their conviction: Jesus Christ is Lord!

The rites of passage in Jesus' experience reveal the realities of the 'world' in which he humbles himself, takes on the form of man, gives himself to death and is raised to new life. Angels and demons, magi and prophets, nature and Spirit— all are involved in and contribute to the significant changes occurring in Jesus' life. The clash with evil is constantly in focus and finds pointed meaning during each rite of passage. In the story of each clash, God takes the initiative. Only he sets in motion and brings through to completion, via those rites of passage, a new hope for mankind. In his Son he provides a radical answer for human helplessness in the face of evil. Beyond a temporary reprieve, beyond a mere warding off of vulnerability, Jesus of Nazareth actually becomes weakness, vulnerability, sin and the Devil's plaything. Through the costly drama of his own rites of passage, Jesus secures a release from satanic bondage for frail human beings: 'The reason the Son of God appeared was to destroy the devil's work' (1 John 3:8).

CHAPTER NINE

TIMES AND SEASONS

Beneath the waterfall?

THE FIRST WEDNESDAY of the feared month was almost upon them. Suddenly, Manisan gave in.

'All right, Father! I will take part in the ceremony. But please don't ask me again next year!'

Alimoud looked up from the rice field. Like his fellow Filipino farmers, he was a skilled rice-grower. It was internal family matters which left him floundering. He gazed at the young woman who had interrupted his work.

'Thank you, my daughter,' he said quietly.

His attention returned to the work at his feet. Inwardly, he breathed a deep sigh of relief. He would not be letting down the Bohebessey community. His family would be safe for another year. What an obstinate girl was young Manisan! Since starting at the secondary school over in Basilan, a big change had come over her. She didn't seem to want to take part in their festivals any more. Every Friday, her wide eyes asked him unanswerable questions as he set off to the village *langgal* for the noon prayers. She was somehow disenchanted with his religion.

Alimoud wondered if it had anything to do with her illness, a year ago. The village herbalist had been sent for on the advice of the imam. Most villagers did not like entrusting their teenage daughters to the wily old *tabib*. Certainly, he had not helped Manisan to recover from her sickness, though he made plenty of visits. In the end, Alimoud paid for the services of the *bahasa*, on his next stopover in Bohebessey. The traditional healer had gone into a trance and diagnosed the problem. Soon Manisan was on the road to recovery.

Even to Alimoud, it had looked like a defeat for the officials of the mosque. From the time of her recovery, a change had come over Manisan. She had become withdrawn, and not at all interested in her father's religious talk. Her respect for the imam and *tabib* had dwindled to almost nothing.

Everything had come to a head over the *magpandi-pandi* ceremony. Manisan had stubbornly refused to be involved in the communal washing rites that occurred during *bulan sapal*, the second month of the year.

'Thank you, my daughter,' Alimoud repeated, as he rechannelled the irrigation water. 'It is best for you, as well as for us and the community.'

Ever since he could remember, Alimoud had taken part in the special rites of ablution at Bohebessey. It was part of the village tradition and, as the imam always emphasised in the mosque at Friday prayers leading up to the month of *bulan sapal*, it was essential for the whole congregation to join together in the rites.

There had only been one difficult year that Alimoud could recall. A strong typhoon had hit the island, and it was impossible for anyone to bathe in the sea on the third Wednesday of the month. Instead, they had had to perform the *magpandi-pandi* inland, at the waterfall, on that Wednesday as well as on the others. Everyone, including the imam, had wondered whether the substitution for the required sea washing would be acceptable. As no one suffered badly in health, or crops, that year, it had obviously been all right.

This year, there was no prospect of a typhoon. They would go to the coast as usual, God willing. That would be on the third Wednesday of the month. Meanwhile, the first Wednesday was fast approaching, and Manisan had at last agreed to participate in the rites of ablution.

Alimoud wondered if Manisan had any idea of what was at stake. She, of all people, needed to take part every year! After all, she had been born in the unfortunate month. Everyone knew that the wicked king of the jinn specialised in attacking people born in *bulan sapal*. It was said by some of the more knowing elders in the prayer-house, that those born in *bulan sapal* were in danger of being eaten by that strong devil after their death, or even at the last judgement.

Alimoud was thankful that he had already performed the *magtimbang*, the balancing ceremony, on Manisan's behalf. He had been tempted to leave it until her wedding day. However, when Jamalud, his eldest son, had completed his study of the Qur'ân, Alimoud had decided to sponsor the two ceremonies together. The family held a *magtammat* to mark the end of Jamalud's Qur'ânic studies, and a *magtimbang* for the girl who had been born in the month of *bulan sapal*.

Manisan had only been four years old, but she had certainly proved a heavy four-year-old! Both children had gone to their uncle's house to have their faces made up, and to be dressed in the traditional, colourful costumes. In the early afternoon, they were carried home on relatives' shoulders to the sound of gongs and fireworks.

The imam had, of course, officiated. He was assisted by some colleagues, invited from other villages. The balance was set up in the main room. It consisted of a bamboo pole hanging horizontally from a beam. As the ceremony began, someone hung a sarong at one end of the pole. Manisan was slid into the sarong. She swung gracefully. At the other end of the pole, family members gradually hung baskets containing rice cakes, pineapples, bottles of oil, even some kerosene. Soon the child was balanced by the collection of commodities at the other end of the pole. Two imams stood by the crude balance, chanting the special prayers for a person born in *bulan sapal*. As they intoned, alternately, they gently rocked the pole up and down. Between prayer cycles, the whole balance was rotated.

Eventually, the praying came to an end and the imams steadied the heavily-laden weighing machine. When the pole was completely still, the child was taken from the sarong, and the counterbalance was removed. The contents of the latter went to the imam, who rewarded his assistants from the bounty. The family rested assured, as they began the *magtammat* ceremony for Jamalud, that the worst dangers threatening young Manisan had been averted. Alimoud was thankful he had gone through with the *magtimbang* ceremony when Manisan was too young to object.

The Bohebessey men had been reminded by the imam, over the last few weeks, that it was essential for those who had been born in the second month to take part in the *magpandi-pandi* rites every year. Others could risk missing the event, but not people like Manisan.

The village was named after its pretty waterfall. That feature of the settlement made performance of the *magpandi-pandi*, on the first two Wednesdays of *bulan sapal*, very easy. The second month of their lunar calendar came regularly during the rainy season in these years. So there was plenty of water on the eastern side of the Island of Basilan.

Hollow bamboo spouts were set into the river at the top of the waterfall to carry the water further out, away from the rock face. The water dropped through the spouts, shower-like, into the river below. The space around the waterfall was somewhat limited, so the people took turns, by groups. First they bathed in the waterfall, or under the bamboo spouts. The men and boys took off their outer clothes; some of the youths went naked. The women tended to bathe clothed, though some stripped to their waists. There was no shame. The group then sat together on a large flat stone in the water, with their backs to the waterfall. Behind them stood the imam. He sprinkled the people, praying as he sprayed the water over them. The *tabib*, acknowledged by some for his ability to cure sickness, and by most for his role in the rice ceremonies, helped him sprinkle. After the ablutions were finished, the first group left the river and dressed, while others took their place. In a week's time, the procedure would be repeated.

On the third Wednesday, the community would go to the sea. The same sprinkling ceremony would be performed there, but it would end differently. When everyone had been sprayed with sea water, they would all gather on the beach around a stone. The imam would sit on the stone to say the special prayer for this month. He would invoke God to protect the congregation against the king of jinn, who roamed the earth especially during *bulan sapal*. Then the feast would begin. The people would separate into small groups to eat the food they had brought with them from home. All made sure that they brought something to the seaside sprinkling ceremony. No one could take part in the sea washing if he hadn't brought some food to share afterwards.

Manisan's hesitations about the *magpandi-pandi* ceremony reminded Alimoud of the argument which had developed at the *langgal* a few years previously. Some visitors had come from overseas. They turned out to be Malay missionaries. They had trained in far-off al-Azhar University in Egypt, and had come, they announced, to convert the Yakan to 'orthodox' Islam. There had been a big fight, and the missionaries were eventually ejected from Bohebessey. The villagers did not want the 'modern' innovations that the Malays expounded in the *langgal*, referring all the time to complicated theological treatises in Arabic. Not long afterwards, they heard from other Yakan, up and down the island, that they were not alone in their reaction to these foreign missionaries.

What foolish 'wise men' these Malays were! How could they attack the *magpandi-pandi* and rice ceremonies and expect to be respected by true Yakan Muslims? Every Yakan knows the power of the king of the jinn! Besides, history supported the Yakan view. There had been no calamity in Bohebessey during the month of *bulan sapal* as long as the *magpandi-pandi* had been faithfully celebrated. The same was true of their traditional rice rituals, and the *mawlid* celebrations. The known way was the best way.

Alimoud knew that the Yakan weren't alone in their convictions. *Bulan sapal* was a bad month for all Muslims. Tausugs, Samals, many Indonesians, even (it was rumoured) brothers in Saudi Arabia—all recognised that sad reality. Different ceremonies took place in many Muslim communities during the second month, in order to avert disaster. Even the most sceptical had to admit that *bulan sapal* was the month in which the beloved Prophet contracted the sickness of which he was to die. The second month was not a month to be dismissed lightly.

Alimoud smiled grimly as he bent over his rice crop. Manisan had agreed to take part in the *magpandi-pandi* this year. Would she next year?

Concepts of time in popular Islam

Many ways of marking time exist in the Muslim world. The variety includes solar, lunar, Julian, Hejiran, seasonal, and high religious festival calendars. One further view of time has a strong motivational effect on ordinary Muslims: hours, days and months are seen as bringing good or evil as life in them unfolds. That concept of time lurks just below the surface in determining what a person does or doesn't do during those periods.

Certain hours of the clock are considered lucky or unlucky. Friday boasts both kinds of hour. There is an unpredictable hour of ill-fortune on Fridays. That day also has a period in which God is especially open to hearing and granting the requests of his servants. In Morocco, the jinn are thought to be active after mid-afternoon prayers. That therefore becomes a time to sleep rather than to work or trade. Among Iranian Muslims, twilight is considered a favourite hour of the jinn. One of the well-known *ḥadîth* relates that God comes down to the vicinity of the earth as dawn approaches. That is consequently a good period for making petitions.

The days of the week are themselves differentiated according to whether they are lucky or unlucky. Egyptian pilgrims to Mecca are encouraged to begin their journeying on a Thursday, because a strong tradition relates that Thursday was the favourite day of Muhammad for setting out on an expedition. In Morocco, Thursdays and Sundays are seen as positive days, Thursday evening being especially good for the consummation of a marriage. In Egypt, also, Thursday is considered the most auspicious night for a man to sleep with his wife. In Iran, Thursday morning is traditionally a good time for composing talismans for protection. In Pakistan, it is thought advantageous to die, and be buried, on a Thursday or Friday. Among the Kabyles of Algeria, a mourning family visits a tomb on five consecutive Fridays, for that is the day when it is believed that a dead person leaves his grave to visit the living. For similar reasons, Muslim Yoruba in Nigeria pour milk on graves every Friday. A tradition states that Friday is the queen of the days of the week, and in God's view is higher than *ᶜîd al-Fiṭr* or *al-ᶜîd al-Kabîr*. Another *ḥadîth* records that Muhammad declared that the gates of paradise are open on Mondays and Thursdays. Prayer on those days leads to assured forgiveness. In Nubia, the evenings of Mondays and Thursdays are believed to be the best times for the performance of *ḥadrs*, or trance dances.

Other days of the week carry a negative, or unfortunate, connotation. In Iran, Tuesday and Saturday nights belong to the jinn, and Wednesday evening is especially the time of evil. On this night the sabbath celebrations of the jinn are held. In Palestine, similarly, Wednesdays and Saturdays are conceived of as dangerous because of the activities of demons.

Figure 8 summarises the positive and negative qualities of different days of the week. Some estimate is suggested as to the intensity of good or evil potential in each day. Important days of the year are highlighted, such as the tenth day of the first month of Muharram. Known as *ᶜÂshûrâ'*, it is believed that on this day the well of Zamzam at Mecca overflows and supplies all the springs in Islamic countries. In that way, each Muslim may have the possibility of drinking the *baraka*-endowed water. The twenty-seventh night of the month of

Figure 8

Days of the Week in Popular Islam

Day	Positive Quality	Negative Quality
Friday	best of all	(one hour)
Saturday		quite strong
Sunday	quite strong	
Monday	quite strong	
Tuesday		quite strong
Wednesday		worst of all
Thursday	very strong	

Rajab is celebrated as the time when the Prophet Muhammad visited Jerusalem. From there, he ascended the heavens to within two bows' lengths of the throne of God. Prayers on behalf of the dead are focused on this night. The fifteenth, or middle night, of Shaᶜbân, the eighth month, is also considered sacred. In Egypt and Nubia, most of the *mawlids* of local saints fall on, or near, the fifteenth of Shaᶜbân. The night of destiny, or power, usually celebrated on the twenty-seventh of Ramaḍân, is thought to be especially auspicious. Angels are present on earth in such numbers that there is no room between them even for a needle. Requests made to God on that night will find sure answers.

Certain days are the most favourable for holding naming ceremonies, circumcisions and weddings. Divination may well be employed to determine which is the best day. In the Egyptian village of Kaum, near the Pyramids, the *mawlid* of its patron saint, Sîdî Ḥamîd al-Sammân, provides the timing for many circumcisions and weddings. Full moons mark auspicious times for wedding festivals. Shrine-visiting is most effective on the *mawlid* of the saint concerned, or else on a Friday or Thursday.

Months of the year are similarly distinguished. Perhaps most significant, at least from the negative viewpoint, is Safar, which follows the first month (Muḥarram) of the Muslim year. (See Figure 4, page 85.) In Iran, it is said that of all the plagues sent by God, nine-tenths of them come in Safar, and nine-tenths of those on the last Wednesday of that month. That marks the night when Hassan and Hussein, grandsons of the Prophet, were lost in the desert. In Nubian communities of Upper Egypt, special ceremonies are held on *Arbah Maidar*, as this last Wednesday of Safar is known. Soup dishes of boiled grain are exchanged, and precautions are taken against the evil spirits prowling around on that day. Malay Muslims mark this last Wednesday with the *Mandi Safar* ceremony, which involves bathing in water consecrated by Qur'ânic verses. The verses are written on pieces of paper and then dropped into the water. The negative view of *bulan sapal*, Safar, among the Yakan of Basilan, in the southern Philippines, has already been highlighted. Interestingly, the Yakan focus their protective ceremony of *magpandi-pandi* on the first three Wednesdays of this second month of the year. Most other Muslim communities seem to place extra emphasis on the final Wednesday of Safar.

Ramaḍân, the ninth month, is the month of fasting and is definitely the 'blessed' month. The jinn are said to be imprisoned during this month. In Egypt, during Ramaḍân, no *zâr* ceremonies take place because the *zâr* spirits are considered to be inactive. By contrast the tenth month, Shawwâl, is traditionally held to be the month for hunting. The eleventh month, Dhû'l-Qaᶜda, is the time for resting, and the twelfth, Dhû'l-Ḥijja, is the time for pilgrimage.

Such concepts of time influence the manner in which ordinary Muslims look on life in general and order the activities of specific days or hours. To travel or not to travel? When to marry? When to pray through the night? What to do during this time or that? When to launch a ship, open a new branch of a bank, or have one's son circumcised?

The point of time

The Old Testament knows a concern for the 'right' time. The change of tenancy of Canaan—from 'Amorite' to Israelite—illustrates that concern. In the biblical revelation, Yahweh's decision that the time had come for the takeover is presented as 'right' or appropriate from the perspectives of both peoples.

The people of Israel had gone down to Egypt during Joseph's premiership. They had grown there, groaned there, and now came time for their deliverance. Within the time of that exodus, sufficient years elapsed in wilderness wandering to allow for the death of all but two of the original escaping adults. Only with the disappearance of those who had no trust in Yahweh as Lord of time and space could Joshua and

Caleb lead the people into their new inheritance across the Jordan.

At that time, the Amorites dominated the seven nations of Canaan. Their name seems often to have been used in a collective sense for Canaanites. The two Amorite kingdoms east of Jordan, those of Sihon and Bashan, were the first to fall, as a result of their offensive against the people of Yahweh. Joshua then dealt a strong blow to the Amorites west of the Jordan. In all, he defeated five Amorite kings, then consolidated his hold on the land with his subsequent routing of the northern Amorite confederacy, near the waters of Merom.

The Old Testament proclaims that Yahweh was intimately involved in these military victories of the late thirteenth century BC. He was behind the dramatic defeat of the 'Amorites' of Canaan and the handing over of the land to the people of Israel at this moment in history (Amos 2:9–10). Such a claim might reasonably be understood from an Israelite point of view. In God's promise to the patriarch Abram of 'seed' who would live in Canaan, the Lord revealed that a 400-year gap would occur between the promise and its fulfilment. In those centuries, the people of Israel would be generated from Isaac, the miracle child of Abram. The people would be bound together as a nation, in a slave capacity, in a country not their own. They would be ill-treated and abused, but held by God's hand until the time came for Abram's descendants, in the fourth generation, to return to Canaan.

What was the significance of the victories of Joshua, from the 'Amorite' point of view? The Old Testament sees those conquests as a much delayed punishment. God hesitated because 'the sin of the Amorites has not yet reached its full measure' (Genesis 15:16). The sin of the 'Amorites' in rejecting the Creator God called forth a reckoning, even if delay after delay was expended in the hope of a change of heart.

'Amorite' is as much in view in salvation history as

'Israelite'. Yahweh is as much the agent behind the coming of Philistines from Crete, Arameans from Kir, Babylonians from eastern Assyria—as he is the deliverer of Israelites from Egypt. His timing underlines both his sovereignty in the affairs of men and his commitment to a relationship with his creation. If a people will live at ease with him, they will enjoy tenancy of his earth. If they reject him, they will die in the wilderness (Israelites) or on the battlefield (Amorites). The Old Testament understanding of time speaks of more than mere human history-making.

The idea of a 'right' moment is repeated in the parallel context of Israel's exile and return to Palestine. In the first year of Darius of Babylon (539 BC), Daniel the prophet undertakes an extended period of fasting and prayer, repenting on behalf of his nation in sackcloth and ashes. He has understood from the word of the Lord, through his contemporary Jeremiah, that the desolation of Jerusalem would last seventy years. The exile came because of Israel's faithlessness to the living God. In Babylon, the people have learned never again to turn to other gods. The time comes for a remnant to return. In Gabriel's words to Daniel about the sure promise of return to Jerusalem for the people of Israel, the timing of the Messiah's coming is also unveiled. In the immediate fulfilment, Cyrus the king of Persia (most probably the same person as 'Darius') becomes Yahweh's 'anointed' instrument. The king is moved by the Lord to make a proclamation providing for the return to Jerusalem of some of the people of Israel to rebuild the Temple.

When the events are subsequently opposed by human forces, the timing of a glance from King Artaxerxes to his cup-bearer brings new resources to bear. Nehemiah confesses the reasons for his sadness to the king and obtains a licence to go to Jerusalem himself and oversee the reconstruction work. The return of a remnant, the rebuilding of the Temple, and the prophecy of Messiah's coming all underline the biblical view of time. Actions on this earth are enveloped in the acts of a holy, but involved, God in heaven.

The Bible therefore has a strong sense of the 'right' time. In the New Testament, the ideas of *kairos,* and *chronos,* would be fully set forth. The supreme focus of *chronos* will prove to be 'the fulness of time' (Galations 4:4, RSV), at which incarnation takes place. Salvation history then proceeds to the ultimate fulfilment of the times (*kairos*), when all things in heaven and on earth will have been brought together under the lordship of Christ (Ephesians 1:10). Like the worldview of ordinary Muslims, Scripture underlines the significance of times and seasons.

The Bible, however, distances itself from the kind of amoral view of time expressed in popular Islam. The biblical view of timing, at both national and individual levels, is dependent upon a relationship between human beings and their Creator. Yahweh is Lord of time, so an Egyptian Pharaoh is disturbed by a dream, or a Persian monarch cannot sleep at night. In consequence, life expectancies change for a faithful Joseph or a Mordecai. In this sense, the biblical worldview does not hand over certain months, days, or hours to evil per se. There is a time for everything, a season for every activity under heaven (Ecclesiastes 3:1–8). Time's unfolding interprets what is going on in the relationship between the Creator and his creation.

The biblical hope to be extended to ordinary Muslims is that evil, or less auspicious times may be radically reversed in a new relationship with the Lord of time and history. Time began as a facet of creation, an expression of God's good will. Time will end in the folding up of heaven and earth; then will come a new time and a new creation. The present time, for all mankind, is the hour of God's favour, the day of salvation (2 Corinthians 6:2).

CHAPTER TEN

KNOWING ONE'S PLACE

Where to look?

'WHILE YOU ARE REPEATING one of the names of God, there should be no interruptions. If thoughts come as you are concentrating on a name, remain seated with your eyes closed. Imagine you are dead and all your mourners have departed. You are alone, ready to face the judgement. Focus all your senses. Direct your mind towards God. Continue to repeat the name.'

'I am such a beginner,' worried Abdullah as he sat barefoot and cross-legged on the prayer mat, listening to the sheikh. He must have spent six months by now on the first name, and he didn't seem to be getting very far.

After each obligatory prayer, Abdullah had begun the practice of repeating the name, *Yâ-Raḥmân*, 100 times. Either he had misunderstood the instructions of his mentor, or he had a long way to go to be free from all kinds of distraction. Repeating *Yâ-Raḥmân* regularly after prayer was supposed to give a good memory, a keen awareness, and to bring freedom from a heavy heart. The opposite process seemed to be going on in Abdullah. How was he ever going to progress to the name *Yâ-Salâm*? The sheikh had taught them a few weeks ago that with this name, whoever repeated it properly 160 times to a sick person, would help that person to regain health. Abdullah seemed far from that kind of power.

The other lessons weren't going too well either. Abdullah had grown up with a keen understanding of the positive and negative values of right and left. He was aware that certain places brought blessing or harm upon people. He was convinced of the powers of numbers and letters. It was in the application of such knowledge that Abdullah seemed to find difficulty. His problems with *salât al-istikhâra*, the prayer for divinatory dreams, was a case in point.

Salât al-istikhâra would be one of the major functions for a spiritual guide to fulfil. Everyone needed to know the best path along which to walk. For the more crucial decisions in life, people would come to him. After all, he was a disciple of the famous Sheikh Rahal. If he grew expert in this art, Abdullah knew that there was promise of power, a famous name and much reward. He applied himself to the method taught by the leader of the order.

'It is well known to all people,' the sheikh had commented one day, 'that if a man refrains from sexual intercourse, and sleeps on his right side, he will have good dreams.' Abdullah had no problem in refraining from relationships with women; his passion in life lay in the realm of the spirit, not the body. He faithfully went to sleep on his right side. But could he remember his dreams? Abdullah wondered if a person's soul actually left the body during sleep and wandered in a way similar to the wandering that occurred at death. Or maybe dreams were simply vivid dramas, happening deep within the mind. Either way, Abdullah had to devise some method of recalling what went on in those unconscious activities. He knew that it was important for him to grow in this fundamental control of his sleep life and he asked the sheikh privately for more detailed advice.

'It is important to have washed properly. If you are married, Abdullah, you must refrain from sexual relations for that evening. Before sleeping, turn to the *qibla*, intone the *Fâtiḥa* and then recite al-Kâfirûn and al-Ikhlâs (suras 109 and 112). You will be given protection from evil and an open door into the future. Next, perform two *rak^cas* and pray the prayer of petition on behalf of the supplicant who has come to you. God will grant you to know whether the course of action he is contemplating will be beneficial for him or not. Go to sleep, and the answer will come clearly in a dream. If you follow this procedure, Abdullah, you will surely recall the dream. Remember to fall asleep lying on the right side. To sleep lying on the left will prejudice the outcome very badly!'

Then there was the question of diagnosis and healing of sicknesses. Abdullah knew that his calling would also involve him in that practice. He watched Sheikh Rahal closely in his preparations and activities. All that the holy man seemed to need was part of the clothing of the sick person. In the evening, he would go through a ritual similar to that required for *salâṭ al-istikhâra*. For more serious problems, the sheikh preferred to make the diagnosis at the shrine of Sîdî ^cAlî bin Ḥamdush or one of the other powerful saints of the past. At the end of the invocation, Sheikh Rahal would curl up on his right side with the piece of clothing from the sick person tucked inside his vest, close to his heart. In the morning he would rise and announce both the cause of the problem and its solution.

There was much to learn, and Abdullah felt very inexperienced. He remembered the last *mawlid* at the shrine of Sîdî Aḥmad Dghughi. The Ḥamadsha had been there, playing. Sheikh Rahal had tried to explain to his disciples, amid all the noise and confusion, the different kinds of affliction which the jinn caused in human lives. It was complicated, but it had gradually dawned on Abdullah that there was at least one major distinction. Some people, fortunate ones perhaps, were only 'struck' by jinn. Others were 'possessed' by them, and became their habitations.

The sheikh had pointed out a man with a distorted face: 'That old man with the paralysis of the face! Do you see him? He is *matrûsh*. The paralysis is on the left side. It came on him suddenly. He was slapped in the face by a *jinnî*.'

Abdullah and the other disciples had nodded sagely.

'Listen carefully to me. To be *matrûsh* is bad enough, but there is one kind of striking that is stronger than *matrûsh*. There are few conditions in life worse than being *madrûb*. The person who is *madrûb* is not difficult to recognise. He is paralysed of course, but not just in the face. His arms and hands, legs and feet are bound as well. Look down and see if a person has a string around his slippers to hold them on. It is likely that he is *madrûb*. Look especially at the left side of his body. Do you see the paralysis all the way up? To be *madrûb* is very dangerous. Such a person may suddenly collapse, and if he is near a road, or by water, it could be the death of him. Happy are those who are only *mushârûn*. A *jinnî* has merely pointed a finger at them. There might come a slight, temporary paralysis; often not. Usually it is a person's first contact with a *jinnî*. There is a general malaise. Someone *mushâr* is easy to help.'

Abdullah had thought that he was beginning to grasp the diagnoses until Sheikh Rahal had turned to the analysis of different kinds of possession. Though the jinn entered the bodies of both the possessed and the struck, it seemed they remained longer with the possessed. They entered those they struck and left almost immediately, but of those inhabited by jinn, *masqût* and *maklûc* were conditions of temporary possession in which the person did not need any special treatment. Other conditions, however, required far more care.

The sheikh had commanded them: 'Pity the person who is *maskûn*, for he is permanently inhabited by a *jinnî*, and is subject to the *jinnî's* will and whims. He is no longer master of his own life. Of course, the most common kind of attack by jinn leaves someone *maqyûs*. He feels absent from his own body. Perhaps the *jinnî* replaces him in his body. Who knows? Some who are *maqyûs* tremble and fall; others sit still, with a faraway look, in a corner. With the person who is *maqyûs*, it could mean an attack in the form of either possession or striking.'

Abdullah's own mind had begun to feel absent from his body. He reeled at the further requirement of recognising different trance states. Although resembling conditions of possession or striking, these conditions were deemed therapeutic in the healing processes of dancing the *ḥadr*. Diagnosis of trouble from jinn would require much training at the hands of Sheikh Rahal.

Meanwhile, Abdullah concentrated on a mastery of the repeating of the names, and on dream divination. Obviously his effectiveness in these arts would be greatly enhanced if his life were increasingly saturated in *baraka*.

As he grew older, Abdullah therefore spent much time at the tomb of Sheikh al-Kamal in Meknes. That saint was well known for his powers, and just being at the site made one aware of the contagious quality of the great saint's *baraka*. Abdullah loved staying there for extended periods. He aimed at building a reputation as an *ᶜarrâf*, one who 'knows'.

Berbers gradually began to make their oaths in front of him at the shrine. He directed them in facing Mecca, and swearing in the name of Sheikh al-Kamal. Others came who wanted his advice on whether a proposed marriage partnership would be propitious or not. Abdullah had a natural aptitude for the science of numerical astrology. He would work out the arithmetic value of each partner's name, and confidently pronounce whether the proposed matrimonial union would be harmonious or not. Magic numbers fascinated Abdullah. He loved to use the threefold magic square attributed to al-Ghazâlî. It featured in many of the amulets he made up, especially in those for conception in the cases of barren women.

Abdullah kept his eyes open, carefully looking for those tell-tale signs in his clientele which would show that they had been visited in some way by the jinn.

'The left,' he often told himself, 'watch the left!'

Concepts of space in popular Islam

Concepts of space are strong in the outlook of ordinary Muslims. They feature in many aspects of both formal and folk-Islamic attitudes and actions.

The right and left differentiation is significant in Muslims' view of space. The *hadîth* suggest that part of the difference between men and women is explained by the fact that woman was created from a rib taken from the left side of man. As a result, the physical and animal side is stronger in woman than in man, and from that follows the necessity for the sexual activity of women to be carefully bounded. In man, the spiritual and angelic attributes are stronger than in woman, and from that follows the importance of men's roles in religious ritual. Women are welcome, but not essential participants, in public worship, whereas men must be present.

In the account of Muhammad's night journey and ascension to heaven, the differentiation between right and left is emphasised within the story of the formal faith of Islam. In the first heaven, Muhammad meets the prophet Adam. A procession takes place comprising the whole human race which would derive from that original man. They are passing in front of Adam at God's instigation. Muhammad and Adam see persons and a gate to their right, from which issues a pleasant odour. Every time Adam glances to the right, to those set in Illiyun, he laughs and rejoices. The prophets then see persons and a gate to their left, from which a horrible stench emanates. In looking to the left, to those condemned to Sijjin, Adam grieves and weeps.

Other *ḥadîth* define the order of washing before formal prayer so that Muslims conform to Muhammad's practice. Right hand, ear and foot are cleaned before left hand, ear and foot. At the end of prayers, greeting is made to the angel of the right shoulder, then to that of the left shoulder.

In some processes of divination, such as that using symbols drawn in the sand by a Sudanese *khaṭṭâṭ*, the right hands of both client and practitioner are employed.

Diagnosis of the kind of jinn attack made upon a person is often guided in Morocco by right and left differentiation. Dreams are highly motivating phenomena among ordinary Muslims. The *Majmac al-Dacawât* by Muḥammad ibn Kiyâs al-Dîn gives rules for sleeping that enable various kinds of dream. In many cases, such as that for sighting deceased relatives in a dream, the special *ducâ'*, or prayer, must be followed by sleeping on one's right side.

Left-handed persons are generally seen as special, either in an aberrant, wicked sense, or else in a positive, supernatural sense. The use of the left hand for certain unclean activities such as picking the nose, or washing the anus after defecating is not just a facet of health etiquette. It reflects a deeper view of the positive and negative potential in right and left.

Another spatial concept that has ramifications throughout the lives of ordinary Muslims is that of *qibla* orientation: facing towards Mecca. In the mythology of Islam, Mecca functions as the navel of the earth. It was created first, and round it the world spread out. The site of the *kacba* (or holy building at the centre of the Sacred Mosque at Mecca) is the central point of the whole universe. Its foundation is in the lowest of the earths, and it stands squarely on an axis joining earth to heaven. That axis passes through all of the created universe to the highest heaven. Of all places, the *kacba* is the place where God is to be met face to face. The earthly Mecca knows a celestial counterpart, where angels congregate in their millions to worship.

Orientation towards Mecca, therefore, speaks of the unity of the community, access to other inhabitants of the created worlds, and potential for touching God's throne. Whenever a sacrifice is made, whether it is that of the *ᶜaqîqa* for a child, or one in honour of a visiting guest, or the great feast marking the completion of the *ḥajj*, everywhere the sacrificer turns the head of the victim towards the *kaᶜba*. Facing towards Mecca adds a strong sanction to oath-making. Would a person dare swear falsely while facing towards the *kaᶜba*? At death, a person is laid to face the *qibla*. Burial is similarly arranged so that the entire body often lies on its side, facing Mecca. Orienting towards the *kaᶜba* occurs at many moments of the Muslim's life, besides the formal rites of prayer and pilgrimage. It speaks of his longing for witnesses and helpers from the unseen world, accessible via that point on earth.

It is important for people to recognise and thus avoid places where it is known that devils or jinn tend to abide. The appreciation of such 'spirit space' will define, for ordinary Muslims, where they should or should not tread. Those who frequently have to step into territory normally inhabited by evil spirits will use amulets for protection.

Just as there are areas of evil influence, so there are spheres of holiness and blessing. Shrines of holy men give sanctity to the area surrounding them. Trees, wells or springs associated with a saint's shrine are held to partake of his *baraka*. Among the Pakistani Baluch, ground that has been consecrated with the *baraka* of a *pîr* can become a *tikkhâna*, or 'house of healing', after his death. Such houses form the focus of cults of healing. Earth from the area is taken home and mixed with water or tea and then consumed, and the *baraka* of the saint is thus transferred to the needy. Saints' tombs become the sites of various rites of passage for the same reason. *Baraka* from such sites is transmitted by some kind of touch. It is the aim of ordinary Muslims to step into 'saint space' whenever *baraka* is required in their lives, either for protection in the vulnerable periods of change of status, or in answer to crises.

Associated with the idea of grids of space is the science of magic numbers and configurations. Even numbers are thought to have something dangerous about them, whereas the odd number five is powerful to defend against jinn or the evil eye. Used offensively, the number five is considered a powerful curse. Seven is the most important number in a positive sense. In Pakistan, in a difficult delivery at the end of a pregnancy, one common remedy is to place a magic square designed by al-Ghazâlî beneath the feet of the woman in labour.

The powers of the letters of the Arabic alphabet are associated with numbers, because each letter in the alphabet has a numerical value. The letters are often divided into those of light and of darkness. The letters of light are used in talismans to produce unity, love and co-operation. The letters of darkness are employed to produce hatred, misunderstanding and war.

Figure 9 illustrates the three-by-three square seal, attributed to al-Ghazâlî (which is actually known as his 'triangle'), shown in both alphabetical and numerical form. The sum of every horizontal, vertical and diagonal line is fifteen. The alphabetical equivalent of the square can be arranged differently to obtain the roots of words such as love (*ḥb*) or

Figure 9[13]

The 'Triangle' of al-Ghazâlî

d	ṭ	b
j	h	z
ḥ	a	w

4	9	2
3	5	7
8	1	6

inclination (*wd*). In such a form it may be used as a talisman to produce love. This square appears in many charms. It features in the well-known seal called the Seven Covenants of Suleiman.

Spatial images in popular Islam are significant and relate in a compatible manner to concepts of relationship and causality. They explain, for example, where jinn or saints abide. Has a person wandered unprotected into places inhabited by evil spirits? That would give a reason for present abnormal behaviour. Should a person visit a shrine? At such a site, *baraka* for healing would be available.

Concepts of space are pervasive in their different forms and help to direct the activities of ordinary Muslims, especially at times of crisis or vulnerability.

Room for mankind

The biblical story of man unfolds within a divinely defined space. It begins in a garden in the East, in Eden. Trees that are pleasing to the eye and good for food spring up in the garden and include the tree of life. Only one place in Eden is forbidden to man. At the centre of the garden, near the tree of life, stands the tree of the knowledge of good and evil. The fruit of that tree is out of bounds.

Eve is created from Adam and, as his wife, hears her husband's warning about the tree in the centre of the garden. It seems likely that she does not hear those words directly from the Creator. Who then is she to contradict the clever misinformation of the serpent? Soon Eve tasts the forbidden fruit of the tree of the knowledge of good and evil and includes her husband in the act of disobedience. Immediately, their eyes are opened. Now the space that had been theirs to roam in innocently is transformed into hostile territory. They desperately try to hide in it from the Lord God, but their efforts are futile. They are banished from the garden.

From this point on, man's space becomes the cursed ground of earth outside paradise. From the dust of the earth he springs, and when he dies he returns to it. Mere dust, excluded from the fruit of the tree of life, will return to mere dust. In the intervening years of his earthly existence, he has to toil to make that earth produce fruit by which he may support himself.

Apart from a sprinkling of hopeful promises throughout the biblical revelation, it is not until the closing vision of Jesus the Alpha and Omega—in the final chapters of the Book—that an alternative living space is provided for recreated man. In the new Jerusalem that comes down out of heaven from God, a redeemed multitude moves into view. That crowd, comprising the bride of Christ, has renewed access to the tree of life. The leaves of the tree are spread for the healing of the nations, and the earth-curse is gone. The centre of existence becomes the throne of God and of the Lamb. There, room for mankind is found.

Such is the ultimate biblical setting of mankind in space. The story that unfolds between creation and recreation frequently underlines the significance of place in man's relationship with the supernatural.

The places of God's self-revealing take on his quality of holiness. Moses at the burning bush in the Sinai wilderness and Joshua in front of Jericho at the borders of Canaan both have to remove their sandals because the ground they stand on is holy. Their parallel experiences are repeated in the lives of prophet after prophet. Encounters with the living God occur in an aura of contagious holiness affecting everything around.

When the completed Tabernacle is finally set up in the desert, the glory of the Lord so fills it that no one can enter the Tent of Meeting. Later, the captured ark of the covenant looks after its own return to Canaan from Philistia. There had been no room in its presence for the Philistine god, Dagon! In its journeying back to Canaan, no person's steadying hand is permitted! Human beings who dare to look into it do so at the risk of their lives! The ark of the Lord displaces all powers, devilish or human, wherever it moves.

When Solomon finishes his prayer of dedication over the newly built Temple at Jerusalem, fire falls from heaven to consume the burnt offering and sacrifices. The priests cannot enter the building because the glory of the Lord completely fills it.

Every now and then, the Bible unveils some of the dominant spiritual occupants of space. There are hints of evil principalities and powers, demonic 'princes' over men, and even over nations, yet despite this unveiling of evil, the ultimate lordship of Yahweh over all space is also strongly expressed.

Ben-Hadad, king of Aram, grows frustrated with the supposed spy in his camp who keeps revealing his military plans to the Israelites. Again and again his strategies are foiled. In the end Ben-Hadad learns that a prophet in Israel by the name of Elisha tells the king of Israel the very words that he speaks in utmost privacy. Ben-Hadad discovers the whereabouts of Elisha and dispatches a strong army with chariots and horses to surround the city. The following morning, when Elisha's servant awakens, he is frightened by the massive force sent to capture them. When he is told about the threat, Elisha suggests that the army on their side is far greater than that arrayed against them. With opened eyes, the servant of Elisha sees the space around him differently: the hills ringing the armies of Ben-Hadad, which surround the city containing the prophet Elisha, are full of horses and chariots of fire. The hosts of Yahweh are present. Space, in a larger dimension, is filled with Yahweh's servants of fire.

Conflict over space finds prominence in the New Testament. Jesus Christ walks into areas seen as unholy by the Jewish religious hierarchy and transforms them. He eats in the homes of publicans and sinners. He touches lepers, unclean women, and corpses. He invades the wilderness to combat the Evil One. He throws moneychangers out of the Temple precincts. He commands devils to leave Legion. He is Lord even of Gethsemane, with armies of angels at hand should he choose to avoid trial and crucifixion. He is commander over Sheol, and spoiler of the grave, for he preaches to the spirits in prison who have been incarcerated from pre-flood days; there are no 'no-go' areas for the Christ. He is finally raised to heaven and seated in God's own presence at the Father's right hand. Angels, authorities and powers now live in submission to him. Christ's victory wins him access to all space on earth and in the heavens.

Part of the good news of being 'in Christ' relates to the question of space. There is no place that a believer cannot enter, protected by the whole armour of God. The believer's role, in a world given over to evil, is that of an overcomer. Testimony to Christ's victory, confidence in Christ's shed blood and obedience to Christ's commands provide a weapon against which no enemy of the believer can stand. What is more, angels surround and minister to those who belong to Christ. Jesus himself intercedes on their behalf before the throne of the Father. The Spirit strengthens them with the same power as was used in Christ's resurrection. Places may be identified as strongholds of evil, but Christ's followers are commissioned to capture them.

The exorcism of places tends to take on significance in Christian mission to Muslims. The ordinary Muslim's concept of space sees certain areas as occupied by evil spirits. Those areas need to be redeemed by cleansing and maybe exorcism if the Muslim is to be freed from fear, in movement around his own home or in the community at large.

In the Old Testament, Yahweh revealed that the defilement of a people would quickly lead to a pollution of the land where they lived (Leviticus 18:25). Such a process actually occurred among the successive inhabitants of Canaan, both 'Amorite' and Israelite. The result for each was a vomiting out of the nation from the land. The exile of the people of Israel was accompanied by barrenness of natural soil, locust plagues and occupation by wild lions (2 Kings 17:25). In consequence, the land, as much as the nation, needed to be reclaimed for Yahweh (Amos 9:13). Part of Yahweh's constant promise through the prophets concerned such reclamation, if only the people would humble themselves and return to him first in a spiritual sense: '...if my people, who are called by my name, will humble themselves and pray and seek my face and turn from their wicked ways, then will I hear from heaven and will forgive their sin and will heal their land' (2 Chronicles 7:14).

In Nehemiah's leadership of the returned remnant, the issues of firstfruits, tithes and Sabbath rest were repeatedly highlighted. Nehemiah's concern was to hold the Israelites to the 'binding agreement' they had made (Nehemiah 9:38). That agreement included a new attitude to the spacious and fertile land which belonged to the Lord but which had been defiled by the people's previous sins. Nehemiah identified a specific polluting of the courts of the house of the Lord; Tobiah, an enemy of the returned exiles, had been provided with a room there by one of the priests and had given himself to evil plans and deeds from that place. Nehemiah threw all Tobiah's household goods out of the room, and then 'gave orders to purify the rooms' (Nehemiah 13:9).

Among Muslims, who see toilets, graveyards and sorceresses' homes as residences of jinn, disciples of Jesus Christ need to reclaim those places in his name. Such ministry probably needs to be learned by Christians from a Western background, for whom the foundational view of space is somewhat different from that espoused by the Bible. Middle Eastern Christians, especially those within a renewed Orthodox tradition, know the need for, and effectiveness of, such reclamation of spaces for Christ. In Jesus' name, places identified as polluted by evil spirits or human rebellion against God are exorcised and cleansed. Often, holy water is sprinkled around the rooms of a home as a sign of the

spiritual cleansing which has taken place. The Lord is invited
to dwell in the reclaimed space. Of course, the major focus
of concern is with the individuals concerned, that they own
the lordship of Christ in their personal lives. For such
believers, the ritual is not a form of magic, but a service of
transfer and dedication.

A significant saying of Jesus himself, in view of such
ministry, concerns the binding of the strong man as preparation for the despoiling of his territory. Only after careful
dealing with the false landlord can the space be spiritually
reclaimed, and the tenants there rescued. Intercessory
prayer in such spiritual warfare must be a major component
of Christian mission to Muslims. Power encounter at that
level, in the space falsely claimed by the Evil One, is a vital
element of Christian witness among ordinary Muslims.

PART 2

CHAPTER ELEVEN

THE WORLD OF
THE ORDINARY MUSLIM

THE FIRST PART OF THIS BOOK has described a world very different from that advertised in most expositions of the Islamic faith. It is nonetheless a real world, one in which ordinary Muslims actually live out their allegiances as religious beings. The task of Chapters Eleven and Twelve is to draw together the material surveyed so far and to suggest how it forms a unified whole.

Contrasting views of reality: 'beings' and 'powers'

The picture of reality emerging from an under-the-surface look at popular Islam is difficult for the Western mind to grasp. Ordinary Muslims see life very much in terms of personal 'beings' and impersonal 'powers'. Westerners also own such concepts, but the boundaries of the concepts and the realms of their operation are very different.

For ordinary Muslims, concepts of 'being' include a large range of both trans-empirical and empirical forms of life. 'Trans-empirical' forms are those which remain beyond scientific analysis; they are intangible and unmeasurable. 'Empirical' forms are those which may be subjected to scientific analysis; they are tangible and measurable. Although the Westerner agrees that humans and animals are examples of empirical 'beings', and may concede that God is a trans-empirical 'being', he does not easily understand the Muslim's recognition of a large range of other trans-empirical 'beings'—including, for example, spirits, ancestors and jinn. Nor does the Westerner agree that foods such as bread actually possess intrinsic life or 'being' of their own.

The identification of 'being' is further complicated in that the ordinary Muslim has definite ideas as to the realm in which each kind of 'being' operates. There are basically two such realms: the 'this-worldly' and the 'other-worldly'. The Westerner perceives God, angels and devils as belonging to the other-worldly realm, precisely because they are trans-empirical spiritual beings; he also sees humans and animals

Figure 10

Western and Folk-Islamic Views of 'Being'

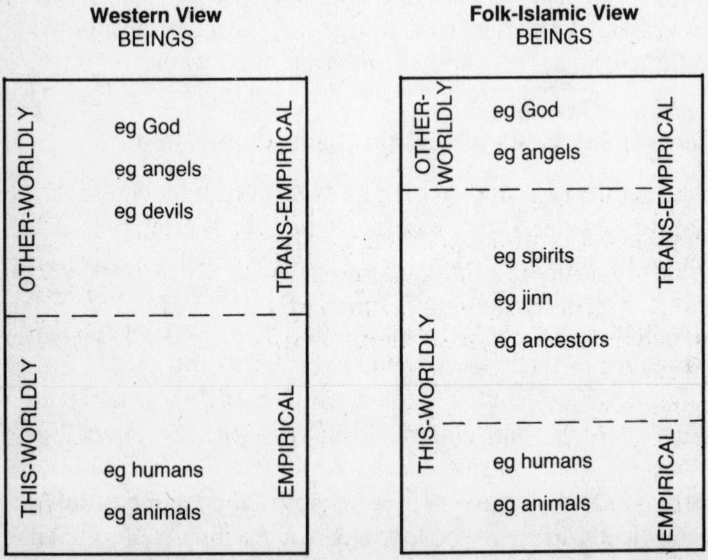

Western View
BEINGS

Folk-Islamic View
BEINGS

as belonging to the this-worldly realm, precisely because those beings are empirical, having bodies of flesh. The ordinary Muslim, however, sees many trans-empirical beings as functioning in the this-worldly realm. Saints, *zâr* spirits, the souls of the recently dead and other trans-empirical beings operate in the same sphere as humans.

Figure 10 contrasts the Western and the folk-Islamic views of 'beings'. Different ideas as to which forms of life may be included in the category of 'trans-empirical' are indicated, as well as alternative perceptions of which kinds of being operate in the other-worldly or this-worldly realms.

The same divergence of understanding occurs in the concept of impersonal 'powers'. The Westerner recognises many natural forces, which are empirical or tangible by nature, functioning in the this-worldly realm. He may concede that

Figure 11

Western and Folk-Islamic Views of 'Power'

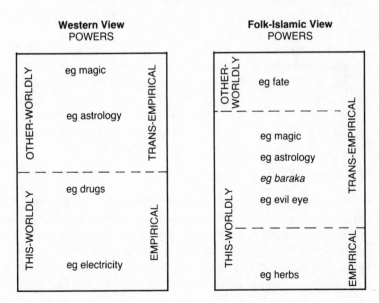

some trans-empirical forces exist, such as magic and astrology. However, if the Westerner does admit the reality of those forces, he sees them as belonging to the other-worldly realm. The ordinary Muslim, by contrast, recognises that a few forms of trans-empirical power, such as fate, operate in the other-worldly realm. He also admits the existence of certain empirical forces, such as herbs, which operate in the this-worldly sphere. His world is filled, however, with trans-empirical forces, such as those of *baraka* and the evil eye, which all function in the this-worldly realm. In other words, the ordinary Muslim recognises many trans-empirical forces which might have immediate effect upon humans' lives.

Figure 11 contrasts the Western and the folk-Islamic views of 'powers', indicating different ideas as to which forms of impersonal force may be included in the category of 'trans-empirical'. Alternative perceptions of which kinds of power operate in the other-worldly or this-worldly realms are also shown.

In concepts of both personal 'being' and impersonal 'power', the folk-Islamic concern is focused on trans-empirical phenomena which operate mainly in this world.

While the rest of this chapter describes the various kinds of personal 'being' as they find definition in the folk-Islamic worldview, the following chapter will analyse the different forms of 'power' and seek to bring both concepts together in an identification of a cosmology of popular Islam.

Concepts of 'being' in popular Islam

Naturally, living humans constitute one of the major categories of personal 'being', subdivided into various classes of humans. Living holy men would seem to command the greatest respect by ordinary Muslims, possessing inherited or innate charisma. They would include the leaders of Moroccan religious orders, or *pîrs* in the subcontinent of India and

Pakistan. Living holy men often derive their special status from their descent, via a complex but complete family tree, from the Prophet Muhammad. Otherwise, by the wisdom they show or the miraculous deeds they do, their unique qualities are acclaimed by all who know them.

Ordinary mortals also comprise part of the world of tangible 'being', though a strong distinction is made between believer and infidel. Among Muslims themselves, there may well be a gradation of respect between the more and less pious, the true and the nominal believers. A difference in spiritual quality and aptitude is made between the two sexes.

Animals are included in this category of tangible or empirical 'being'. Again, distinctions are made. The pig is formally proscribed as an unclean animal, and its flesh is tabooed for eating. Another animal, however (in the Middle East at least), is viewed with the greatest abhorrence. The dog is perceived as the dirtiest beast and, because of the principle of metamorphosis, it is seen as a likely carrier of a metamorphosed *jinnî*. To call someone 'the son of a dog' is a great insult, for it casts doubt on the true humanness of the person being insulted. Horses are a protected species by virtue of their association with the winged Burâq, who features in the story of Muhammad's visit to Jerusalem and ascension into the heavens.

Certain natural products are considered to possess life of their own; hence the view of nature differs considerably from the standard Western one. Whereas the Westerner has no scruples about subjugating nature, ordinary Muslims most often prefer to live in harmony with nature. Natural products such as herbs and drugs are believed to cause effects on human beings or even on spirit beings. The treatment given by ordinary Muslims to bread is significant and exemplifies this view of nature.

In the trans-empirical realm, there are many forms of 'life', as the preceding chapters have illustrated. The souls of the recently dead are seen as present or near at hand, both initially after death and then at certain recognised intervals, or on specific festival days of the Islamic year. Such a view is especially to the fore in cultures where the faith of Islam has rested largely as a veneer over more traditional views of the world. In many African communities, where ancestor veneration is an intrinsic part of tribal and clan relationship, Islamisation has allowed for a continuance of this relationship under the aegis of a formal adherence to Islam.

The concept of *qarîna*, or some kind of double of the human individual, is another expression of 'being' in the trans-empirical realm. That double is seen as responsible for a variety of occurrences in the life of a human being.

Named jinn such as the Moroccan A'isha Qandisha or the Iranian Al exemplify another powerful form of 'life'. Usually, such named jinn are female and their involvement is with male humans. The description of a man as being 'married' to a *jinnîya* is not uncommon; in some rarer instances, women are held to be captured by male jinn.

Unnamed jinn comprise another genus of trans-empirical 'being'. They are feared as very powerful beings, usually malevolent, and strongly operative in relation to mankind. All sorts of harm are attributed to the activities of jinn, whose existence finds authentication in the Qur'ân itself, and many Muslims wear some kind of protective device on their account.

A specialised species of trans-empirical 'life' is discovered in the *zâr* spirits and their equivalents. These possessing spirits are seen as malevolent only to a certain degree. When a give-and-take relationship is established between them and their female habitations, the women concerned are enabled to live in equilibrium. They are also guaranteed regular, enjoyable occasions for their unguarded self-expression as religious beings. *Zâr*-type spirits are not exorcised but become part of everyday life and decision-making. They give motivation and meaning to home life and determine the form of feminine spiritual experience. They are a powerful species of 'life' in the world of ordinary Muslims.

Deceased saints provide another potent form of 'being' in the view of ordinary Muslims. Both their corpses and their shrines—even the ground, water, or foliage surrounding their graves—are endowed with large deposits of *baraka*. In return for honouring such dead saints, Muslims may receive help from them. Vows, visits and saints' day celebrations comprise the main occasions for giving honour to dead saints. In return, the saints render specific services, either in intercession with God on a higher spiritual plane, or else in the dispensing of *baraka* on a more mundane level. Many Muslims, even the most orthodox, relate to saints at times of crisis or need in their lives. The highly educated, for example, often take the added precaution of vowing at a saint's shrine before examinations, in the hope that the *baraka* may benefit them. For far more Muslims, the process of vow-making has brought pragmatic changes. The Muslim world, both urban and rural, is comprehensively filled with saints' shrines.

Prophets, apostles and messengers are also seen as strong personalities in the trans-empirical world of 'being'. Charms appeal to them and intercession is addressed to them. Along with certain female relatives of the supreme prophet (such as Fâṭima and Nafîsa) they are seen as potential mediators with God. In some cases, they may be directly petitioned. In other cases, God himself may be addressed, but asked to apply their merit to the benefit of the petitioner. Prophets are seen as human beings with proven acceptance by God, and therefore as strong potential helpers of the afflicted. Veneration of Muhammad, including his relics and artifacts, is high on the agenda of religious devotion for multitudes of Muslims.

Led by Iblîs, devils comprise a further category of 'being' and are always evil. Some specific devils are identified by name, others by the effect they have on their victims. Walhân is said to preside over ablutions and prayer, al-Haffaf over deserts, Zalambûr over markets and Bathr over misfortunes. A *mârid* is identified by its characteristic habit of rolling victims in the dust, as its name in Arabic suggests. This type of devil is seen as a very strong personality among Egyptian Muslims, and appeasing such devils, especially at times of vulnerability (particularly childbirth) is common practice in many communities.

All, or nearly all, of these forms of 'life' ground their existence in the world of human beings—the terrestrial world. It may be true that devils originate from a netherworld, and it might be argued that the *qarînât* actually inhabit a world that mirrors that of human beings. The arena of their common operation, however, is this world. All beings, both empirical and trans-empirical, described thus far vie for room to manoeuvre in the space that comprises this earth. The Muslim therefore lives his life in company with a large number of other often hostile beings. Since the tangible universe is replete with varying forms of life, one cannot be too careful in one's relationships with other inhabitants of this world. Is a certain sentence or action going to offend some of them? Might it bring repercussions upon oneself? How did I treat that piece of bread I noticed on the pavement today? Did I respond in a healthy way to a stray dog? Is my child sick because a *jinnîya* or a twin spirit has struck him? Should I go on to the local saint's shrine, after seeing the government doctor, to get a remedy for this chronic illness of mine? Where can I find *baraka* to redress the balance in my threatened marriage? To whom can I appeal, that I might lose my barrenness, and conceive and bear a son? Such questions arise in a world full of many co-inhabitants with positive, neutral or negative intentions towards human beings.

Other concepts of 'being', also trans-empirical, make up the rest of the ordinary Muslim's worldview. These forms of life, however, belong to the other-worldly area of existence.

Their centre of operation is not on this earth, but elsewhere; such are angels and archangels. Like devils, so certain angels and archangels are carefully distinguished. Angels preside over the days of the week, each having a special associated perfume which is used when a Muslim approaches a specific presiding angel. One angel holds the balance on the Day of Judgement, while another executes the divine decrees of death at the appointed hour. Munkar and Nakîr (identified by function in sura 47:29 of the Qur'ân) subject men to the fearsome questioning about their faith in the tomb after death. The earth is affected by angels who cause the winds to blow, who bring down the rain by hand, who watch over unborn babies, and who care for nursing infants. Gabriel, spoken of in the Qur'ân as God's medium of revelation (sura 2:91ff) and, implicitly, as Holy Spirit (sura 16:104), brought the sacred word to Muhammad. The being closest to God, closer even than Gabriel, is Sarafiel. The archangelic throne bearers provide focus for much intercession, as their mediation would gain a hearing with God himself. The ranks of angelic beings, dwelling in the heavens and closer to God, offer the ordinary Muslim the hope of benefactors, mediators, and intercessors with a most remote Lord.

God himself, of course, heads the list of Muslim concepts of 'being'. The focus of his dwelling is in the heavens, beyond the seventh heaven. With some recognition of his immanence, the main picture of God for most Muslims emphasises his other-worldly character and residence. He is an almighty, all-knowing God, far off. None shares his divinity, though some have access to his dwelling place.

Such, then, are the more significant concepts of personal 'being' recognised by ordinary Muslims. We turn now to their understanding and categorisation of impersonal 'powers'.

CHAPTER TWELVE

POWERS, PATTERNS AND PROCESSES

I F THE ORDINARY MUSLIM'S concept of varieties of 'being' is complex, so also is his idea of the possibilities of 'power' or 'force'. While the Western mind by and large recognises the reality of natural forces in the empirical world, and (with faith) supernatural power in the other-worldly realm, the ordinary Muslim perceives a whole intermediate range of powers. Those powers are neither empirical on the one hand, nor other-worldly on the other. They are trans-empirical, consequently not scientifically measurable. At the same time, they are this-worldly, therefore accessible to mortals.

Concepts of 'power' in popular Islam

Of the strictly empirical concepts of 'power' recognised by ordinary Muslims, herbs stand out as one of the major kinds. Natural drugs constitute a major medicinal source in many communities. Several cultures know categorisations of food and herbs on a hot/cold basis. Others know the power of certain kinds of plant to deal with evil spirits. In many large Islamic cities, a common vendor is the itinerant incense burner who for a few coins will fumigate the premises. The goal is not so much to perfume the place as to make it impossible for evil spirits to lodge there.

Dreams and visions are examples of a genus of 'force' which falls on the borderline between the empirical and trans-empirical worlds. What actually happens in sleep? Does the soul leave the body temporarily and wander? Are the visions seated in the mind, or in the emotions, or externally, in space/time? Certainly, ordinary Muslims perceive dreams and visions as highly significant forces. They function in a strongly motivating way in most Muslim cultures.

Muhammad's initial receiving of revelation came in a dream or vision, during sleep. So too in contemporary times the call to be a practitioner of some sort often comes through the medium of a dream. Among the Tausug of the Philippines, for example, most medicine men begin a practice through a dream in which they are visited by *shayâṭîn* (devils). The Malayan *bomor*, a curer specialised in trance-healing, usually receives the *alamat* or 'sign' of his new calling in a dream.

Divination by dream interpretation is a ubiquitous practice in popular Islam, often concentrated into a science of interpretation (*cilm al-tacbîr*) as, for example, in the Sudan. In Afghan Turkestan, the *bakhshi* will spend a night sleeping in the house of his patient; the dream he then receives during the night enables him to diagnose the patient's ailment and to select the appropriate therapy.

Dreams are sought as a means of communicating with the dead. The Kabyles of Algeria put food on the graves of deceased relatives if they dream of them. Visitational dreams are common throughout the Muslim world and may feature dead relatives, saints, jinn, angels or other spiritual beings.

Many saints' shrines are established as the direct result of dreams. A large number of shrines in Pakistan, for example, are dedicated to certain saints, although the saints themselves are not buried at those sites. Such a saint is considered to be present as a *shaykh mu^câshir*; that is, he has revealed himself to a holy man in a dream, indicating his desire to be venerated in a particular place.

A vast inventory of various kinds of 'power' fills the trans-empirical—though this-worldly—sphere of folk-Islamic thought. Amulets, charms and talismans are believed to protect from harm, to cancel offensive magic, and to undo sickness derived from various attacks. Different amulets specialise in achieving different ends, as the Arabic words used to describe them indicate. They may be *^cûdha* (from 'to protect'), *hijâb* (from 'to shield like a curtain'), *hirz* (from 'to guard against evil'), *nafra* (from 'to flee'), *wadh* (from 'to make distinct') or *tamîma* (from 'to be complete').

The Seven Covenants of Suleiman is a favourite amulet among Middle-Eastern Muslims, and may be found on sale in the market places of such cities as Amman, Beirut and Cairo. A child's shoe suspended from the rearview mirror of a taxi, truck, or private car is thought to be a powerful insurance against accident. Blue beads abound on infants, or vulnerable animals, to protect them against the devastating harm of the evil eye. Amulets containing the names of Muhammad, the names of the archangels Gabriel, Michael, Azrael and Israfel, the call to prayer, and verses from the Qur'ân are also worn to ensure safety from disease and harm.

In Iran, *du^câ's* (amulets) are composed of occult words and symbols, interspersed with sacred oaths and Qur'ânic verses, usually written in ink on long, narrow strips of paper by a *jadoogar*. They are often rolled and worn by the purchaser in a small cloth or leather bag around the neck. Known in Afghanistan as *ta^câwîdh*, amulets are commonly woven into the wearer's clothing.

Curses are a species of 'power' recognised in the give and take of community life. To have 'five in the eye' thrown at one, especially by a woman, would not be the best way to end a day. Cursing works by employing the powers of the occult world. In effect, oaths are conditional curses, compelling assistance. Jinn, or dead saints, are obliged by an oath to assist, or else suffer the consequences of the curse. In certain situations, living saints attributed with supernatural power have used the threat of cursing as a sanction against internal clan warfare.

Vow-making is one major way in which ordinary Muslims relate to saints, usually making their vows at the site of a saint's tomb, at auspicious times. Many motivations drive Muslims to this practice. Strict silence is kept over precisely what is vowed, and the fulfilment of vows is usually held as an important priority. Upsetting dreams experienced by someone who has not fulfilled a vow will lead to quick, corrective action. One form of vow-making is that of fulfilled vowing, in which the person fulfils his part of the bargain first, for example, by making a sacrifice, or by going on the *ḥajj*. Then the saint is morally obliged to fulfil his part of the bargain in meeting the request or desire of that person.

Augury comprises the art of divination by omens. Animals, birds, days, months, or varying circumstances are seen to augur good or ill. Among Malay Muslims, a broken pot at a wedding festivity portends ill for the bride and groom. In Algeria, to dream of losing a tooth, or to see a toothless person, indicates a death in the family. For the Tausug, a black butterfly entering a house is an omen of mourning, and a group of stray dogs howling in a certain section of the street warns of the coming death of a sick person. For many Muslims, certain days are good or bad for travelling, cutting new cloth or undertaking other tasks. A common belief among Arabs is that by simply uttering the name of disasters, or diseases, a person can evoke them.

As we saw in Chapter One, the evil eye is seen as a powerful 'force' and appears as a significant factor in ordinary Muslims' views of causality. A Pakistani captain of one ship may seriously accuse the captain of another of ruining his fishing by means of the evil eye. The Jats, a Muslim group in Pakistan, eat their food quickly and privately to prevent its possible exposure to the evil eye. A new sewing machine in Morocco, stopped from working by the evil eye, is set going again when the power of that eye has been recognised and dealt with in a magical way. It is, of course, taboo directly to accuse an individual of having the evil eye. A polite ruse exists in the Middle East which secures protection but avoids the insult of accusation. The five fingers of the human hand, or *khamsa*, arrest the influence of the evil eye. To extend the open hand, palm foremost, toward a person, is normally the grossest insult, for it is a direct accusation that that person has 'the eye', so the ruse consists in wiping one's forehead with the back of the open hand. This natural gesture incidentally directs the *khamsa* at the feared eye without openly insulting the onlooker.

Another kind of 'power' is concentrated in the ritual act of *dhikr*, or 'remembering' God. In the origins of this word, as far as it applies to Islamic religious practice, focus is brought to bear on the trans-empirical and other-worldly arena of activity in front of God. The word comes to the fore in the Qur'ân when revelations establish Mecca instead of Jerusalem as a focus for prayer for Muhammad and his Medinan followers. The new orientation, at this point, expresses many significances for the young community of faith. Included is a concept of worship in the form of *dhikr*: 'So remember ye Me and I shall remember you; show thankfulness to Me and do not act ungratefully towards Me' (sura 2:147). That *dhikr*, or 'remembering', is made facing the place where a celestial host, in the absence of the exiled human Muslim community, worships God. *Dhikr* puts the Muslim in the presence of other worshipping beings, at a level beyond the mundane. The repetition of certain words or formulas in praise of God finds local adaptation in the *ḥadrs* of ordinary Muslims. In these public expressions of trance worship, the 'power' of *dhikr* in transporting human beings into another world is a recognised reality.

Baraka is largely interpreted by ordinary Muslims as a 'power' or 'force' similar to the *mana* of Polynesian societies. *Baraka* concentrates into an almost tangible form the experienced reality of positive power. It has been suggested that the concept of *baraka*, along with the more aggressive motivation of *jihâd*, or holy war, has comprised the strongest Islamising force in Berber North Africa. Certainly in that part of the Islamic world, the very word *baraka*, in a multiplicity of permutations, fills everyday speech from sunrise to sunset: living holy men and dead saints own repositories of *baraka*; the Qur'ân is supremely a source of *baraka*. Much of the activity of ordinary Muslims, both in the everyday round of their lives, and also in their response to crises, concentrates on accumulating as much *baraka* as possible.

Divination is seen as a powerful 'force' giving access to the future. Various practitioners of the folk-Islamic world have authority because of their abilities in the arts of divination. Astrology is a related field and functions strongly in the processes of charm preparation and in the belief that individuals are moved by the stars. Comets and rainbows have varying significance, according to the zodiacal sign in which they appear. The stars are consulted in some communities when crops are about to be sown.

Magic and sorcery are recognised as potent 'forces' in the folk-Islamic world. Though magic is understood to be either spiritual or satanic, both benevolent and malevolent purposes are largely achieved by the same means: the use of the names of God, invoking angels or jinn, quoting sentences of the Qur'ân, and forming mysterious combinations of letters, figures or numbers. The end in view becomes the determining factor of the moral quality of the magic employed. Magic books are frequently attributed a high importance. Among many Malay Muslims, for example, the magic book *Tâj al-Mulûk* is revered as a *kitâb* (religious book). Magic may be used for healing or (often) to produce or cancel love; it may also be used to give supernatural strength to warriors. Sorcery, always evil in intent, is seen as a sinister power in the folk-Islamic concept of causality. Its power is used by certain people and feared by many.

There are some 'powers' which are not only· trans-empirical but also other-worldly, for example, holy books. The Qur'ân supremely, but also other special writings (*kutub*), is seen as having an intrinsic power. Such a view usually finds expression in bibliolatry and divination through a holy book. The holy book is seen to have power to protect people or precious possessions. Many Mercedes, BMWs and Volvos driven around cities in Muslim countries exhibit a Qur'ân on the rear shelf. The *kitâb* is there to preserve the vehicle and occupants from accident.

Fate is viewed as an almost ultimate force in the Muslim world. *Qadr*, or *qisma (kismet)* as it is commonly known, is blamed for many crises ending in death. The pronouncement that a calamity has been *maktûb* or 'written' indicates that a higher power, yet not somehow God himself, has been responsible for the calamity. There is no redress against fate, before which a human being can only be silent.

A cosmology of popular Islam

It is time to bring together our examination of the concepts of 'being' and 'power' in popular Islam. Figure 12 expresses a possible cosmological 'map' for popular Islam, defined in terms of the personal and the impersonal. At the same time, this figure makes a distinction between the empirical and the trans-empirical spheres: the empirical comprises animal and vegetable life—phenomena seen and touched, and therefore measurable; the trans-empirical is composed of non-physical beings, from the souls of the recently dead to God himself.

It is important to recognise that the seat of activity of trans-empirical beings (jinn, etc) may not necessarily be

Figure 12

Cosmology of Popular Islam

	Concepts of 'power' (Impersonal)	Concepts of 'Being' (Personal)	
OTHER-WORLDLY REALM	qadr	God	
		archangels: Sarafiel / Gabriel / others	
	books: especially Qur'ân	angels: no gender; created of light	
THIS-WORLDLY REALM	magic	devils: Iblîs / others	**PHENOMENA**
	sorcery		
	astrology	jinn: have gender usually bad	
	divination	prophets: apostles / prophets / messengers	**TRANS-EMPIRICAL**
	baraka		
	dhikr	dead saints: good	
	evil eye		
	omens	zâr spirits	
	vows	named jinn	
	curses	qarînât	
	blessings	ancestors	
	prophylaxes	souls of recently dead	
	{ dreams / visions / sleep }		
		living holy men	**EMPIRICAL PHENOMENA**
		humans: Muslim: male / female	
		others	
	herbs		
	drugs	animals	
	other natural forces	plants: wheat (bread) / others	

limited to the supernatural world. Indeed, as has already been made apparent in this book, much trans-empirical activity takes place in the natural world of humankind. The figure therefore also distinguishes between this world and that beyond. A few kinds of 'being' and certain 'powers' are seen as trans-empirical by nature and operating in an other-worldly domain. Equally, a few kinds of 'being' and certain 'powers' are seen as empirical by nature and operating in the world of living mankind. The majority of 'beings', and the majority of 'powers', however, are identified as trans-empirical in nature, yet operating in the world of living mankind. That intermediate sphere of 'beings' and 'powers' forms the core of the cosmological outlook of ordinary Muslims.

Metamorphosis

One major element of thought influencing such categorisation of concepts of 'being' and 'power' is that of metamorphosis. The fact that certain beings can appear under alternative guises makes the boundaries between the types of 'being' fluid. All too often, trans-empirical beings exchange their forms for those of empirical phenomena. Angels, for example, are thought to be capable of assuming any shape or form, except those of dogs or pigs. The *ḥadîth* contain many stories of crises in which angels appear as the allies of men. Gabriel, for example, comes in the guise of Jacob to comfort Joseph when the latter is trapped down the well.

The more common subjects of metamorphosis are the jinn. They may appear as humans, animals, or even inanimate objects such as stones. Human manifestations are found in the named jinn personalities of the folk-Islamic world. However, exaggerations in the jinn/humans' eyes, or feet, or vital statistics, betray the metamorphosis. Dogs and cats are the most likely animal manifestations of jinn, hence such animals normally receive special care, because of the possibility of other identities. Jinn may deliberately take the form of hairs swallowed in human foods; they are then able to cause internal discomforts.

The aim of the jinn is thus to impinge on the human and creature worlds and to entangle them in their own whims and desires. They may do this, as we have seen, by sexual inter-course with humans. Such intercourse, it is often reported, is far more pleasant than that with mortal women, but jinn women tend to be insatiable. 'Marriages' may be thought to occur between jinn and humans. Indeed, among the Hadan-dawa of the Sudan, tribal folklore includes a myth of origin that explains the tribe's existence as the outcome of the union of jinn with Abyssinian girls. Jinn babies play with human babies. A child having a fit may be believed to be undergoing torture from a *jinnîya*; such jinn are visible to children and animals while remaining unseen by human adults.

Some Muslims think a human being may undergo meta-morphosis. Such an extreme situation would only occur at the instigation of strong forces from the spirit world, but stories are told of individuals who take on characteristics of the jinn after being somehow involved with them.

In a world in which all of creation is to a certain extent dynamic and interrelated, the added dimension of meta-morphosis adds further complexity to the picture. When a Muslim sees a dog, is he looking simply at a carnivorous quadruped, a member of the genus *canis*? Or is he seeing a metamorphosed *jinnî*? If it is merely an animal, he may throw a stone to shoo it away. If it might be a *jinnî*, he does not want to risk harming it, lest it avenge itself upon him. Rather, he invokes God to protect him and leaves the animal alone.

Or when a Muslim meets another human being, is he greeting only another individual of the genus *homo*? Or are there tell-tale marks suggesting that this 'human' is some-thing else? Is he 'married' to a spirit-woman? Is he the embodiment of a twin spirit? Is he tormented by a devil? Has he become *majnûn* (literally 'possessed by jinn')? Perhaps he is a manifestation of an angel? Maybe he is a *murâbiṭ*, a saint? Village half-wits are often thought to be the favourites of God because their spirits are already in paradise, their minds are elsewhere, and the lunacy of their speech reveals that they are conversing with angels. Depending on the observer's interpretation, he enters into specific relationship with, or avoidance of, the individual concerned.

Figure 13 expresses some of the potential effects of the process of metamorphosis on the human race. Various beings of the trans-empirical world, from souls of the recently dead to angels, may alter the life of a human being. For example, an angel may be metamorphosed and appear as a man on earth. A *qarîna* of a person may be transported from the trans-empirical world into the empirical world so that people will mistake that metamorphosed *qarîna* for the real person. Ancestors may be reborn in their grandchildren

Figure 13

The Effect of the Process of Metamorphosis on the Categorisation of Human Beings in Popular Islam

'Spirit beings' identified as:	Metamorphosis	'Human being' identified as:
angels→	→	→–angel on earth
devils→	→	→–*majnûn*, a maniac
jinn→	→	→–becoming a *jinnî*
dead saints→	→	→–carrying *baraka*
zâr spirits→	→	→–possessed
qarînât→	→	→–'double' of person
named jinn→	→	→–'married' to *jinnîya*
ancestors→	→	→–medium for forbears
dead souls→	→	→–embodiment of dead

Trans-empirical world ← | | → Empirical world

or great-grandchildren. The possibility of metamorphosis clouds the normal ease with which people assess one another. Beings from the trans-empirical world may also affect other forms of life, such as crops, plants and animals, in the empirical world.

In the complex worldview of ordinary Muslims, categories are fluid, and empirical and trans-empirical forms of 'life' may be exchanged. As a result, definitions of causality, for example, include the possibility of such mutation in their exploration of reasons for calamity or sickness. Ideas of space and time are also informed by this potential for interchange among the coinhabitants of the world. Which spaces are safe and which are dangerous? When would certain activity be likely to expose a person to harmful, metamorphosed occupants of the trans-empirical world?

A vast range of 'powers' both to bless and to harm, potentially affect the ordinary Muslim in the vagaries of human life among so many forms of 'being'. To rectify an uncomfortable situation, he needs to have the true cause identified, and an alternative, stronger 'force' enlisted in his aid. He might make appeal, in such a process, to various living 'beings' who are ready and waiting to get involved on his behalf.

In a formal sense, Islam is about submission; in a philosophical sense, the details of existence for Muslims are *maktûb*, or 'written'. In actual reality, however, ordinary Muslims spend hours of the day and night, as well as a significant proportion of their income, seeking to change their destiny. Beneath the surface of formal religion exists a busy, pragmatic complex of activities designed to rewrite what is presented as 'written'.

CHAPTER THIRTEEN

OFFICIAL AND
POPULAR ISLAM

THE WORLD OF THE ORDINARY Muslim
is complex and self-justifying. It makes holistic sense
to the person who sees himself as one among a great
number of 'beings', and who finds himself confronted by a
plurality of 'powers'.

Such a view of reality seems far removed from the world
of formal Islamic faith. What have magic and *baraka* to do
with submission and trust? Why are *zâr* practitioners not
forbidden to operate? How are shrines of saints permitted to
dominate the landscape? We have discovered an unusual
kind of 'Islam'!

Of course, the world of official faith is most advertised as
Muslims relate to the world around them. Consequently
official faith is the only aspect of religious belief and expression likely to be studied by those seeking, from outside, to
learn about Islam. Simple reflection, however, reminds the
Christian that, within the household of his own religion, a
similar 'contradiction' exists. A significant role is often
played by those committed to allegiances which the
upholders of the official faith would condemn. Within 'Christian' communities occur many religious expressions which

mirror the kind of phenomena described in this book with regard to popular Islam.

The aim of this chapter is to describe and explain the subject matters of formal and unofficial religious belief and practice, as they apply to theistic faiths. Out of such explanation will arise a clearer understanding of what is meant by 'official' and 'popular' Islam.

Official and popular religion

In every expression of monotheistic faith a gap has developed, almost inevitably, between faith as defined theologically and faith as it finds expression in ordinary people's lives. Such a distancing seems to occur more easily where monotheistic faith is presented in deistic—as opposed to theistic—terms. The deist tends to see God as responsible for creation, but far removed from it. The theist tends to see God as responsible for creation, and continuing to be involved with it. Deism, consequently, presents God as far off. Needy humans easily fill the gap with alternative 'beings' to whom they can appeal for help.

This common feature of divorce between what might be called religious imagination and theology is as true of Judaism and Christianity as it is of Islam. Various terms may be used to describe the official aspect of a particular faith. They include the ascriptions 'formal', 'high', 'ideal' or 'theological'. That official form contrasts with the 'popular', 'informal', 'low', 'non-official' or 'folk' aspect of religious expression.

Official religion tends to deal with universal issues underlying ideas of origin, destiny and ultimate meaning in life. It codifies and conserves written texts of revelation about such issues. Those texts fix an authoritative body of beliefs. As time passes, commentaries are written to make the original record meaningful in new situations, though these do not replace the original revelation. That revelation continues as normative.

Official religion finds its social expression in complex institutions. Within such organisations, religious authority is invested in a hierarchy. The specialists who fill those positions derive their authority from the knowledge they have of the data of revelation. They are experts in the 'word', protecting the prestige of the revelation, and interpreting its implications for the lives of human beings. Within the religious organisation, then, emphasis is placed on specialisation, leadership, orthodox belief and practice, bureaucracy and self-preservation.

Official religion also provides a moral and ethical motive for its adherents, derived from the data of revelation in which clear commands and expectations are expressed by God. Such guidelines are normally codified and protected with sanctions in the religious community.

Popular religion, by contrast, tends to deal with the problems of immediate everyday life. Disease, flood, barrenness, drought, war and accident claim its attention, though few authoritative written texts relate to these problems. Beliefs are enshrined in myths (especially those of origin), folklore, proverbs and epics; hence continuity of tradition is maintained by entrusted heritage, whereby a grandmother or grandfather passes on to a younger relative the secrets of her or his expertise. Some special texts such as books of magic or astrological charts may constitute part of the paraphernalia of unofficial religion. They, too, devolve on select individuals who will use them and protect their secrets.

Again, popular religion is not highly institutionalised. It is instead based on the needs and customary rites of passage of the people. The religious masses of any faith tend to manifest elements of popular religion in their allegiances. Those masses contrast with the relatively small community of official hierarchical specialists, who remain the protectors of the official status quo. Authority within the world of popular religion—as we have seen—depends on each practitioner's proven power, rather than on a place in the official hierarchy. Popular religion is as a result informally organised, localised and closely linked to places or persons possessing intrinsic power.

Often, popular religion is amoral in its attitude towards life. There is a pragmatic approach to questions of involvement with the 'beings' and 'powers' of the world that provides it with its context. Spirit beings, for example, may be perceived officially as innately good or bad. Ordinary believers, however, invoke or involve them in their own causes, irrespective of whether they are officially 'good' or 'bad'. Their interaction with such spirit beings rests on an alternative analysis of those spirits' value. If the spirits can assist or appease, ordinary Muslims will appeal to them.

The perception of those spirits' attitudes to the world of man is ruled by the same pragmatic sense. If human beings serve them well, or co-operate in their purposes, the spirits bring benefit to the mortals concerned. If human beings offend them, for example by intruding unwelcomed into their 'space', the spirits hurt them.

I am making a somewhat artificial delineation between the theological, sociological and ethical aspects of official and popular religion. In fact, within any major monotheistic faith, both views of religious reality tend to be operating, in tension, together. Sometimes that tension is very much on the surface, as with the continuing debate about the role of Mary within Roman Catholicism. Often, the tension is ignored or suppressed, at least in any outward exposition of the faith concerned. Both views of the world may indeed reside within a single member, or group of members, of a monotheistic faith. What is certain is that those within any particular faith who live more in the popular world, and who may be denounced by the upholders of the orthodox faith as aberrant, heretical or marginal, rarely view themselves as deviating from what is seen as substantial by the official faith. They still see themselves as genuine Jews, Christians, or Muslims.

The 'great' and 'little' traditions of Islam

Such a distinction between official and popular religion is as applicable to Islam as to other monotheistic faiths. Anthropologists have described a major contrast in Middle-Eastern Islamic society as that between the great and little traditions. Whereas the great tradition embraces the structures and personnel of official Islam, the little tradition comprises the associations and practitioners of popular Islam. The former are focused in mosques and theologians, the latter in shrines and holy men. It is in the operation of both traditions that society acquires strength and wholeness, for in Middle-Eastern society, religious allegiance sits at the very core of people's worldview. Both traditions, therefore, are of considerable significance. 'Little' does not imply fewer in number.

In the Islamic cultures of West and East Africa, various culture fields overlap and include traditional social, political, economic and religious culture; Islamic culture in its particular African forms; and Western culture in its African forms. As far away as the Philippines, a similar pattern is observed, wherein indigenous beliefs and practices coexist with more recently accepted, formal Islamic creed and practice. Official and popular religious allegiances equally are part of the 'Islamic' faith as it finds expression in various cultural contexts around the globe.

Figure 14 summarises and contrasts various aspects of official and popular religion in the world of Islam. The analysis portrays the extensive areas covered by both aspects of the faith, including theology, law, mores, ethics, politics, speech, structures and emotions. The two worlds are essentially different in the sense that they hold alternative views of reality. Though they may coincide at various points along the

Figure 14

Official and Popular Islam

Aspect	Official Islam	Popular Islam
Issues	Questions of life, death, heaven, hell, salvation, eternity, believers, non-believers From preaching of Muhammad	Questions of fear, sickness, loneliness, guilt, revenge, shame, powerlessness, longing, meaninglessness, disease, crisis From everyday life
Text	Qur'ân, kept up to date by commentaries *(tafsîr)*	No basic text is handed on except books of magic applicable to some situations
Institution-alisation	Formal: – sheikh or imam, down through heirarchy; does not include women – Sunni orthodoxy; others are sects within the great tradition (Shîᶜah) – major mosques in Mecca, Medina, Jerusalem, Damascus, Istanbul, etc – university-type education; textual sources – associations: Islamic League, Muslim Brothers – Sufism in formal *tarîqas*	Informal: – specialists may be imam, medicine man, *pîr*, witch-doctor; includes women – groups built up around persons of power; sects as new persons of power emerge – no central edifices, but local places of power: trees, shrines, streams, etc – education by dream or apprenticeship – associations: practitioner and dependants for *baraka* transfer – Sufism as maraboutism, ḥadrs
Authority	Ulema (ruling theologians) and hierarchy of religio/political officials	Lies in the *baraka*-possessed, proven power of practitioner
Language	Classical Arabic; form not changeable	Colloquial Arabic or local language

Morality	System provided, based on the Qur'ân; legal and societal sanctions	Amoral 'fitting in' with the spirit world; appeasing jinn that are angered, using those whose favour is won
Rites	Cyclical, reinforcing rites taken care of; socio/ religious function	Crisis rites supremely taken care of; often involvement in local, cyclical rites

way, their constructs are different, even largely opposed to each other.

Christian mission to Muslims

The material surveyed in this book raises a major, and perhaps embarrassing, question for Christian missions to Muslims. With which 'Islam' is Christian witness familiar? Which 'Islam' is known, or maybe even knowable, by most contemporary missionaries to Muslims? Is it Qur'ânic, institutionalised, orthodox and official Islam? Or is it everyday, everyman, non-publicised, local and popular Islam?

It *is* important for Christians to research, study and assess the composite facets of official Islam. One of the major trends in the Islamic world today, brought about by certain pressure groups from within the official religion, is the application of a more puritanical interpretation of the formal tenets of the faith. The crusade of such groups is against the popular religion of so many Muslims worldwide. Al-Ashᶜarî and Ibn Taimîya are their exemplars and provide their theological foundation for condemning popular practices. The insistence of a variety of fundamentalist movements is on a more disciplined, orthodox expression of Islam.

Such knowledge is accessible to most enquirers. Muslim theologians and others in the official hierarchy welcome such investigation. The Qur'ân needs to be read, understood and evaluated on its own terms by missionaries to people who see it as God's final word to them, and to all mankind. There is a definite sense in which Christians need to be involved in a mission to Islam—to official, orthodox Islam.

It is, however, equally important for Christians to get to know the less advertised but just as pervasive world of popular Islam. That world is discovered in the *hadîth* literature, in the folklore of local communities, and in myths of origin. It is visibly worked out in rites of passage and at times of crisis. It surfaces in the reinterpretations given to certain beliefs and practices of the orthodox faith. It is a world well researched by anthropologists and by some Christians who have lived with Muslims.

It is at this intimate level and in this 'popular' world, that ambassadors for Christ must learn to recognise what is going on, and how to address the issues. Behind the facade of established ritual worship lie beliefs and practices which reveal a strong commitment to an alternative view of the world.

Intellectual discussions about the historicity of the crucifixion may not communicate well with the Muslim who believes that because his local magician has been to Mecca on *hajj*, that man's magic has greater power. The issue of power, not information, thus tops the agenda for most ordinary Muslims. Does the missionary for Christ have any stronger antidote for evil spirits in the home than the local incense burner? What of exorcism and healing? Do Christ's ambassadors have any expertise, on behalf of their King, in these ministries?

Missionaries must not be deceived by the seeming Westernisation of many of the Muslims to whom they relate. Of course, there are degrees of Westernisation! The context of encounter, also, will largely determine the kind of Muslim the Westerner meets. Even so, it is false to assume that because a Middle Easterner is educated in the West, or seems to operate easily in a materialistic, technological society, he has no residual commitment to a different view of the world. Christian missionaries have not been alone in their failure to understand Muslims, for political, commercial and philanthropic concerns have consistently made such a false assumption.

In Christian mission the aim must constantly be to get beneath the surface and discover the assumptions of ordinary Muslims in their complex, unpredictable and largely hostile world. The earlier chapters of this book have suggested some points at which possibilities of 'seeing' and then exploring that alternative world arise for those seeking to share Christ with such people. The ordinary Muslim's concern for equilibrium leads to activities and allegiances— even reinterpretations of the meanings and functions of orthodox beliefs and customs—which provide clues for understanding and communication.

CHAPTER FOURTEEN

BELIEF AND PRACTICE:
WHICH INTERPRETATION?

THE RELIGIOUS ACTS of Muslims appear to be identical, whether being expressed in Marrakesh or Mombasa, Damascus or Delhi. The common statement of belief and common practice makes the outward image of the faith consistent throughout the Islamic world. Yet beneath the surface, a divergence of view is discernible. That divergence does not primarily take place on national or cultural lines, as one might expect, yet it touches the foundational aspects of Islam.

The major difference arises in the functions and meanings ascribed to orthodox confession and deeds. It is a difference of understanding about the universally agreed statement of faith and summary of practices.

Statement of faith

The Muslim creed (*îmân*) includes a statement of belief in the only God, his angels, his books, his apostles, the Last Day and predestination: '...virtuous conduct is (that of) those who have believed in Allah and the Last Day and the angels and the Book and the prophets...' (sura 2:172).

For many Muslims, belief in the only God devolves largely into a magical use of the names of God. The ninety-nine Beautiful Names (*al-'ismâ' al-ḥusnâ*) mostly derive from the Qur'ân. That there are specifically ninety-nine is known to all believers, whether or not they are acquainted with the Qur'ân. The number is written on the hands of each human being. The major creases of the left palm form the figure ⋀\ (or 81 in Arabic numerals). The corresponding creases of the right palm form the figure \⋀ (or 18 in Arabic numerals). Combined, the two yield ninety-nine.

Fig 15

Certain formulas 'compel' God to do what is requested. Those formulas usually include some of the Beautiful Names. Similarly, most amulets make use of the names of God. The handbook *Shams al-Maᶜârif al-Kubrâ* of al-Bûnî (died AD 1225) continues to influence contemporary magic in the Arab world. A large part of the book deals with the Beautiful Names of God, identifying the specific results to be obtained by using different names. Figure 15 is taken from that book. It forms a talisman made up from the first two names, al-Raḥmân and al-Raḥîm. Four spokes of a wheel are made from those two names. The spokes support a double rim on which is written the following declaration:

Outer Rim
In the name of God, the Merciful, the Compassionate:
O God, I implore you in your goodness.
In the name of God, the Merciful, the Compassionate;
Truly you will preserve the one who carries this
composition of mine from the evil of all that might
harm him and you will appoint over him its angels and
servants and assistants who are entrusted with its
service to guard him by day and by night.

Inner Rim
Muhammad is the Apostle of God and those with him
are stronger than the unbelievers. Among them are
merciful ones whom we see bowing and kneeling,
seeking kindness and favour from God. Their marks
are on their foreheads, the effect of prostration,
and that is their likeness in the *Tawrât* and the *Injîl*.

On sale in Lagos, Nigeria, is the English handbook *Ninety-Nine Names of Allah*. The Islamic Publications Bureau offers to its African readers the opportunity of learning and using the ninety-nine Beautiful Names. The introduction to the book seeks to warn against abuse of the power contained in the names by quoting the following story:

▸ Osman Baba repeated Ya-Qahhar (Oh Destroyer) many times until he became obsessed by this Attribute. If he threw a piece of cotton at someone and it hit him, he would die. The people complained to Waliyuddin 'Kuddisa Sirruh' who told them to take a piece of cotton and throw it at the back of Osman. When it hit him he turned and said, 'Oh Waliyuddin, you have killed me', and he died. The power was given to him by Allah because he repeated the Name.[15]

Intention may be positive or negative, but the names remain powerful.

Associated with the names of God is the practice of composing magic squares. Different names or attributes of God may be represented by various letters or numbers. The number one, for example, stands for the unity of God. Figure 16 illustrates a magic square based on that number. The figures on the horizontals, verticals and diagonals each add up to sixty-five (or five times thirteen—both significant for combatting offensive magic).

Figure 16

Magic Square Centred on the Unit 'One'

15	2	19	6	23
16	8	25	12	4
22	14	1	18	10
3	20	7	24	11
9	21	13	5	17

The prayer beads (*subḥa*), are designed to assist Muslims in their recitation of the ninety-nine Beautiful Names. In folk-Islamic practice, however, the prayer beads are more commonly used in that form of divination known as *ist-ikhâra*. Oaths carry strength because of the appeal they make to God as witness. In such an attitude towards the Islamic doctrine of God, the approach appears to be manipulative rather than submissive. Highlighted are the forms of appeal rather than the divine person named in the process. An appropriate use of a suitable divine name will automatically achieve the desired end; the motivation is pragmatic and self-centred.

The doctrine of angels (*al-malâ'ik*) authenticates a species of 'being' to whom ordinary Muslims may appeal for assistance. Angels live in the other world, closer to God than

Fig 17

human beings, and are seen as agents of power, so their names are commonly used in protective talismans. Men are protected by angels, ten by day and ten by night. Riḍwân, the guardian of paradise, and Mâlik, the guard at the gates of hell, are often invoked. Nineteen special angels have charge of the fires of hell while north, south, east and west each have guardian angels.

Figure 17 is a reproduction of the famous amulet known as the seal of the Seven Covenants of Suleiman. It purports to protect against jinn and other evil influences, to win love, to bless the activities of selling and buying and to produce good health and prosperity. The amulet proceeds from the word '*Allâh*' at the top right to 'Muḥammad' at the bottom left. At the first circle enclosed in a rectangle, on the right, the four diagonal words spell out the names of the archangels Gabriel, Michael, Azrael and Israfel. There follows a long introduction describing the horrific powers of Umm al-Ṣub-yân (some of which was quoted in Chapter Two) and her eventual submission to Prophet Suleiman in terms of the seven covenants. The 'first covenant' serves as an example of them all:

> In the name of God the Merciful and Compassionate. By God and there is no god but He, the Seeker, the Sought-after, the Victor over the vanquished, the Intelligent, the Destroyer, the Holder of dominion and Master of this world and the next, the Restorer of rotting bones, the Guide to the misbelievers, the Despiser of him who follows his own caprices, the Conqueror, the Ruler, from whom no one can escape, and whom no one can overcome or outwit. I shall not come near the person upon whom this amulet has been hung, neither in travel nor in rest, neither in studiousness nor in stupidity, neither in sleep nor in solitude, and God is witness to what I say. Here is its seal...

The amulet concludes by quoting the verse of light (sura 24:35) and the verse of the throne (sura 2:256). The naming of angels, or archangels, at the beginning of the talisman carries protective weight.

The doctrine of God's books (*al-kitâb*) is turned largely into a practice of bibliolatry and bibliomancy in popular Islam. The Qur'ân, above all, is a repository of *baraka*. The word itself, with its derivations, appears thirty-one different times in the text. The attempt to transfer this inherent *baraka* guides much of the Muslim use of the Qur'ân. Various chapters and verses are reputed to be powerful for such problems as headaches, fevers, swellings, aches, blindness, insanity, toothache, and the protection of property.

The Qur'ân, like the prayer beads, is used in *istikhâra*. A practitioner (if it is a big decision), or the head of a household (if it is a less crucial issue), will close his eyes, utter God's name, maybe recite the *Fâtiha*, and draw his fingers from the back of the Qur'ân up among its pages. He opens

Fig 18

the book where his fingers enter and reads the first sentence or part of a sentence on that page. From the nature of the words he will draw a conclusion as to what to do (or advise) in the matter under consideration.

Throughout the Islamic world, the Qur'ân is used as a charm in itself. Figure 18 shows miniature copies of the Qur'ân on sale in Cairo alongside ordinary and large print volumes. Such miniature replicas are pinned on to children's clothing as talismans, as illustrated in Figure 19.

Fig 19

Daily recital of the Qur'ân, either by special Qur'ân readers, or by radio broadcast, is considered to be a protective activity. One saying common in Egypt asserts that Satan does not enter the house in which the Holy Book is recited every day. The act of recital keeps evil at bay.

Such unorthodox views of the Qur'ân are exaggerated among Muslim populations for whom Arabic is a foreign tongue. Although the reading of the Arabic Qur'ân may be encouraged as an act of piety, its obscurity in non-Arabic societies helps promote an alternative view of its effects, where it is seen as powerful and efficacious in a magical sense.

In popular Islam, the doctrine of God's apostles (*al-rusul*) revolves largely around their dealings with the supernatural world. Both Suleiman and Muhammad stand out in the popular mind, because of their reported interaction with and power over demons and jinn. For many Muslims, prophets are more appealing than most angels, because of their reputed willingness to intercede with God on man's behalf. Prophets have also been weak mortals themselves, and therefore understand human frailty.

The names of Muhammad are treated in a manner similar to those of God, being powerful for protection, and for enforcing charms. *Qasîdas*, traditional Arabic poems such as the famous *Mu^{c}allaqât* collection of the eighth century, extol the Prophet and companions and are used in festival devotion around the Islamic world today. Other prophets' names are used in talismans, the most important being Adam, Abraham, Isaac, Ishmael, Jacob, Moses, Jonah, David and Jesus. Associated with such veneration of Muhammad, and others of God's apostles, is the respect paid to relics throughout the Muslim world.

In the popular mind, the doctrine of the Last Day (*yawm al-dîn*, or sometimes *yawm al-âkhira*) relates to death and spirit life. It is often reinterpreted to offer hope of salvation on that final day. The apostles are viewed as willing mediators with God, on behalf of Muslims, at the final judgement; Muhammad, it is commonly believed, will intercede for his community at that time. Such hope sometimes militates against a present living by conscience, since it is confidently expected that, despite all, and on account of their own merit, the apostles will rescue to paradise members of their own community. The careful living which the doctrine of the Last

Day is intended to inspire is thus annulled in a reinterpretation of that doctrine's implications.

The doctrine of predestination (*al-taqdir*) is similarly and radically undermined in much of folk-Islamic belief and practice. Although ultimately explaining the humanly unalterable and inexplicable, *al-taqdir* or *al-qadr* is often pushed to the bottom of the Muslim's awareness. Above it come his many attempts to reshape his own destiny. On auspicious occasions, both within the religious calendar (for example, during *Ramaḍân*), and within the rites of passage (for example at birth), and via certain 'beings', attempts are made to alter what is determined. *Laylat al-qadr* operates within Islam in a manner somehow similar to April Fool's day in the West. On April 1st, institutionalised lying is condoned in a Western society that normally upholds the telling of truth as important. In Muslim countries, *laylat al-qadr* provides a period when God listens either directly, or via the angel Gabriel, to the requests of Muslims concerning their 'fate'.

Practices

The specific practices (*dîn*) of Islam comprise the confession of faith (*al-tashahhud*), the prayer ritual, legal almsgiving, the annual fast, and pilgrimage to Mecca. The last four of these practices are referred to, collectively, as *al-ᶜibâdât*. As with the confession of faith, the significance of these 'pillars' of Islam (*arkân al-'islâm*) for ordinary Muslims differs from the meaning formally expressed by the religion's theologians.

The words of the confession (*kalimât al-shahâda*) are commonly believed to be supernaturally able to drive away evil. They are frequently on Muslims' lips, along with the *bismillâh'*, as they traverse areas which are acknowledged as the territory of hostile trans-empirical beings.

The prayer ritual (*ṣalât*), facing Mecca, is seen partly as a protective measure against incursions from the spirit world. Demonic pollution may be removed by the process of ablution. A well-known *ḥadîth* records that Muhammad insisted on the nose being included in the pre-prayer washing process, because the Devil spends the night inside people's noses. Another *ḥadîth* emphasises that sin is washed away by the ritual ablutions before prayer. The title of the particular section in Muslims' collection of *ḥadîth* dealing with that topic is 'Purging of Sins with Ablution Water'. Among Muslim Hausa in northern Nigeria, more emphasis is placed upon the ablutions, which are performed assiduously, than upon the actual prayers, which may be only partially performed.

The Muslim at prayer often places an object (*sutra*) on the ground between himself and the *qibla*. The *sutra* is intended to prevent an unbeliever, or an evil spirit, passing between himself and the *qibla*, thus invalidating the prayer. *Ḥadîth* listed by al-Nasâ'î include one forbidding gaps in the ranks of worshippers at prayer, lest Satan mingle with them. Another *ḥadîth* in his collection commands the moving about of fingers during prayer, so that no nestling place for demons is afforded.

In many Muslim communities, the worship at Friday prayers includes elements of popular devotion. The *dhikr* ritual, for example—consisting of prayers, ecstatic chanting, drumming, Qur'ân recitals and incense burning—has traditionally been an integral part of congregational prayer among Nubian Muslims.

Almsgiving (*zakât*) finds its own rationale in the folk-Islamic world. Performing the act may be seen as a means of bringing *baraka* into the donor's life. Beggars thus provide opportunities for healthy Muslims to accrue merit to themselves. Equally, the act of giving alms may be sanctioned by the concept of the evil eye. Beggars comprise one group of people perceived as possessing a strong 'eye'. Fear of being hurt by the evil eye of a beggar is a motivation for giving alms among many Muslims.

There are several occasions for fasting (*ṣaum*) in Islam. The most exacting fast is that of Ramaḍân. *Laylat al-qadr* occurs in the last ten nights of that month and commemorates God's first revelation to the Prophet Muhammad, which is usually thought of as the twenty-seventh night of Ramaḍân. On that occasion the gates of heaven are open, and the possibility exists of altering human destinies, for prayers are then carried to the throne of God. Many acts of popular devotion occur during Ramaḍân, including detailed and enthusiastic veneration of Muhammad.

During the beginning of the month of Dhû'l-Ḥijja and in the two months preceding it, pilgrimage (*ḥajj*) to Mecca is enjoined on Muslims who can afford, once in their lives, to make such a journey. Associated with the rituals of the *ḥajj* are many elements that find meaning in a folk-Islamic outlook on life.

Sight of the *ka*^c*ba* is accompanied by an opening of heaven, so that prayers are heard and accepted. Muhammad is reported to have rebuilt the *ka*^c*ba* to the design of the edifice originally placed there by Abraham. One corner of the building is known as the Yemenite corner, where activity in prayer brings angelic help to the intercessor. At that corner, seventy angels say 'Amen' to the prayers of the believer.

Between the black stone corner and the door of the *ka*^c*ba*, stands a part of the wall known as *multazam*. Meaning 'that to which one is attached', it is the focus of attempts, by pilgrims, to become literally united with the *ka*^c*ba*. Muslims flatten themselves against this portion of the wall, rub themselves against it, and try to attach themselves to it. In some *ḥadîth* it is suggested that stroking of the walls of the *ka*^c*ba* is an atonement for sins. *Baraka* is certainly transferred, also, in a physical embrace of this solid symbol of the faith's centre. Figure 20 illustrates such activity at the *ka*^c*ba*.

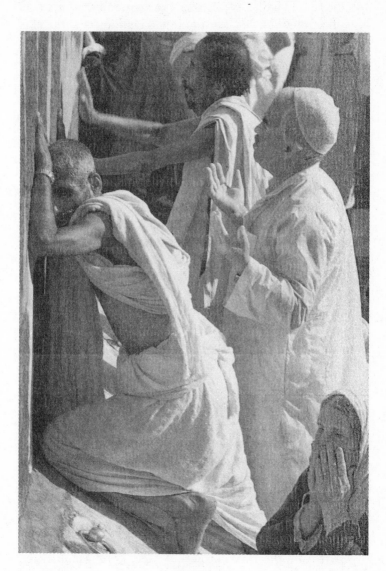

Fig 20

The black stone (*al-ḥajaru'l-aswad*) figures as the centre of specific ritual kissing as pilgrims move around the *kaᶜba*. In his collection of *ḥadîth*, Muslim Ibn al Ḥajjâj (see Appendix 1) includes a chapter on the excellence of kissing the black stone, emphasising that the stone is to be kissed as an act of similitude to that of Muhammad, not as an act of worship in itself. Other *ḥadîth*, however, suggest that the pilgrim relates in a somewhat more dynamic manner to the black stone. It would seem that the stone has 'life' of its own. Thus Ibn ᶜAbbâs passes on that Muhammad said that the black stone originated from paradise, at which time it was whiter than milk. The sins of the children of Adam gradually turned it black as they touched it. On the Day of Resurrection, when it will have two eyes by which to identify all those who will have touched or kissed it, and when it will be given a tongue by which to speak, it will offer evidence in favour of those who have honoured it.

The 'stoning of Satan' is an integral part of pilgrimage procedure. Pillars symbolically representing Satan are subjected to stone throwing on the morning of the day of sacrifice. The pillars stand at Minâ and are known as 'the first', 'the middle', and 'the last'. They mark the successive spots where the Devil in the guise of an old sheikh appeared to Adam, Abraham and Ishmael; and where he was forced away by the throwing of stones. The last pillar is commonly called *al-Shayṭânu'l-Kabîr* (the Great Devil). Satan is alive and well in the contemporary Muslim's cosmology and may even appear, by a process of metamorphosis, as a respected religious elder. A connected *ḥadîth* concerning the use of seven pebbles for each stoning emphasises the importance of the use of odd numbers in the *ḥajj* rituals.

Drawing of Zamzam water offers the prospect of *baraka*-endowed refreshment, for relatives or sick people, when the pilgrims return home carrying the specially collected water.

Apart from the two mosques at Mecca and Medina, the mosque of al-Aqṣâ in Jerusalem is perceived as the third most important pilgrimage destination in the Muslim world. It was from the site of al-Aqṣâ that Muhammad reputedly made his ascent to the heavens. The impression of his footprint in the *ṣakhra* (rock) on the Temple site is the focus of veneration for Muslims at this significant centre of the faith.

From whatever pilgrimage, a *ḥajjî* is seen as endowed with extra *baraka* or power, especially if he is already recognised as a practitioner in some folk-Islamic sense; the *ḥajj* confers much authority on such a person.

In the *ḥajj* context, folk Islam comes especially to the fore in substitute pilgrimages made, throughout the Muslim world, by those unable to visit Mecca and Medina. Such pilgrimages involve shrine visitation and saint worship on a massive scale.

Figure 21 identifies some of the essential differences between official and popular conceptions of fundamental beliefs and practices of Islam. The forms adhered to are the same, but their meanings are vastly different. Muslims with a folk-Islamic view of the world maintain a radically reinterpreted understanding of *îmân* and *dîn*. That conceptual reinterpretation tends, in turn, to reflect on the functions which the forms fulfil in those Muslims' lives. Still, whichever meaning is foremost in any particular context, those involved see themselves as validly Muslim. There is no question of difference of interpretation implying more or less allegiance to the Islamic community. Indeed, the two worldviews often coexist within the same Muslim; in their differentiated meanings and functions, the forms have differing goals, both of which may be seen as valid, and sought after by an individual Muslim.

The fundamental fact that needs recognition is that both worldviews do exist, even within the foundational formulas of the Islamic faith.

Figure 21

Function, Form and Meaning in Official and Popular Islam

Intended Function	Form	Meaning in Official Islam	Meaning in Popular Islam	Reinterpreted function
EXPRESSION OF SUBMISSION TO GOD	Creed			**TO MAINTAIN EQUILIBRIUM IN LARGELY HOSTILE WORLD**
	Only God	monotheistic confession of faith	magical use of the names of God	
	Angels	servants of God at his pleasure	possible mediators and powerful in charms	
	Books	encoding of God's self-revelation	bibliomancy and bibliolatry	
	Apostles	vehicles of God's word to man	possible mediators and veneration, relics	
	Last Day	ethical focus of man's life	acts to gain merit for dead relatives	
	Predestination	ultimately, all in God's hands	*laylat al-qadr* to try and change destinies	
EXPRESSION OF BELONGING TO COMMUNITY OF FAITHFUL	Pillars			
	Confession	proves one is a true Muslim	protection in spaces inhabited by evil	
	Prayer	bodily purity for worshipping God	removal by water of demonic pollution and sins	
	Alms	reponsibility to fellow-Muslims	precaution against the evil eye	
	Fasting	sign of communal commitment	veneration of Muhammad and *laylat al-qadr*	
	Pilgrimage	visit epicentre of the faith	obtaining of *baraka* and alternative shrines	

CHAPTER FIFTEEN

'WORLDS' IN CONFLICT?

I T. IS PLAIN THAT THE BELIEFS and practices of ordinary Muslims contradict many formal
aspects of Islamic faith. They indicate a commitment by
the masses to popular religion. Unfortunately, that commitment has remained mostly hidden from or ignored as irrelevant by Western missionaries to Muslims.

Such beliefs and practices are, however, common and
permeate the everyday life of human beings from Morocco
to Malaysia. They persist—even where formal religious
ideals (especially of *îmân* and *dîn*) are nominally adhered
to—in an alternative interpretation of the meanings of those
ideals. They direct and control much of the festival devotion
of Muslims, especially where such rituals deal with rites of
passage or crises. They are the heritage of a complex, unofficial world of practitioners, where gifted men and women
direct Muslims' lives, and maybe also their deaths, in intri-
cate detail.

Behind such popular beliefs and practices lie existential
assumptions which make holistic sense of a particular way of
looking at the world. This worldview sees the universe as
living, complicated, and composed of various kinds of

'beings' and 'powers'. It is a world in which mortals contend with many other competitors for control of their lives. As such, the folk-Islamic model of the universe is vastly different from that which supports the assumptions and behavioural activities of the official faith.

The result should be a clash: alternative views of the world mocking each other. The surprising truth is that there is relatively little dissonance between the two domains. Official and popular expressions of Islam tend to live easily with one another. Indeed, both views may operate in veiled partnership within any one single Muslim.

This is not to suggest that there has never been any objection to popular Islam by members of the formal, official hierarchy. One of the early, vigorous condemners of popular Islam was the purist, Ibn Taimîya. Nor is it to underestimate the strength of contemporary reform movements, such as those pioneered or supported by the Wahhâbîs, the Ikhwân and others. It is, however, to remember that almost immediately after his own death in the early fourteenth century, Ibn Taimîya himself became an object of veneration. It is also to point out that the evidence of contemporary Islamic societies suggests that deep commitment to alternative worldviews exists within them, yet without severe dissonance.

The lack of such obvious dissonance is, perhaps, the main reason why Western investigators, including Christian missionaries, have often failed to recognise the existence of the folk-Islamic world. At the surface of internal Muslim debate, relatively little reference is made to a dichotomy between two views of the world held by those claiming status as faithful Muslims. Islam's outward image appears consistently as that of an official, ideal religion.

Official Islam: host to popular Islam?

The truth would appear to be that the worldview of popular Islam is (for the most part) accepted, and even nurtured, within the embrace of the alternative, official worldview. In certain respects, the formal faith couches in its own codes and condoned practices elements of folk religion. In the historical extension of Islam, too, the faith is heavily indebted to many of its own missionaries who have been motivated as much by their experience of Islam in its popular expression as by their desire to advance a formal, monotheistic book religion.

At the same time, part of the ethos of the official religion militates strongly against an insistent and singular dogmatic orthodoxy and orthopraxy. This ethos may be summed up in the Qur'ânic saying *lâ ikrâha f'il-dîni* ('There is no compulsion in religion...' sura 2:257). It is certainly encouraged by the fact that Islam has grown to be a world religion, with adherents from a variety of non-Arab backgrounds. Islam has necessarily endeavoured to accept as validly Islamic a multitude of variations on the major theme. As long as the outward forms are expressed faithfully the world over, that is what matters. The meanings attached to those forms, for the most part, tend to be viewed as secondary.

The Qur'ân and popular Islam

The Qur'ân presents itself as the embodiment of the revelation delivered to Muhammad in a clear and pure Arabic (sura 16:105), sent down to be 'a guidance and a mercy' (sura 16:66) to a people who believe. As such, it deals predominantly with the ultimate issues of official religion, and with the working out of those concerns in the details of human belief and practice.

Perhaps a significant facet of the very coming of the Qur'ân via Muhammad is found in the way in which, through it, formal religion is brought to bear upon a people lacking such a dimension to their religious experience. In that sense, the Qur'ân, in its historical evolution, may be read as a commentary on the changes occurring as men from a deeply pagan background become truly Muslim in an official, religious sense. Law is increasingly codified, ritual and religio/ ethical commands are explained and inaugurated, as the details of truly monotheistic faith become defined in the process of revelation. At the same time, calls are made concerning internal commitment to the one God of formal faith, in an explanation of the revelation's claim to be superceding the book religions of Judaism and Christianity.

In the development of such an official religion for largely pagan Arabs, certain concessions are made (perhaps inevitably) to their more animistic or folk beliefs and practices. The Qur'ân retains such concessions within its embrace, sometimes by heaven-sent inclusion, at other times by comment on situations met with by Muhammad.

In terms of cosmology, the heavens are spoken of as being seven in number (sura 78:12), created one above another 'in storeys' (sura 67:3). The lowest heaven is adorned with lights functioning as 'projectiles for the satans' (sura 67:5). This concept of shooting stars as designed to pursue and destroy evil spirits (*shayâtîn*) which try to penetrate above the heavens to the throne of God is repeated several times in the Qur'ân (suras 15:16–18; 37:6–10).

Angels fill the 'stairs' of heaven (sura 70:3f) and witness of themselves that they are ranked in progressive degrees (sura 37:164–166). Those of highest standing sustain the throne of God, singing praise and glory to their Lord (sura 40:7) and interceding on behalf of human beings. In this life, each person has two recording angels noting his good and evil deeds (sura 50:16f,22). Two other interesting angels in the cosmology of the Qur'ân are found in Hârût and Mârût (sura 2:96), who have access to the power of *shayâtîn*, and provide the knowledge of magic to man.

The jinn feature significantly in the Qur'ân's cosmology. They are created by God (sura 6:100) from 'fire of burning heat' (sura 15:27), are good and evil (sura 72:11), usurp men's worship of God (sura 34:40), and will be judged on the Last Day (sura 72:14,15). Hell is said to be filled with jinn and men (sura 11:120). Suleiman and Muhammad both play important roles with regard to the jinn. Suleiman is known as Lord of the *shayâṭîn*, having control over them (sura 38:36). His authority emerges strongly in the story of his contest and dialogue with Bilqis, Queen of Sheba (sura 27:22–45). One interpretation of this passage explains that Suleiman was seeking to determine, with his sea of glass, whether the queen was in fact a *jinnîya*. Hairy legs would have given her away! The power of Suleiman over an authoritative demon, the wicked and crafty *ᶜafrît*, is openly confessed in verse 39 of this sura.

The idea of *qarîna* as referring to a twin spirit is also present in the Qur'ân. Dialogue is mentioned as taking place between a man and his *qarîna* or 'companion' (sura 50:22–26).

The concept of dead prophets being able to act as recipients of blessing finds implicit justification in the Qur'ânic injunction to salute Muhammad: 'Verily Allah and His angels pronounce blessings upon the prophet; O ye who have believed, pronounce blessings upon him, and give (him) the salutation of Peace' (sura 33:56). It is only a small step from such a vision to a view of blessing moving from dead prophet to followers. Certainly, friends (*awliyâ'*) or saints of God find a place in the cosmology of the Qur'ân (sura 10:63). Reference is also made to Muhammad's night journey to Jerusalem and through the heavens. The concept of the special blessedness of Jerusalem, and the importance of pilgrimage to it, is built upon Qur'ânic reference to the special blessing associated with that area of land (sura 21:71,81).

With regard to time, the idea of sacred months appears within the Qur'ân. There are four months during which no fighting is to occur among the Arabian tribes (sura 9:5). *Laylat al-qadr* is the subject of a complete chapter (sura 97). In that night, angels and the Spirit descend for every matter, and the channels of communication are uniquely open between heaven and earth. In sura 44:2, *laylat al-qadr* is called the 'blessed night'.

With regard to orientation, the Qur'ân emphasises the importance of the *qibla*, at first in the direction of Jerusalem, and later facing Mecca (sura 2:143,145). That latter designation includes reference to angels' worship there at the heavenly equivalent to the earthly *ka^cba*.

Some pre-Islamic occult practices are specifically condemned in the Qur'ân (sura 5:102). Others, however, although implicitly denounced, would seem to have been given reinforcement by the Qur'ân's admission of their potency. The 'evil of the blowers among knots' (sura 113:4) is specifically mentioned in that sura of protection. This form of witchcraft, in which women specialised, was viewed as very powerful. Knotting of a rope caused the intended victim to be 'bound' and helpless. Despite the Qur'ânic promise that '...Allah will defend thee from the people...' (sura 5:71), a sound tradition acknowledges that Muhammad was himself bewitched by Labîb Ibn A'şam so that, for a year, the prophet was impotent.

Magic, although usually presented in the Qur'ân as a kind of deception (sura 20:64,69), is confessed in some contexts to be a real force. This is especially the case with the angels Hârût and Mârût (sura 2:96).

Oaths, or abjurations, are quoted freely throughout the Qur'ân, although an effort is made to condemn perjury (sura 16:93).

The intention of the Qur'ân to provide a focal point and guide for the development in an idol-worshipping society of a high religion must not be minimised. For millions of Muslims, from Muhammad's Companions to today's Muslim populations, the Qur'ân has done precisely that. However, in its concessions to certain pagan beliefs and practices, and more especially in the details of its cosmology, the Qur'ân also contains within its precious pages the seeds of an approach to faith which is far removed from its idealistic position. This alternative approach has developed among ordinary Muslims, from the *hijra* (exodus) until today, and has found its ultimate justification within the very Book of Wisdom.

Pre-Islamic practices incorporated into official Islam

It would seem that many of the beliefs and practices of popular Islam that have found acceptance in what began—in intention at least—as a revolution to an ideal religion, derive from two main sources. Various animistic practices were prevalent throughout Arabia when Muhammad emerged as the founder of a new religion. Many of his followers continued with some of the practices and most of the beliefs with which they were already familiar. A second major source has been the underlying continuation of ideas and practices, current among other peoples who have gradually become Muslims, as Islam has spread. Such 'converts' have tended to retain many of their previous concepts beneath a veneer of conformity to orthodox Islam.

Some of the practices of Arabian tribesmen which continued, officially or unofficially after their Islamisation, included the *ḥajj* to the *kaᶜba* with various of its attendant ceremonies, rituals in such activities as paring nails or washings after certain kinds of defilement, the use of amulets for protection, the use of hair and fingernails for offensive magic, the protective measures taken against the *qarîna*, the evil eye and jinn, and various kinds of divination. New believers tended to carry into their worldview as Muslims previous ideas about the soul, death, spirit world, blessing and cursing.

In the progressive expansion of Islam, proponents of the faith have often been representatives not of the orthodox, ideal religion, but rather of various expressions of the unorthodox, popular religion. The Turks, for example, began to convert to Islam shortly after their first contacts with the Ummayad armies, at the Oxus river, by means of the Sufi mystics of Persia who went across the Oxus with the liberating message. Later, it was the converted Turkic leaders who assumed control of the orthodox Muslim states. As a result, within orthodoxy, it was demonstrated that ideal forms of the faith would be a gentle and accommodating host to the more exportable and successful expressions of popular religion.

Such expressions were an important element in the Islamisation of the Malay archipelago, where practices of magic and healing combined with the fundamental dogmas of Islam to attract the indigenous peoples.

In many ways, it would appear that the Islamisation of the Indo-Pakistan subcontinent owed as much to the religious fervour of 'saints' as to the activities of Muslim generals. Such holy men performed miraculous deeds, such as confining town demons to water-pots, and in the process won the Hindu governors and people to Islam.

Among Africans south of the Sahara, in more recent times, a similar process has occurred. Muslim missionaries, often medicine men, tended to identify pagan spirits with Muslim jinn, by which process the native Hausa *iskoki* cult, for instance, found continuance under formal allegiance to the religion of Islam. Among the Yoruba, Islam has been adapted to meet the indigenous need for divinatory and manipulative control of time and events. Fulani Muslims in the Cameroun use spirit possession and necromancy in a syncretistic mix of traditional and Islamic approaches to healing.

In western Sudan, among the Molsi, Islam's inclusion of the African's central concern for ancestor veneration broke the lengthy resistance shown to the new religion. In Tanzania, where Islam was embraced by the Bantu Wazaramo, the possession phenomena in both religions provided the bridge to conversion. Thus expansion of the formal faith has often been courtesy of adaptations made at a popular level to accommodate the major beliefs and practices of the convert peoples.

Muhammad veneration

A further major factor in the link between official and popular Islamic belief and practice is provided in the person of Muhammad. During his life, Muhammad laid repeated stress on his mere humanness. He was simply an unlettered Arab (sura 7:158), whose words were the result of divine inspiration (sura 18:110). He was only a messenger, nothing more (sura 3:138). Indeed, the Qur'ân condemns the veneration of saints in former religions, where priests and ascetics were often deified (sura 9:31).

The reality of the seventh century, however, was such that foes expected of Muhammad supernatural acts, miracles and transcendental knowledge (cf suras 2:112; 6:109; 10:21), if his claim to prophethood was to be believed. Equally, friends were only too anxious to ascribe to their human leader such signs of prophethood. The biographers of the generation following Muhammad made the miraculous picture of the prophet rich and all-embracing. Mûsâ Ibn ᶜUqba, a contemporary of Ibn Isḥâq, is typical of third-generation biographers who deliberately accelerated the process of idealising Muhammad. Even the more conservative Ibn Isḥâq himself passed on stories of miracles, such as those in which Muhammad melted a rock with a drop of water, or produced water from a dried waterhole with an arrow.

Within a few generations of his death, Muhammad had acquired many special names by which he could be invoked, several of them the same as names applied to God himself: *Nûr al-Nûr* (the Light of Light), *al-Ra'ûf* (the Merciful) and others. Collections of Muhammad's names are sometimes referred to as the Noble Names, in order to distinguish them from the Beautiful Names of God. The formula 'God bless our Prophet and lend him salvation' was expanded and elaborated into litanies of praise and appeal.

Fig 22

Translation

This is a prayer for signs of blessing. In the name of God, the Merciful, the Compassionate. Oh God, I have intended to pray for the Prophet (may God bless him and grant him salvation); obeying your command and believing your prophet Muhammad (may God bless him and grant him salvation); and out of love for him and longing for him and exalting his might and being and worthiness; so accept this prayer from me in your favour and goodness and remove the veil of negligence from my heart and make me one of your upright servants.

Oh God, increase him in honour upon honour with which you have invested him; and in greatness upon greatness which you have given him; and in light upon light from which you have created him; and raise his position in the company of those you have sent and his rank in the ranks of the prophets....

Typical of such litanies is al-Jazûlî's *Dalâ'il al-Khayrât* (Signs of Blessing). Al-Jazûlî's poetic paean develops from the opening prayer presented in Figure 22. Muhammad is exalted, blessed and prayed for by the reciter of the litany. The goodness of both God and his apostle are appealed to in a supplication for forgiveness. In later sections of the work, Muhammad is explicitly acclaimed as the sole intercessor and channel of communication between the Muslim and God. Prayer is addressed directly to him. *Dalâ'il al-Khayrât* and al-Mirghanni's *Mawlid al-Nabî*, a *qaṣîda* subtitled 'The divine secrets about the birth of the most honourable human creature', are popular at celebrations of the Prophet's birthday.

Addressing the Prophet with blessings and prayers constitutes an important facet of daily religious life for most Muslims. It takes the form of pronouncing the *taṣlîya*: the words *ṣallâ Allâh ᶜalayhi wa sallam* give the sense of 'God bless him and grant him peace'. The *taṣlîya* is traditionally said every time a Muslim enters or leaves a mosque. It is also believed to help in finding lost articles. Muhammad is especially venerated in two festivals of the Muslim year: *Mawlid al-Nabî* and *Laylat al-Miᶜrâj*.

Relics of the Prophet are highly revered by Muslims. Footprints of Muhammad are commonly venerated. The twelve such markings, identified on *al-ṣakhra* in the Dome of the Rock at Jerusalem, are world famous. The tomb of Muhammad, in Medina is perhaps one of the greatest objects of veneration associated with Muslim devotion today. On the wings of such veneration of Muhammad himself, the whole theme of sainthood and *pîr* worship has more generally flown undeterredly into the accepted historic and orthodox expression of the faith.

Unwilling host at times, orthodox religion has usually yielded to the imagination and needs of the ordinary Muslim's heart concerning an object of devotion, a mediator with God, and a powerful answerer of prayer.

Ḥadîth literature and popular Islam

Often ignored by Western investigators of Islam, perhaps because of its lesser accessibility, *ḥadîth* literature provides an important key to the puzzling lack of dissonance between the worldviews of official and popular Islam. Sunnîs (including the Wahhâbîs) and Shîʿahs accept that, besides the Qur'ân, Muhammad received an 'unread revelation' (*waḥy ghayr matlûʿ*) whereby he was enabled to render authoritative declarations on various matters. A *ḥadîth* from Ibn Anas authenticates this lesser form of revelation:

> I have left you two things amongst you, and you will not stray as long as you hold them fast, one is the book of God, the other the laws [*sunna*] of the Prophet.[20]

The *ḥadîth* in which the *sunna* were enshrined were of importance from the very outset of Islam. Among both pre-Islamic and post-Islamic tribes of the Arabian peninsula, it was considered a virtue to follow the *sunna* of one's forefathers; to accord authority to inherited tradition was therefore normal. After Muhammad, new content was given to the accepted form. That such recalling of Muhammad's words and deeds took place on a massive scale is indicated by al-Bukhâri, seven generations after the Prophet, who examined over 600,000 potential *ḥadîth* of the Prophet and retained 7,397 as authentic.

The purpose of the *ḥadîth* (both authentic and unreliable) seems to have been to comment on appropriate action in various political, societal and moral circumstances, to give expression to distinctive theological emphases among different groups of Muslims, and to elucidate obscure parts of the Qur'ân. (Appendix 1 explains the *ḥadîth* collections in more detail.)

The *ḥadîth* literature deals explicitly with areas largely untouched by the Qur'ân, and expounds quite fully those facets of folk-Islamic belief and practice only vaguely hinted at in the Qur'ân. The al-Bukhârî and Muslim collections, plus the later *Mishkât* (an eclectic arrangement of traditions used extensively by Sunnî Muslims in the Indo-Pakistan subcontinent), elaborate on the nature of the spirit world. In the Muslim collection, for example, such elaboration comes out in the chapters on the excellent qualities of the Holy Prophet, on the Day of Judgement, paradise and hell, on details of life in paradise and on the turmoil and portents of the last hour. The role of angels at the battles of Badr and Hunayn, and the command of Ishmael, in charge of the Gate of the Watchers at the entrance to heaven, are defined in *hadîth* concerning Muhammad's terrestrial and extraterrestrial activities.

Apart from reinforcing a folk-Islamic cosmology, the *hadîth* also justify many popular practices. They record, for instance, the kind of action considered appropriate when sickness is diagnosed as the result of the casting of the evil eye. Incantation is the treatment recommended by Muhammad.

The *hadîth* give a rationale to folk-Islamic saviourship. They contain many references to the intercession of prophets on behalf of the sinful in their communities.

Figure 23 lists some of the issues dealt with by al-Bukhârî in his comprehensive collection of *hadîth*.[21]

The *hadîth* stand with the Qur'ân as authoritative in the eyes of all but the most strict Islamic theologians. Their study comprises part of the curriculum of theological schools. The neo-fundamentalist reform movements of the present decades uphold them (perhaps to their own cost) as authentic and important. In other words, the official religion of Islam embraces, as part of its own heritage, the very collections of sayings and customs that incidentally deal so intimately with the beliefs and practices belonging mostly to popular Islam. That strong inclusiveness in fact reduces the (expressed) dissonance between the alternative views of reality.

Figure 23

Al-Bukhârî's Contribution to Folk-Islamic Thought

Subject	Reference
Ablutions	Vol I, Books 4 and 5
Wet dreams	Vol I, Book 5
Menstruation	Vol I, Book 6
Use of a *sutra*	Vol I, Book 9
Eclipses	Vol II, Book 18
Satan's tying of knots	Vol II, Book 21
Funeral beliefs	Vol II, Book 23
Kissing the black stone	Vol II, Book 26
Laylat al-qadr	Vol III, Book 32
Angels, jinn	Vol IV, Book 54
Virtues and merits of the Prophet	Vol IV, Book 56
Precautions in sexual intercourse	Vol VII, Book 62
cAqîqa sacrifice	Vol VII, Book 66
Incantations, evil omens, magic, soothsaying	Vol VII, Book 71
Invocations	Vol VIII, Book 75
Oaths and vows	Vol VIII, Book 78
Dreams	Vol IX, Book 87
The ninety-nine names of God	Vol IX, Book 93

Felt needs and popular Islam

Perhaps the most important factor militating against strong dissonance between two opposing views of the world concerns the needs of Muslim peoples. In ideal Islam, the focus of revelation is upon a word 'sent down'. The God who sends that word remains mostly remote, even unknowable. The formal, theological expression of Islam presents a view of reality maintainable in pure form, perhaps, by only a few intellectual   theologians   or   highly   motivated   neo-fundamentalists. But for ordinary mortals, reality is seen very differently; they require help close at hand, on a daily basis.

The continuation and development of folk-Islamic belief and practice by the Muslim masses represents not a deliberate erection of an alternative worldview to that proposed by ideal Islam, but a simple maintenance of life as they construe it. Where ideal Islam has accommodated that world, well and good. Where it has not, influence has been brought to bear on the upholders of official religion, persuading them to soften their stance. Thus, at times, the orthodox expression of Islam has been consciously softened to include some of the burdens of popular Islam. The contribution of al-Ghazâlî in this regard is significant. Al-Ghazâlî was a revered orthodox theologian. He is still known by the title 'The Proof of Islam'. Al-Ghazâlî was also a committed Sufi (mystic). At the end of his life, al-Ghazâlî combined his practical mysticism with a professorship at a college in Nishapur. His major aim in his magnum opus was to show how a careful observance of Islamic law could be the basis of a genuine Sufi life. After al-Ghazâlî, the all-important *fuqahâ'* (jurists) of Islam had more or less accepted Sufism within their concept of orthodoxy.

Where the needs of ordinary Muslims have been excluded from the theological expression of Islam, as under radical reform movements, folk-Islamic belief and practice have frequently been tolerated because Islam is, in itself, more than simply a religious system. As a way of life, accommodation to the needs of adherents is inevitable. Although excesses such as evil magic may be spoken against, no theologian will define for the mother of a sick child what she may or may not do in her efforts to seek healing for her infant. Typical of such mothers might be a wife from Upper Egypt who had lost fourteen out of her twenty children, including two sons who died at eight and nine. This mother had reached the conclusion that demons sent by Satan had strangled the youngsters. To prevent further deaths, and possible resulting divorce, she sacrificed a sheep, bought amulets and magic written charms, consulted sorcerers, Sufis, and even Coptic Christian priests, because everything was at stake. For too long, and in too many central issues, the formal faith of Islam has played host to the beliefs and practices of such a suffering woman. There is no going back on that accommodation now, whatever the neo-fundamentalists may pronounce in their immediate enthusi-asms.

The worldview of popular Islam is built upon and inte-grates with the everyday stresses and joys of ordinary people. There is a lack of dissonance with the alternative, official Islamic worldview simply because the popular view of the world is more appropriate, more mundane and more pervasive. Without a dynamic, divine involvement, contra-dictory of its own systematic tenets, official Islam cannot hope to compete for the uncompromising patronisation of most Muslims, for it cannot meet their most fundamental needs. Ideal Islam has few resources for dealing with the everyday concerns and nightly dreads of ordinary Muslims; popular Islam, on the contrary, knows an abundance of remedies. Each local community recognises practitioners who can provide the charms or ceremonies necessary to effect peace of mind and to restore equilibrium.

The folk-Islamic view of the world thus has little argument with that of official Islam. It operates in the realm of human beings with needs and fears that inform and are informed by their outlook on life. It is no problem for ordinary Muslims to adhere to the formal facets of official Islam, and ordinary Muslims certainly perceive themselves as being true Mus-lims. It is simply that their personal and local needs find solution within another worldview: that of popular Islam.

CHAPTER SIXTEEN

POWER ENCOUNTER

Taha

THE YOUNG MAN TREMBLED with anxiety. His shaking fingers dialled the international, country and town codes. Then they picked out the number of his parents' home in faraway Khartoum.

'Hello! Hello! This is Taha! What has happened to my father?'

There was a stunned silence at the other end of the crackling line. After what seemed like an eternity, Taha's mother released the flood of grief that had been momentarily shocked into silence by her son's incredible question.

'Your father has just died, Taha! The doctor is here now, and the washers of the dead are on their way. Your uncle is being brought early from work to take care of everything. Your sisters and I are trying to think about the food we need to prepare for all the relatives and neighbours who will come to pay their respects. We miss you now, Taha. Your father died with your name on his lips. But, Taha, how did you know?'

That was one of many questions in Taha's own mind. He had long realised that there was something special about his relationship with his father. There was some peculiar force within his father that had both attracted and scared him. As he returned the telephone to its cradle, he thought back over the years of his relationship with his father.

His first conscious awareness of a strange power in his father dated from the time when his mother had been so ill. Her legs had been badly burned in a kerosene stove accident. The hospital had done an inadequate job and she was in constant pain. One night, Taha's father had taken him into the room where his mother was sleeping fitfully.

'We are going to deal with your mother's legs in our own way, Taha,' he said.

As the woman slept, Taha's father began to intone strange words. At the same time, he made stroking movements over his wife. The next moment, the hair bristled on Taha's back. For his mother began to speak, not with her own voice but with a deep, masculine sound. Taha's father seemed to control the conversation and stopped the session after a while. Taha thought he looked exhausted. Next morning, his mother's legs were radically improved. Taha's father warned him not to say anything to his mother about the details of the evening before.

Other, smaller instances came to Taha's mind. He always seemed to be strongly 'in tune' with his father. Even though he had come to England five years previously and had worked hard in his adopted land, his spirit felt bonded to his father in the Sudan.

Taha had noticed that he himself also possessed strange powers. He had first begun to discover them in England, in situations where he was caught in a difficult position. One of the first times had been when he was working as a cook in a small London hotel. Through some mistake, the kitchen had ended up with one chicken too few for an important business lunch. Taha's boss had taken a chicken out of the freezer, but was at a loss for what to do.

homeland, he felt free to indulge in all that the West had to offer. And there was plenty on offer in places like London. Taha assumed that fast girls and drugs were part and parcel of what a Christian country like Britain was all about. His experience of English society showed just how inferior the Christian nations were in comparison with his homeland and its strict behavioural codes.

Then, through one of his many temporary jobs, Taha met some unusual British youths. They were Catholics, and they seemed to know a peaceful, joyful power which didn't need drink or sex for stimulation. He went to church with them. Gradually, he started dropping into churches on his own. The buildings seemed to be places of peace. In them Taha sensed a different kind of presence from the one that had invaded his home since his father died.

Eventually, Taha met some Christians from a Protestant church down the street on which he lived. They befriended him, began to introduce him to Bible study, shared with him their lives and testimonies of what Christ meant to them.

One evening, a lot of things came to a head for Taha. Two of the local Protestants brought round a friend from their church who had lived for many years in the Middle East. After tea, talk, and questions, the visitor commented quietly to Taha: 'Your father was a medium, Taha, wasn't he?'

'Yes.'

'There is a power, Taha, which can break the strength of your father, and of this evil spirit which keeps bothering you. That power belongs to Jesus Christ. But you will have to confess your sinfulness and need of Jesus' forgiveness in your life.'

After a while they stood to pray together. As the three Englishmen were praying, Taha's vision blurred. He felt faint. The Englishmen sat him down, then went to prayer again. Authoritative, commanding words were spoken in Jesus' name. Taha repeated words of confession and from

Suddenly Taha had an inspiration. 'Leave it to me,' said excitedly. He sat down in front of the chicken and 1 one solid minute concentrated everything in him on th frozen bird.

'Put it in the oven now,' he declared at last.

'Don't be silly, it's not defrosted yet!' argued the chef.

'Put it in the oven!' Taha insisted. Incredibly, in less thar five minutes the chicken had become tender, cooked, beautifully hot, just how these British liked it.

'Weird foreigner!' had declared the chef, and promised Taha a drink in reward.

That had been the beginning. Then there was the bank loan for the new car. The loan should have been impossible, humanly speaking, but for Taha it worked. There had been other things. Taha knew a strange power in his life, somehow linked to his father. And at the moment when his father died, suddenly, 3,000 miles away, Taha knew.

It was after his father's death that Taha paid the price for his unnatural talents. Someone disturbed him at night—not just any 'someone'—it was someone big, heavy and determined. Taha would wake up in a sweat because there was a presence in his room. A British friend learned one evening that Taha wasn't joking. They had both been in the living-room downstairs, talking late into the evening. Suddenly they became aware of a person upstairs, above them, in Taha's bedroom. Then the heavy footsteps started coming downstairs. Quickly the friend came to his own conclusion. 'I'm getting out!' he declared. 'There's something horrible in this house!'

Taha felt compelled to stay. What difference would it make to him if he moved? The visitations worsened as Christmas approached.

That reminded him of something else. A confusion in his life needed to be resolved. Taha was from a Muslim background and was as faithful as other Muslims he knew, in Khartoum, at saying his prayers. Of course, once out of his

his own heart invited Jesus to live in him. Later, they moved upstairs and exorcised the bedroom in Jesus' name.

The road of discipleship for Taha is a long one. Many aspects of his life need Jesus Christ's continuing attention. But the bondage in his daily experience is broken. He sleeps at night now. No evil presence dominates his flat or his mind.

Temal

Temal lived in a remote town in the south-western corner of Turkey. What a bus journey to get home from Izmir! People only made that kind of trip on special occasions. Now, here were these strangers, Englishmen, come to visit him, not from Izmir but from Istanbul!

Quickly, Temal learned the reason for their visit. These foreigners, who—it turned out—spoke Turkish well, were friends of someone with whom Temal had been corresponding for a number of years. They had met Mr Johnson in London, it seemed. Mr Johnson had given them Temal's address and had asked them, on their return to Turkey where they were studying Turkish, to look up Temal on his behalf. Mr Johnson sent his greetings via them. Could Temal give them some account of his present situation for them to pass on to Mr Johnson?

Temal decided to trust them. If they really knew Mr Johnson, they were probably good friends. They seemed clean and transparent enough, not like some of the other foreigners whom he had met, drifting east along the drug route. Clearly these men had made a special journey to come and see him on Mr Johnson's behalf.

'I suppose it all began many years ago,' he began. He paused to sip the hot, sweet tea he had made for them all. The foreigners settled to listen, relaxing from their long journey. 'I had a dream.' Temal thought back over the years to those first stirrings of hope for some answers to his spiritual questionings. 'A figure dressed in white appeared to me and said very gently, "Your heart is right, Temal! Keep on seeking!" I was being given some guidance, some encouragement. My quest for something real in my heart was not just escapism, or unfaithful disbelief. Here was a white-robed being telling me to go on searching.' Temal paused, his mind leaping forward by months.

'Then he appeared to me again. It must have been months, maybe a year or so later. The same white-robed creature came in another dream. "Your heart is right, Temal!" he said again. "Keep searching! The true way is in Jesus!" So he spoke to me. And as I listened in my dream, I knew that he was right. When I woke up, I still knew that he was right.'

The foreigners were listening attentively. They must be trustworthy. Temal had noticed the tears coming to their eyes as he had spoken of those dream visions.

'Not long afterwards, I was listening to my radio. By chance, I turned to a waveband I don't normally use and I caught the word "*Injîl*", then "Christ", and then "Jesus". I tuned in. It was a programme talking about who Jesus is...I mean was...well, was and is, too! It was peculiar. I knew a little, from my younger years, of the Christians' false view of Jesus as divine. I knew that Christians had also changed their scriptures. But I had never heard those scriptures actually read by anyone. Nor, come to think of it, did anyone who spoke so strongly against them ever point out when, and by whom, they had been corrupted. Anyway, over the radio the Gospels about Jesus were being read. They certainly didn't sound very forced to me. They sounded very natural, as if the people who had written them were talking of events which they, or their friends, had seen.

'I noticed, in the Gospels, that Jesus didn't stand up and shout "I am the Son of God!" He seemed to act in wonderful ways and let the people around him draw their own conclusions. I felt very attracted to this person who seemed to know what was inside people, and who seemed to have an answer for their spiritual hunger. I listened regularly to the broadcasts. At some stage, I heard Mr Johnson's name mentioned as being willing to send a copy of the Gospels, in Turkish, to anyone who wrote. I wrote. I received the Gospels and other good books. Most recently I have been studying the Gospel of Luke by correspondence. I send my answers to Mr Johnson in London. I have so enjoyed studying the Gospel of Luke. I am convinced it really is good news! I know now that the true way for me is in Jesus!'

Temal's English visitors beamed and embraced him. 'We want to pray with you, brother Temal,' they said.

The evening visit was a wonderful experience for Temal. At the end of it he felt that he'd been recognised and accepted as part of a worldwide family. He'd learned also that there were other Turkish members of that family. Perhaps one day he would meet some of them!

Basma and Soheir

It was a mess! If only Basma had known six months ago what she knew now, maybe things could have been different. Half a year ago, life had been bad enough!

Her mother had been stuck across town in a cheap, private hospital for a major operation. How thankful she had been for the Christian family for whom she worked part-time. They were foreigners, but they had made the effort to learn Arabic. They were people of prayer too. She enjoyed working in their home. It seemed to be a place of peace, despite the numbers of people who came and went. They had gone to the hospital with her to lay hands on her mother and to pray for her. No one in her own family had been interested. She had to admit that that wasn't surprising, considering the way in which her mother only managed to make enemies rather than friends. Basma certainly knew what a sharp tongue her mother could wield. Thanks be to God, her mother had got over the operation and recovered her strength. There was power in these Christians' praying. They seemed to trust the Lord with whom they spoke in Jesus' name.

On reflection, that must have been the time when Soheir, her young half-sister, got into trouble. Typical of Soheir! Now who knew whether the girl was alive or dead?

Just a few days ago, the English woman for whom Basma worked had taken Soheir to a doctor in the city centre. It turned out that the pains that Soheir had been having were due to one awful problem: she was pregnant! She was unmarried, and in three months she was going to have a baby! Basma had quizzed her distraught sister on the way back from the clinic. Soheir wailed that she didn't know how it happened. How could she be pregnant? She had never been near a man. What had fate brought into her life now?

There had seemed to be only one clue, and Basma had pursued that vague possibility relentlessly. She and her husband had gone to confront the tailor to whom Soheir had gone, during the time that their mother was sick in hospital, to choose material for a new dress. That was six months ago, and Soheir was now six months pregnant. Because of the family circumstances, Soheir had gone alone. One thing Soheir had admitted in the taxi to Basma on the way back from the doctor was that she had accepted a glass of tea at the tailor's and had then felt quite ill. Basma's husband had argued hard with the tailor. The man had a reputation in the neighbourhood. When the words 'pregnant' and 'prison' were mentioned one after the other, the tailor had grown frightened. Basma's husband had felt sure that he was on the right course. He involved the police. The tailor disappeared. When the police had found him and finished with him, the story came out in the open. He had spiked Soheir's tea with a strong drug, and then had raped the virgin as she lay unconscious in his shop. The whole neighbourhood was electrified by the story. Tailors became very suspect people.

Meanwhile, the pregnant Soheir had disappeared. She didn't know of the confession of the wicked tailor. All she knew was that somehow she was pregnant, or so the doctor said. And her swollen abdomen? And the kicking movements within her body? Yes, she must be expecting a baby. But how? And how could she ever go home again? Her brother, who hated her anyway, would surely kill both her and the life within her. What should she do? Where could she turn? Go to her father? Go to Basma's home? In all the dark thoughts and questionings, Soheir was aware of just one thin strand of light, holding her back from doing anything really drastic, at least for the time being.

Basma's English friend had whispered to her at the doctor's on that awful visit, a couple of days previously, 'It's all right, Soheir. Jesus knows your heart. He knows the truth. We will pray for you.'

That was about the last thing anyone had said to her. Now she hid, dazed and shocked, waiting for another evening to bring darkness. Perhaps this night would bring an end, or a beginning.

Basma was worried out of her mind, as well. She felt responsible for her younger sister. She dreaded their brother's quick temper. She longed for everything to work out somehow. A similar glimmer of hope flickered on the horizon of her spirit. Would Jesus come and help them in their need?—the Jesus she had asked into her heart? the Jesus she had begun to learn about and relate to? the Jesus who had definitely healed her mother?

Basma left her children with her nearby aunt and crossed the city to her English friend's home. 'Soheir disappeared three days ago. I've come to pray with you to Jesus.'

The hunger of the heart

Beneath the surface of conventional religious behaviour, huge needs expose the disequilibrium many Muslims know in their lives. Such lack of peace may be due to direct involvement in the occult world, as with Taha. It may be part of the longing for a true relationship with the living God, as in the case of Temal. It may be due to the breakdown of relationships in families and communities, the effect of sin and abuse of trust, as in the tragedy of Basma and Soheir.

In each instance, some focus of power encounter took place in the lives concerned. For Taha, it was a battle against the spiritual forces that manifested their hostility towards him; it was a battle against the involvement Taha had had, through his father, with the powers of the satanic realm. It was a battle for freedom from a spirit that constantly invaded Taha's home after his father's death.

For Temal, the encounter was concentrated in a battle against the enemy of his soul which had starved Temal of the true way to peace with God. That battle was first engaged, sovereignly from above, in Temal's dream-life. There, in a vision, an angel underscored and encouraged a search that took shape in Temal's mind. The battle involved the spiritual energy necessary to envisage, produce and air a radio broadcast specifically designed for the ears of Turkish Muslims. It took a correspondence course ministry and follow-up visitation. Years of spiritual warfare provided the bridge over which Temal walked to faith in Christ.

For Basma and Soheir, the encounter focused considerably in a battle of consistent Christian witness over a period of five years. It took the learning of Arabic. It took public prayer for healing in their mother's sickness. It took the building of confidence and mutual trust. Finally, it took the prayer of faith in a crisis, so that, in the human impossibilities, the Lord Jesus might speak and act.

In each instance, the Muslims concerned made an active response to the processes going on in their lives. Taha had to yield control of his life to Jesus and ask him to be Lord. Temal had to choose to follow the angel's words of advice, and seek for the true way in Jesus. Basma (and perhaps one day Soheir) had to invite Christ to change her life, to live within her as Saviour.

In whatever manifestation, and with whatever personal details, the resources of Christ are specifically given to enable his church to prevail against the gates of hell. The battling is a positive—as opposed to a defensive—action. At the time of their need, many of the 'gates' which the Devil would hold hidden and closed become visible in the lives of ordinary Muslims. The channel for advance is commonly some sort of power encounter.

The kingdom, the power, and the glory

In the biblical view, popular religion most often demonstrates the allegiance of a people to the 'powers' of a second kingdom—one of darkness, bondage, deceit, non-fulfilment and fear. In God's self-manifestation, both as the covenant God of the Old Testament, and more fully as the Saviour of mankind in the New Testament, the focus of encounter between the kingdoms of light and darkness frequently takes the form of a battle between the 'powers'.

In the Old Testament, the essence of the problem is often pointed in terms of confrontation. Is Moses' God stronger than Pharaoh's magicians? Is Elijah's God greater than the Canaanite baals?

Similarly, in the New Testament, the clash of the kingdoms frequently finds focus in spiritual warfare. Is the Holy Spirit more powerful than Elymas' spirit? Do the seven sons of Sceva (Acts 19:13–16) really speak with authority, or can they be 'overpowered' by a possessed man? The apostle Paul's commissioning involved a direct statement of the centrality of encounter in his life's task. Jesus was sending him to Jews and Gentiles 'to open their eyes and turn them from darkness to light, and from the power of Satan to God' (Acts 26:18).

A significant factor in such power encounters, at least as they are documented in the Bible, is that the power for good belongs to a sovereign holy God. It is not the property of the agent. Indeed, the Power is a divine Person! So, it is not a setting of Christianity against the religions, nor of one world-view against another, but of the Spirit of God against the powers of evil. To err here is to risk engaging in the idolatry which leads to triumphalism. The kingdom bespeaks a King. Let no ambassador or soldier usurp the glory which belongs only to Jesus Christ!

Jesus' own ministry of reconciliation begins with an announcement of the coming of the kingdom of God (Mark 1:15). As far as God is concerned, the gospel is preached to herald the kingdom of God. Conversion, or repentance and belief, provide entry into that kingdom (Matthew 4:17). Jesus' teaching ministry is filled with parables of the kingdom. Miracles are 'signs' of the kingdom. As risen Lord, at the post-resurrection end of his earthly ministry, Jesus continues to speak intensely about the kingdom of God (Acts 1:3). After Jesus' ascension, the kingdom of God is announced by the apostles, is master-directed by the Holy Spirit, and is headed from glory by the King of kings himself.

The biblical context for mission, therefore, is one of two kingdoms. Whether in Old Testament Egypt or New Testament Ephesus, the powers of the kingdom of darkness remain unalterably opposed to the establishment on earth of the kingdom of God. A biblically informed theology of mission has to face the question of the kingdom of God and the alternative kingdom.

Perhaps it is partly due to an idolatrous, rationalistic spirit from the kingdom of darkness at work among Western believers that many missionaries to Muslims are blind to the real issues at stake. Mission to Muslims is not necessarily so much a matter of trying to convey primarily intellectual information, against most of which the Muslim is already 'inoculated'. It is a question, rather, of preaching the gospel with power, with the Holy Spirit, and with deep conviction, as well as with words (1 Thessalonians 1:5).

The calling of the church immersed in or skirting a vast sea of some 935 million Muslim souls is that a will might be done and a kingdom come on earth. Paul was allowed to stay less than three weeks in Thessalonica. Nevertheless, a strong convert church grew quickly there. That church was soon involved in widespread mission to the west, and ecumenical love to the poor and persecuted Jewish Christian brothers and sisters over in Palestine. According to Paul, the model fellowship in Thessalonica resulted because, under God's sovereign working, the gospel came to the people 'not simply with words'.

Our look at popular Islam pushes the issue of kingdom-power very much to the forefront. In so doing, it confronts the Christian evangelist (especially if he is a Westerner) with a dilemma. In their beliefs and practices, ordinary Muslims focus attention on the same issues that brought about so many dynamic encounters in the ministries of Jesus, Paul and others. People are sick and in need of healing: by magic, or by Christ? People require help in a world of hostile, occult 'beings': by alliance with evil spirits, or with the Holy Spirit? People desire guidance in making important decisions about the future: by fortune-telling and divination, or by Holy Spirit revelation? In popular Islam, there is almost complete allegiance to the kingdom of darkness in the search for such assistance.

At the same time, however, the very view of reality that gives rise to the beliefs and practices of ordinary Muslims is in many respects far closer to the biblical one than to the missionary's own mechanistic, scientistic worldview! If the Western believer ever comes to be faced with the details of folk-Islamic belief and practice, is he able to deal with those phenomena as real entities? Or does he view them as invalid, because his worldview claims that there are no such things as jinn, *qarînât* or zodiacal influences? Perhaps he sees the ordinary Muslim as 'primitive'; after all, sickness is explicable simply by germs, not by the evil eye or sorcery. Will his ensuing activity be one of spiritual power encounter or Western education?

For too long, it would seem, in Christian witness among Muslims, there has been no power encounter because there have been no power bearers. The sad situation of the poor Gadarene demoniac (Mark 5:1–13) has been often repeated. 'No one' could bind him, and 'no one' could release him. The beliefs and practices of popular Islam bespeak the need for power encounter. Their foundational worldview makes sense of such a process for, as we have seen, it understands 'power'. The heart of the matter lies in Muslims coming to know Jesus Christ as King over all. If the essence of that introduction to Christ occurs in their experience, perhaps there is a chance for Muslims to bypass the normal miscommunication in learning about Jesus. To 'know' the Lord, who has confronted and changed their disequilibrium, provides the possibility for Muslims to 'know' that Lord in his true lordship. Their cosmological map may be transformed as they discover, from the Bible as well as from their own experience, that Jesus is more than a prophet. He is divine; he bears in his body the marks of the cross; he is indeed God and Saviour.

There consequently needs to be a major emphasis on the teaching of the word among those Muslims whose relationship with Jesus Christ begins in power encounter. The fruit of genuine encounter in experience will be an openness to new realisations at a cerebral level. Grounding in the faith, anchoring of experience in biblical truth, will be crucial for new believers in Christ who come to faith via the process of power encounter.

The fact that official Islam hosts folk-Islamic beliefs and practices offers the possibility that something of the relevance of power encounter for ordinary Muslims might be appropriate also for proponents of the ideal form of the faith. Certainly in Indonesia, in recent decades, inroads made against the secret spiritism of many Muslims has broken through to the hearts of orthodox Muslims in a manner previously unknown.

The way of the cross

In its coming and powerfulness, the kingdom of God centres paradoxically upon the one act of ultimate weakness: the cross of Christ. In that act is expressed the tension for both servant and Master. The kingdom comes in power, yet the kingdom comes in great weakness.

The New Testament expounds a clash throughout the complex realms of creation. As Christ ushers in the kingdom of God, as the hope of the Old Testament begins to become a reality, all creation is jarred. It agonises like a mother about to give birth to a baby (Romans 8:22). There is pain in renewed hope.

The created world has in some special sense been apportioned to a whole spiritual hierarchy of angelic beings, according to the Bible. Christ came to a world where men were 'following the course of this world, following the prince of the power of the air, the spirit that is now at work in the sons of disobedience' (Ephesians 2:2, RSV). Satan himself is exposed as head of this hierarchy. The last book of the New Testament prophesies that 'the great dragon was hurled down—that ancient serpent called the devil or Satan, who leads the whole world astray' (Revelation 12:9). Until then, the Devil claims the whole of humanity for his parish. In Satan's employ are 'guardians' of specific nations who carry considerable authority over the affairs of the earth. The universe of folk-Islamic thought is only slightly removed from the picture presented in the Bible.

With Christ's advent, this evil claim to authority is fundamentally challenged. In every major event of Christ's life on earth, the spiritual crisis of the hour is highlighted in the New Testament. The veil is drawn aside, and conflict is exposed in the heavenly places. Both in its unfolding and in its wake, that conflict brings immense suffering.

The birth of Christ is heralded by the activity of the Holy Spirit, by angelic visitations and by cosmological signs. Equally, there follows an ugly display of the powers of darkness, as Bethlehem mourns the slaughter of the innocents.

The miracles of Jesus are full of significance in the arena of spiritual conflict. The Synoptic Gospels describe the wonders of Jesus as *dunâmeis*, foretastes of the 'powers of the coming age' (Hebrews 6:5). Jesus' specific reference to the 'finger of God' (Luke 11:20) in his exorcising shows us his view of his ministry as a battle. Nevertheless, wonderful healing for men and women is inextricably connected with 'stripes' for Christ (Isaiah 53:5, AV).

The cross provides the pivot of the conflict. Jesus' death is accompanied by all manner of supernatural manifestations. Yet it is his very death, the apex of his suffering which unleashes those contortions of the created universe (Hebrews 2:10); the unimaginable suffering of the abandoned Christ constitutes the definitive victory over the kingdom of darkness.

The resurrection and ascension become the unchallengeable statement of Christ's achievement in this conflict. Yet again, suffering is concomitantly mentioned. For 'we see Jesus...crowned with glory and honour because he suffered death...' (Hebrews 2:9). Victory and suffering are closely linked for Christ, and in some mysterious way they are also to be linked for his church.

Christ's call to Saul of Tarsus is to conflict and suffering. He confides to Ananias that the transformed Pharisee is 'my chosen instrument to carry my name before the Gentiles and their kings and before the people of Israel: I will show him how much he must suffer for my name' (Acts 9:15,16). In turn, the apostle passes on the same message. He writes from prison to the believers whom he has founded in the faith: 'For it has been granted to you on behalf of Christ not only to believe on him, but also to suffer for him, since you are going through the same struggle you saw I had, and now hear that I still have' (Philipians 1:29,30; Colossians 1:24).

The *koinonîa* of believers embraces those who rejoice and those who mourn, those who live in plenty and those who suffer for Christ's sake. In the holism of such fellowship lies hope for mutual bonds, with brothers and sisters coming to Christ out of a process of power encounter. The gospel does not promise prosperity so much as persecution. In holding out that truth to believers from a Muslim background, the fellowship of believers does well to identify with such brothers and sisters in their submission to Christ's lordship, whatever the human cost. It is in pressured moments that power encounter is actually provoked (Acts 5:29,30). And out of power encounter, as much with evil human structures as with spirit beings, comes the cross for the church of the Saviour. That cross is to be willingly borne by all would-be disciples.

An exposition of the world of popular Islam, if it does nothing else, surely demonstrates the reality of the kingdom of darkness. It provokes us to the conclusion that the kingdom and its powers have to be addressed, if those in its bondage are to be released to faith in the Lord who loves them and died for them. Such encounter needs to take place in the wisdom and under the authority of Christ, so that it be a dealing with the real issue, not with the missionaries' culturally-coloured perception of the problem. A fuller recognition that 'witness' (*marturîa*) include suffering, lends biblical holism to the understanding of mission among ordinary Muslims.

One of the visions of Christ left with his hard-pressed disciples, as the canon of the New Testament closes, depicts exactly this paradox of immediate suffering and ultimate victory. A Lamb that is 'slain' is seen 'standing' victoriously between the throne and the four living creatures (Revelation 5:6). Wounds of the cross single out the world's greatest missionary; marks of death are transformed into tokens of triumph in the profoundest power encounter of all time.

CHAPTER SEVENTEEN

THE GOSPEL AND THE ORDINARY MUSLIM

O NE OF THE APOSTLE PAUL'S defences of his life and good faith began with the assertion 'I am a Jew...' (Acts 22:3). Well into the later years of his apostleship, Paul still thought of himself as a Jew.

As he went on to describe his Damascus road experience, Paul recalled the message he received from Ananias, a highly respected fellow-Jew living in Damascus. That message conveyed how the 'God of our fathers' had chosen Paul to know his will, and to see his Righteous One. The God of the Jews opened the eyes of a Jew to the Jewish Messiah, Jesus of Nazareth. Now, having tramped the mountains and plains of Asia Minor and Greece, Paul still answers both the commander of the Roman troops and the angry Jewish mob with the same words: 'I am a Jew...'

By the same token, it was Paul who argued most strongly that gentiles could become believing Christians without first having to become Jews. After his missionary work in Galatia, Paul had reported this conviction to the church leaders in Jerusalem, taking Titus with him. The point was proved. There was no requirement that Titus be circumcised (Galatians 2:3). Indeed, Paul's ministry to the gentiles was strongly affirmed. Not long afterwards, Aristarchus from Thessalonica was accepted as a valid brother and partner in mission with Paul, without his being circumcised or forced to identify himself with the Jewish people.

In his preaching to Greeks, Paul proclaimed to them 'what you worship as something unknown' (Acts 17:23). He accepted that they were already 'worshippers'. He quoted their own poets to get across his message about all mankind being made in God's image. He emphasised the concepts of 'ignorance' and 'thinking'. Paul in fact sought to communicate within the terms of his audience's worldview.

Christ himself seemed to accept that a Samaritan could remain a Samaritan, experience fulfilment as a Samaritan while believing in him, and worship the Father, not on this mountain or that, but in spirit and in truth. A Syro-Phoenician, a Roman, or a Greek could all begin and enjoy a relationship with God by faith, without needing first to become proselytes to Judaism.

At the same time, each individual, from whatever background, knew judgement and transformation in becoming part of the Lord's family. The Pharisee Saul had to become the messianic Jew, a true 'Jew' in his heart. He had to learn to live by the Spirit of Christ, not by the dead letter of the Law. This proud man had to have burned deep into his soul the fact that, in Christ, there is 'neither Jew, nor Greek, slave nor free, male nor female' (Galatians 3:28).

Believers from gentile backgrounds had to face facts about their previous worship of idols. The images were effectually nothing but a front for the worship of demons. Gentiles 'in Christ' needed to respond to prophetic views on their communal relationships. Aberrant liaisons had been condoned, before, by the demons they had served. Just because the gentile ethos encouraged plural sexual relationships did not mean that believers could. Their stand had to reflect the holiness of their new Lord (2 Corinthians 7:1).

A Samaritan had to face the reality, declared from above, that she worshipped what she did not know, for salvation was truly from the Jews (John 4:22). Believing in the Messiah brought transformation to an empty life whose worship was a waste, and whose sequential adultery was not the joy for which she was created.

Syro-Phoenicians, seemingly involved in the occult world, Romans, an occupying force with a view of their Caesar as a god, and Greeks, with their mythologies and false ideas of salvation—all came in for some degree of judgement as the light of the gospel touched their lives.

The tension portrayed in Scripture is a tension highlighted in mission, especially cross-cultural mission. On the one hand there is a continuity: God is prepared to take the initiative in approach; he is willing to begin relating to human beings wherever those human beings may be; he reads human hearts and brings unspoken longings to fulfilment. On the other hand, there is radical discontinuity: God, who is truly holy, is concerned about a transformation of our human cultures. His goal is that they should more faithfully honour Christ the King.

Western culture and mission to Muslims

Undeniably, in bringing a message from a sovereign God, Christian missionaries are agents of culture change. There can be no meeting of a divine Christ with culture-bound mankind without a shift in the human worldview. The gospel of the kingdom of God will have ramifications throughout a culture as allegiances are transferred, as the demonic is exposed and dealt with, and as assumptions are confirmed or transformed by the Author of absolute truth.

Equally, Christian missionaries, in bringing a message they have heard and received from within their own cultural constructs, tend to colour the manner in which that message is passed on. They speak out of what they know. The mark of others' understanding and acceptance of the message, for which they look in their audience, tends to be formulated in terms which they dictate and expect. The Jerusalem Council, whose deliberations are recorded in Acts 15, was the proto-type 'missions conference', in which this issue was deliber-ately faced.

Our look at the lives of ordinary Muslims has prompted some uncomfortable questions about our success or failure as missionaries to such people. For the most part, perhaps, we have not even recognised the 'world' in which many Muslims are living.

Western Christian witness among Muslims tends to pro-mote a mono-cultural outlook on life. Too often the Bible has been interpreted via a Western worldview that refuses to be informed by that source text itself. The fact that the New Testament begins with a genealogy and a dream is lost on most missionaries to Muslims. Instead of the declared real-ities of a Middle Eastern inspired word, Western values such as individualism, rationalism and naturalism have tended to determine the approach made in mission.

Western culture's overemphasis on individualism, for example, prejudices many of us into seeing conversion on a one-by-one, 'personal' basis as the most important priority, but there are significant scriptural examples of multi-individual decisions, whereby whole groups of people repented and believed on Christ.

Again, the biblical idea that man should live in harmony with the world around him is, to a large degree, a concept alien to the Westerner. In our view, nature is to be subju-gated or put to use—what do you mean, 'bread has life of its own'?

Perhaps most significantly, Western Christian faith tends to be cognitively oriented. Evangelism often becomes a mat-ter of communicating propositional truths. Intellectual assent to such truths is taken to equal 'conversion', whereas the New Testament emphasis appears to be far more holistic, expecting conversion to issue from a proclamation in miraculous act as well as word. The resulting 'converts' are ordinary people whose lives have been totally transformed. Together, they know a radically new kingdom style of living. In explaining why Muslims are so seemingly resistant to the gospel, the Western Christian's cerebral bias possibly goes as far as any special innate hardness of that particular brand of human heart.

Such Western categories of thought and ways of looking at the world are, paradoxically, uninformed by the Bible itself. They tend only to separate the Western missionary from people such as ordinary Muslims, who function from within a more dynamic or experience-oriented view of reality.

The changing of worldview?

If the gospel brings about fundamental change in worldview, and if, with regard to missions to Muslims, increasing understanding is shown for the human being who is the subject of such change, what guidelines are to be given to the missionary as agent of change? What kind of transformation in worldview is the missionary to seek? 'Seeing' the world of popular Islam is only half of the problem, though it is a very necessary first step. A deeper problem lies in the matter of response to that 'seeing'.

In a power encounter, an unrecognised temptation exists to inject a Western worldview along with the spiritual dynamic that deals with the offending 'powers' and 'beings'. When a missionary is involved in such ministry in the life of a Muslim, it is easy for the Muslim to transfer his allegiance to that missionary. Such teacher/disciple roles inevitably involve implicit learning of the missionary's cultural perspective. A transformed Muslim may thus be quickly alienated from his own culture.

Jesus was often careful when he had been involved in power encounter to insist that the released persons stay *within* the bounds of their own cultures. A healed leper was to go through a cleansing ritual with a priest and be reintegrated into his society. An exorcised Legion was to remain with his townfolk and recount in the Decapolis what Christ had done for him. A healed and forgiven paralytic was sent home. Often, Jesus refused permission to such people to follow him. He wanted them whole within their own cultural settings. At the same time, those 'cultural settings' would be infiltrated by the yeast of transformed lives. The 'harvest' at Sychar illustrates, in a cross-cultural situation, the effectiveness of such an approach to power encounter (John 4:39–42).

In mission to Muslims, the essence of power encounter is not a war against the particular culture pattern of the Muslim concerned but a commitment to battle, from within the culture pattern, against the spiritual forces which bind men, women and children, and keep them at a distance from their Creator.

Some examples follow of patterns of thought within folk-Islamic culture which need careful appraisal if the kind of deep-level changes brought about by processes of power encounter are not to bring societal disintegration as well.

Baraka

The concept of *baraka* pervades Muslim minds. It matters not whether it is a question of fulfilling the formal, religious duty of *ḥajj*, or the more magical attitudes towards *baraka* as a power for healing.

Baraka is seen as 'good'. It could, however, be 'too good' for one. At the very centre of Islam, in Mecca itself, is a very dangerous possibility that must be avoided. If a pilgrim were to look up into the sky right above the *kaᶜba*, he might have a glimpse into paradise and thus suffer mental derangement; he would have been exposed to too much *baraka*. That is why, if you look carefully, you will see that doves never fly across the roof of the *ka^cba*. *Baraka* is at its greatest intensity at the *ka^cba*. It is, consequently, the place pilgrims choose to walk round and round constantly. If human pilgrims are not available, then angelic ones replace them. The gate to heaven is above the *ka^cba*. Never could a believer be physically closer to God. Precisely there, however, where *baraka* exists in its most concentrated form, it is also unpredictably dangerous. *Baraka* is not to be played with.

Who or what holds *baraka*? Certain persons or objects may be possessors of *baraka* in their own right. Muhammad, of all human beings, is most endowed with *baraka*. Holy men and their graves are huge repositories of *baraka*. The Qur'ân itself is full of *baraka*. Little children, seen as innocents, may possess *baraka*. Bride and bridegroom are possessors of *baraka*. Certain animals, such as horses, sheep, bees, doves, and so on have *baraka*. Animal products and certain plants and vegetables contain *baraka*. Rain and sunshine dispense *baraka*. Certain periods of the year, such as the month of Ramadân, are replete with *baraka*. Actions, names, numbers and places may each hold *baraka*. As may be seen, the supernatural 'force' is held both by human beings (alive or dead) and by inanimate objects.

Baraka may be gained or lost. Some persons and things possess *baraka* in themselves. Other persons inherit *baraka*. Those in line to Muhammad, the *sharîfs*, inherit the blessing. Marabouts are also inheritors and passers on of *baraka*. Transfer of *baraka* may occur by biological means, or by smearing with saliva, spitting on someone, or even sharing a meal with someone. Positive actions, for example fulfilling the *dîn* of formal faith, bring *baraka* into peoples' lives. Equally, *baraka* can be stolen or taken without the holder's consent. It can also be lost by contamination, or breaking of taboos.

In everyday greeting, *baraka* is passed to and fro. One common speech pattern of North Africa simply says, 'May *baraka* be on you!' The response is, 'May *baraka* be on you as well!' In the relationships of host and guest, there is *baraka* involvement. To refuse hospitality is to oppose the *baraka*, to act like an enemy. In accepting hospitality and drinking the coffee, *baraka* is brought into the ceremony by both the host and guest (acting as brothers) and the coffee (a symbol of surplus and prosperity). *Baraka* is the goal in view in the celebrations of the birthdays, or 'deathdays', of holy men. The activity is designed for people to '*khudh al-baraka min al-mawlid*' ('take the *baraka* from the *mawlid*'). The effectiveness of charms and amulets increases by the amount of *baraka* put into them by their maker. The most widely used amulets derive their *baraka* from the Qur'ânic words written on them. Methods of healing, and especially the use of pieces of paper inscribed with verses of the Qur'ân and soaked in water, aim to bring *baraka* to bear on behalf of the sick. In the latter case, the *baraka* is transferred to the patient when he drinks the water.

The concept of *baraka* is fundamental to the worldview of most Muslims. It appears in the context of formal faith. It is validated and exegeted quite considerably in the Qur'ân. The *ḥadîth* describe its potential for movement through contact and touching. *Baraka* explains much of the activity of holy occasions, on both an official and popular level and finds expression in magical practices, including those of protection and healing. It is seen as a power inherited by certain people and objects, and transferable to others. It operates as a cohesive force in social interrelationships. In its earliest derivation, the word *baraka* conveyed the idea of the kneeling position of the camel. It described the position of rest. In that sense, *baraka* expresses the need and goal of Muslims as human beings. In a world of activity and stress, disturbed by many 'beings' and 'powers', they need the blessing that will bring peace.

In the Muslim context, such a glimpse into the world of *baraka* lends a vista of hope to the relating of the good news of Christ. Missionaries need a willingness to work within the culture pattern: to sit down and drink coffee; to take a new look at the Old Testament and its concepts of 'blessing'; to recognise the Christian possibilities, both formally and informally, of blessing one another. Followers of Christ from a Muslim background in northern Nigeria come to church services at the 'time' dictated by their own view of temporal space. In Westerners' terms it is late, but they are always there for the most important part of the ritual—the blessing! Perhaps we can begin to see why.

The evil eye

The evil eye has been presented in this book as a strong component in the ordinary Muslim's cosmological view. The Muslim is not alone in this experience. Studies made in Latin America, the Indian subcontinent and Europe have isolated the evil eye concept as a significant factor in societal makeup. The question emerges from all such studies: what is there, in those societies, that requires this vigorous expression of powerful effect-without-touch among its members? For, as we noted in Chapter One, *baraka* seems to require some kind of contact for transference, whereas the evil eye works with just a glance.

Perhaps the evil eye concept expresses a response to fear. People in well-defined family or clan groups fear 'outsiders'. Fear of harm derived from outsiders' envy may be personified in the evil eye. The fear thus becomes institutionalised and helps set boundaries, for example as to who is to be considered an 'insider' and who an 'outsider'.

The fear of the evil eye also helps society to handle 'abnormality'. Certain groups of people are recognised as likely casters of the evil eye. They are those who are generally perceived to be atypical, consequently in some way 'jealous' of normalcy. Examples include women with traits such as barrenness that prevent them from living the normal roles of womanhood; beggars, or people with unusual eye colourings. As we have seen previously, the sanction works both ways. The duty of *zakât* (almsgiving) tends to be reinforced by the fear of beggars throwing the evil eye on ordinary people if they don't give them money.

Perhaps the evil eye makes most sense from a socio-economic perspective. Often, the syndrome focuses on the delicate matter of potential increased wealth in a peasant community. In such a community, a sense of the 'limited good' exists. Unlike the Western mentality which claims, for example, unlimited wealth for anyone to obtain, the limited good psychology says that wealth is limited. If one person takes more, someone else loses. Consequently, in many villages, the principle objects of envy are livestock. Healthy and fertile buffalo cows could mean more wealth for one particular family. Others would then be receiving a decrease in the 'good' available to them. For this reason, such animals are carefully hidden in the inner courtyard of the village home. Less at stake, but also susceptible, might be children, food, or things such as water-pumps. All such animals, humans and objects constitute a potential for increase of well-being in the families that own or acquire them.

The evil eye concept brings direction and sanction to a community that operates within the bounds of the 'limited good'. It helps maintain the tension between potential for growth at others' expense, and accepting a self-limiting norm. How does the individual household relate to the larger society? What happens if one household is tempted to claim more of the defined, limited good at others' expense? The evil eye concept provides a strong corrective. If a family goes for too much, someone's eye of envy will touch it somewhere, and the imbalance of that family within the community will be rectified.

In trades such as weaving or pottery, the evil eye enables an excess of tradesmen competing in a limited market willingly to restrict their output to an agreed amount per day. Those who deviate from this self-limiting, in order to produce more cloth or pots for the market, are subject to ostracism. They take the precaution of surrounding their artifacts of production (looms or wheels) with talismans to fend off intervention by their companions. The evil eye syndrome operates within the structure of such a trading network to discourage individuals from exceeding the limits of their socially prescribed roles.

In Christian witness to people for whom the evil eye is not only a surface belief, but also an expression of deeper assumptions or processes, the question must be asked: what are the ramifications for the whole worldview, as the surface phenomenon is confronted? Can a peasant society survive without the sanction of the evil eye belief? (Is Christ against peasant societies?) Is there an alternative sanction, in Christ, which will effectively regulate interpersonal behaviour?

Could the evil eye belief help explain why some development programmes introduced by well-meaning Western missions meet with considerable lack of interest? The story seems to be common: aid projects designed to install electric pumps, mechanical tractors, or education programmes, all to enable villagers to control their own possibilities of increase (including perhaps lower mortality rates through health care), are opposed by the villagers themselves. Such seeming negative responses will possibly remain unexplained, unless an understanding of the function of the evil eye concept within the community is reached.

To exorcise or not?

Possession cults like the *zâr* phenomenon explained in Chapter Seven occur in many parts of the Muslim world. By and large, the *zâr* spirit or its equivalent is not exorcised. Attention is focused, rather, on establishing a give-and-take relationship between patient and possessing spirit.

It would seem that the *zâr* ritual provides more for the participants than simply a spiritual experience. The ceremony can take anything from a few hours to all day and night. The function is normally patronised by women who enjoy the social interaction, the gossip and banter, as well as the opportunity to let inhibitions go. There is often sexual involvement in the erotic nature of the trance dancing, and in the views the women have of the *sayyids* possessing them. The cathartic element of the ceremony is enhanced by the belief that, when a woman enters a trance, she is basically lending her body to the *sayyid*. She is therefore no longer responsible for her actions, and 'self expression' can take a form normally unacceptable within the society of which she is a part. The transfer of money in exchange for music, divinatory diagnosis and interpretation ensures the possibility of future *zâr* ceremonies. Often the clientele is regular. Various special coloured costumes are worn to please the *zâr* spirits—and their human models!

There would seem, therefore, to be a variety of motivations behind *zâr* ceremonies. If women are worried, or under some kind of emotional strain, the *zâr* ceremony will help them to relax and be at peace. If they have a guilty conscience, the blame can be transferred, at least temporarily, to the *zâr sayyids*. Certain social pressures also find release in the intensive group interaction. In some instances, it would appear that the *zâr* ceremony provides an effective means of identifying and treating actual mental illnesses. In the case of patients suffering from *waswasa*, or a compulsive obsession, the dancing becomes an outlet for the discharge of pent-up emotion. In some respects, the acting out of the obsession, or the 'untying' of the *waswasa*, appears to take the form of a dramatised dream.

Exorcism of the spirits possessing Muslim women in their *zâr* rituals by a Christian missionary bent solely on power encounter would thus leave a large gap in the social and psychological make-up of the women's world. As much attention would need to be paid to the discovery of alternative Christian customs that fulfil women, as to the spiritual confrontation involved in the power encounter itself. Sensitivity to the unspoken needs beneath the surface of the *zâr* ritual will assist the Christian missionary both in addressing the demonic in the Muslim woman's world, and also in providing meaningful alternative expressions for her social, psychological and spiritual longings.

Communication within worldview parameters

What is in view, therefore, is dynamic, experience-oriented gospel sharing with ordinary Muslims. Those ordinary Muslims, however, do not live in a vacuum; they are immersed in a web of societal meaning and implication, part of an interacting whole.

The objective in mission to Muslims must be to render the unchanging gospel, as relevantly and comprehensibly as possible, to these people. It is not a question of altering the content of the gospel itself. The message of the cross will constantly be a stumbling block to proud mankind (1 Corinthians 1:23). It is a question, however, of 'preaching' that gospel in power, from within the constructs of Muslim reality, and beginning with Muslims' needs.

How often have Muslims especially 'rejected' the emissaries' culturally-loaded presentation of Jesus Christ, rather than the Saviour himself? Winning the responsive Muslim requires a new baptism in humility among today's Christbearers. Introducing the Jesus who can truly meet every need, who can miraculously change affairs in the everyday Muslim world, who judges, or accepts, or transforms, their cultural habits to bring new wholeness to society, as well as to individuals—such must be the goal of those called to minister to today's Muslim masses.

The channels for such sharing might be many. Dreams, for example, offer a viable entrance to the centre of the worldview of popular Islam, for dreams already function in a significant way within their lives. Dreams are in fact strongly visible in the Old Testament, and considerably so in the New

Testament. History records the importance of dreams in effective evangelism of Muslims (as with Temal) where care has been taken to note their significance. Do we pray for Muslims to dream and dream of Christ? Do radio broadcasts, films, video and audio cassettes, records, testimonies, tracts and other communication forms designed to reach the hands of ordinary Muslims mention dreams? Or does the Western categorisation of thought prevail, declaiming such a channel as inappropriate for the proclamation of truth? How many Muslim equivalents of a Pharaoh or a Babylonian monarch have woken with a dream pounding in their minds? And where are the Josephs and Daniels of today to affirm and interpret God's word to them?

Missionaries are tentatively exploring other channels of proclamation to Muslims with a folk-Islamic view of reality. Some are emphasising the concept of 'blessing', as it finds expression in Old and New Testaments, as a means of potential communication with *baraka*-conscious people. Music and drama, with careful deference to the Muslim hesitancy in portraying holy prophets, are tried as ways through 'gates' other than the purely mental one to people's hearts. Ministries of deliverance and healing find strong opportunity for bridging the gap, over which many Muslims are joyfully leaping and jumping to faith in Christ. Emphasis on the mediatorial role of Christ, the presentation of the 'mystery' of the gospel and other approaches—all are encouraged in an attempt to hold hands out to Muslims deeply influenced by an Islamic mystical tradition. Others are endeavouring to 'go the second mile' in making the outward expression of Christian community as near to indigenous Islamic forms as is faithfully possible. The call, in such situations, is not to faith in Jesus via Western culture, but is much more direct.

Many channels can carry the Christian gospel to the centre of the folk-Islamic worldview. When the Christian evangelist meets a Muslim who sees life from a folk-Islamic point of view, will the common ground of discussion be the heart of the matter, according to the Muslim? Or will the longings raised in the Muslim's immediate circumstances, answered only partially by his current beliefs and practices, be ignored in favour of the presentation which the missionary feels is important?

Some of the needs felt by ordinary Muslims have been depicted in previous chapters of this book. Such needs, it would seem, all too often outweigh theological niceties in the experiences of ordinary men and women. As a result, those same needs provide opportunities for the communication of a Christian gospel which speaks relevantly to them.

From private intercessory prayer to public healing in Christ's name, power encounter offers a biblical point of contact in which the demonic is exposed and dealt with. The experiential knowledge of Jesus offers hope of a receptivity to new, faithful information about who he is. To know him, experientially, as Lord, breaks open the closed cosmology of popular Islam and offers the possibility of a life lived in safety and love, because it is lived in the strength of an indwelling, divine person. The Holy Spirit who thus 'comforts' the child of God also bears witness to the truth.

In such a strong meeting of needs, there need be no destruction of healthy worldview. Ideas about the causes of sickness, for example, may continue as valid, only now there is a new perspective, as the demonic in the worldview of popular Islam is exposed, and the light of Christ shines in the darkness. Illness resulting from magical, or devilish, activity may be resisted and rebuked in Christ's name. Instead of fear of numerous evil beings, there may be spiritual authority over them, and a personal filling with the protective Holy Spirit. A responsive relationship with nature may continue, except that it will be man as whole man, rather than as helpless victim, who will interact with nature. Divine gifts of wisdom will substitute for satanic forms of divination. Concepts of time and space may still revolve around what is right to do, where, and at what moment. Appeal will be made, however, not to the zodiac, but to the Lord of the heavens.

Ways in which folk-Islamic concepts and assumptions help maintain societal relationships will need to be carefully considered in any compassionate proclamation of Christ to ordinary Muslims. Are there functional substitutes for attitudes and activities which were part of people's lives before they gave their allegiance to Jesus? Are there ways in which radical change brought about by power encounter is unnecessarily destroying societal dynamics previously controlled by elements in folk-Islamic belief and practice? What roles are assigned to women in the emerging, believing community? Is there recognition and room made for the expression of gifts of power resting on Christ's new people from a folk-Islamic background?

Lest we be overwhelmed by some of the questions and suggestions raised in this book, we need to be reminded that the Lord of the harvest, including that part composed of ordinary Muslims, is the Holy Spirit. He is the one who sends out labourers into the harvest (Acts 13:2). Amazingly, he uses the weakest instruments to gather his crop. He does not withhold his breath until we rid ourselves of all those deeply imbedded traits that displease him. He graciously uses us, even though we may be steeped in a culture which, in many respects, must grieve him.

Three final questions conclude this study. They arise out of our detailed examination of the world of popular Islam and are addressed to Christians who know a calling to share the glorious gospel with Muslims. Can such ambassadors for Christ recognise as real the folk-Islamic genius of the ordinary Muslim's worldview? Do they have the relationship with Christ to be able to provoke the encounter between the kingdoms experienced by the ordinary Muslim? Do they possess the faith, patience and humility to trust Christ to produce the ensuing transformation of worldview at the deepest level of the Muslim's life?

As far as the Christ of that glorious gospel is concerned, the open invitation originally made in the towns of Galilee holds true for today's Muslim masses. The One who is gentle and humble in heart offers rest for wearied souls. The Son will be yoked with burdened human beings, carrying their loads, teaching them his Father's ways. The Lord of heaven's hosts stands where the ordinary Muslim stands. His sovereign, costly offer is addressed to them: 'Come unto me.'

It would be best for our exploration of the unseen face of Islam to conclude in prayer. The following collect is offered as a model.[22]

Almighty God,
who called your Church to witness
that you were in Christ
reconciling men to yourself:
help us so to proclaim the good news of your love,
that all who hear it
may be reconciled to you:
through him who died for us and rose again
and reigns with you and the Holy Spirit,
one God, now and for ever.
Amen.

APPENDICES

1

THE *HADÎTH* LITERATURE

The Sunnî sect of Islam accepts many records of *hadîth*, but those referred to as 'The Six Books' gradually won universal recognition and remain authoritative today. Outstanding among these is the compilation made by Muhammad Ibn ᶜAbd Allâh Ibn Ismâᶜîl al-Bukhârî (AD 810–870). Al-Bukhârî's comprehensive collection of *hadîth*, known as *al-Jâmiᶜ al-Sahîh al-Musnad min-Hadîth Rasûl Allâh*, is divided into 97 chapters and 3,460 sub-chapters. It was rapidly approved as a work second only to the Qur'ân itself. Abû'l-Hasan, Muslim Ibn al-Hajjâj (AD 817–875) wrote his *al-Jâmiᶜ al-Sahîh*, containing 12,000 *hadîth*, modelling his work on that of his mentor, al-Bukhârî. Muslim and al-Bukhârî are together referred to as *al-Shaykhân* (the Two Sheikhs), and their books as *al-Sahîhân* (the Correct Two), emphasising their authority in the Islamic literary heritage.

A 40-chapter collation of some 4,800 *hadîth* is given by Abû Dâwûd, Sulaymân Ibn al-Ashᶜath (AD 817–888) in his *Kitâb al-Sunan*. Another disciple of al-Bukhârî, named Abû ᶜîsâ, Muhammad Ibn ᶜîsâ al-Tirmidhî (AD 820–892), arranged his *al-Jâmiᶜ al-Sahîh* of 4,000 *hadîth* into 46 chapters, each with sub-chapters. Abû ᶜAbd al-Rahmân, Ahmad

Ibn Shuᶜaib al-Nasâ'î (AD 830–915) produced a collection of 5,000 *hadîth*, divided into 51 chapters, entitled *Kitâb al-Sunan*. The sixth compiler, Ibn Mâjah, Muḥammad Ibn Yazîd (AD 819–886), recorded some *hadîth* not previously mentioned in his 4,341-*hadîth* work, entitled *Kitâb al-Sunan*.

Apart from these six main works, the compilation of Ibn Hibbân (died AD 965) should also be mentioned, for it is considered by many Muslim authorities as third in importance, after the collations of al-Bukhârî and Muslim. It contains some 2,600 *hadîth* not existing in the collections of those two foremost compilers.

The *Mishkât al-Masâbîh* is a well-known book of Sunnî *hadîth*, used by Muslims in India. It was originally compiled by Imâm Ḥusayn al-Baghâwi (died AD 1116 or 1122), and entitled *Masâbihu'l-Sunna* or 'Lamps of the Traditions'. In AD 1336 Shaykh Walî al-Dîn al-Tabrîzî revised it, added on an extra chapter to each section, and called it *Mishkât al-Masâbîh* or 'Niche for Lamps'.

The Shîᶜahs accept the authenticity of three of their collators of *hadîth*. The records of Thiqat al-Islâm Muḥammad Ibn Yaᶜqûb Kalaynî (died AD 940) are regarded as the most important. This arrangement, known as the *Kâfî*, contains some 16,000 *hadîth* and is the best known among Shîᶜah Muslims. Other collections were made by the jurist Shaykh-i Sadûq Muḥammad Ibn Bâbûya Qumî (died AD 991), who entitled his the *Man-lâ-Yasthazira al-Faqîh*, and by Shaykh Muḥammad Tusi (died AD 1068), who produced his in two books called *Kitâb al-Tahdhîb* and *Kitâb al-Istibṣâr*.

Traditions containing the sayings of the imams, such as those collated by Sayyid al-Raẓî (died AD 1015) under the title *Nahj al-Balâgha*, are also received as authentic by the Shîᶜahs. They are recited on suitable occasions today.

The *hadîth qudsî* comprise sayings of the Prophet which are in fact direct words from God through him, recorded by those who heard them spoken. They do not form part of the Qur'ân. There are several collections of such *hadîth*. A two-volume work, published in Cairo in 1969 by the commission for Qur'ân and *ḥadîth*, is entitled *al-Aḥadîth al-Qudsîyya*. Such *ḥadîth* are viewed as important and authoritative in giving direction to mores and customs.

Interestingly, contemporary neo-fundamentalist Islamic movements tend to undermine their own ideological stance since they appeal to the authority of the *ḥadîth*, as well as the Qur'ân, in proposing changes to the modernist Islam of many of today's Muslim countries. In emphasising the authority of the *ḥadîth*, those reactionary movements also reinforce the cosmology that the *ḥadîth* expose and affirm, and in which so many of the Muslim masses live and move.

2

THE MAJOR SECTS OF ISLAM

The first leaders of the Islamic community were strongly related by blood, as Figure 24 demonstrates. Even the early caliphs who do not qualify for inclusion in this more immediate web of relationship (such as Abû Bakr and ᶜUmar) were still related to Muhammad, though more distantly.

A major division of the Islamic community occurred soon after Muhammad's death. Abû Bakr followed the Prophet as first 'successor', or caliph. He was an old man, but he had been one of the first converts. In the two years of his leadership the Bedouin tribes of Arabia, who had sworn loyalty to Muhammad, and who had since begun to break away, were recovered for Islam. Abû Bakr was succeeded by ᶜUmar, who in turn was followed as caliph by ᶜUthmân, and he by ᶜAlî. Each of these latter three met a violent death. ᶜAlî was cousin, and son-in-law, of the Prophet, but he was opposed by Muᶜâwiya, who claimed the caliphate for himself. A major split in the Islamic community followed. The Shîᶜahs, or 'followers' of ᶜAlî, separated from the Umayyads.

It is said that there are seventy-three sects of Islam. The Shîᶜahs are the largest breakaway group and today form the major religious community in Iran, with large followings in

Figure 24
Quraysh (Selected) Line of Descent

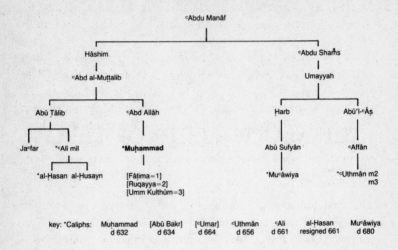

Iraq, Syria, Yemen, Pakistan and elsewhere. Most Shîᶜahs are known as Twelvers, because they follow the first twelve imams, or 'leaders', from ᶜAlî and his sons. Other Shîᶜahs are Seveners, or Ismâᶜîlîyas, because they hold to only seven imams, concluding with a different seventh imam, called Ismâᶜîl. They believe that Ismâᶜîl will return as the Mahdî. Seveners are found today among the Muslim communities of India and East Africa. Still other Shîᶜahs are Fivers. They hold that the imamate passed to Zaid, a second son of the fourth imam. Today much of the Shîᶜah population in North Yemen adheres to the Fiver sect.

Further divisions include the Druze, named after al-Darâzî, who formed the separate community in the tenth century. The Druze are now found mostly in Lebanon and

Syria. In the nineteenth century, the Mahdî expectation gave rise to the Bahais. Also in the nineteenth century, the Ahmadîyas arose in India, their founder Ghulam Ahmad Mirza being regarded as both Mahdî and Messiah. The Ahmadîyas, sometimes known as Mirzâis, are viewed as non-orthodox by most Muslims.

The great majority of Muslims call themselves Sunnî, followers of the *sunna* or 'pathway' of their forefathers. The Sunnîs have known fewer divisions than the Shîᶜahs. In the nineteenth century, a certain Wahhâb started a Sunnî reform movement in Arabia. Today, the Wahhâbîs control the holy places of Mecca and Medina, and inspire indigenous reform movements throughout the Islamic world. Also in the nineteenth century, the revolt of a Mahdî in the Sudan was aimed at setting up a new Muslim kingdom. Figure 25 illustrates some of the major sub-divisions of Islam.

Figure 25

Major Sub-Divisions in the History of Islam

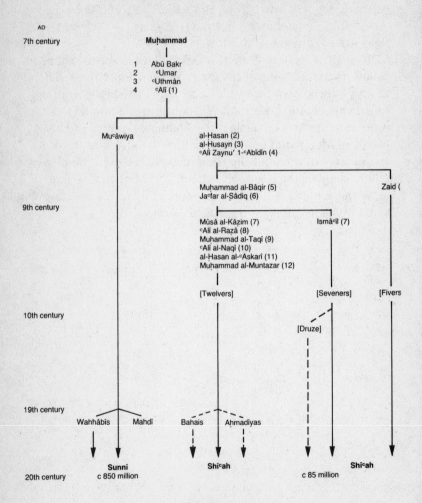

Key: 1 → 4: the four 'rightly guided caliphs'.
       (1) → (12): the twelve 'imams' descended from ᶜAlî

3

AN INTRODUCTORY BIBLIOGRAPHY

Widow Aziza's Eye

Ghosh, Amitav. 'The Relations of Envy in an Egyptian Village.' *Ethnology: An International Journal of Cultural and Social Anthropology.* Vol 22, no 3 (July 1983): pp 211–223.

Lindquist, Eda W. 'Rue and the Evil Eye of Persia.' *Moslem World.* Vol 26 (1936): pp 170–175.

Maloney, Clarence (ed). *The Evil Eye.* Columbia University Press: New York, 1976.

The Night Belongs to the Jinn

Alberts, Robert Charles. *Social Structure and Culture Change in an Iranian Village.* Two volumes. University Microfilms: Ann Arbor, Michigan, 1963.

Collante, Jose R. 'Jinn among the Moros.' *Moslem World.* Vol 26 (1936): pp 240–245.

Crapanzano, Vincent. 'Saints, Jnun and Dreams: An Essay In Moroccan Ethnopsychology.' *Psychiatry.* Vol 38 (1975): pp 145–159.

Saints and Sons

Andrzejewski, B W. 'The Veneration of Sufi Saints and its Impact on the Oral Literature of the Somali People and on their Literature in Arabic.' *African Language Studies*. Vol 15 (1974): pp 15–53.

Eickelman, Dale F. *Moroccan Islam: Tradition and Society in a Pilgrimage Center*. University of Texas Press: Austin, 1976.

Geijbels, M. 'Aspects of the Veneration of Saints in Islam, with Special Reference to Pakistan.' *Moslem World*. Vol 68 (1978): pp 176–186.

Lings, Martin. *A Moslem Saint of the Twentieth Century*. Shaikh Aḥmad al-'Alawî: London, 1961.

Unravelling the Future

Epton, Nina Consuelo. *Saints and Sorcerers: A Moroccan Journey*. Cassell and Co: London, 1958.

Fernea, Elizabeth Warnock. *A Street in Marrakech*. Doubleday: New York, 1975.

Makal, Mahmut (Deedes, Wyndham trans). *A Village in Anatolia*. Vallentine, Mitchell and Co: London, 1954.

Osman, Mohammed Taib Bin. 'Indigenous, Hindu, and Islamic Elements in Malay Folk Beliefs.' PhD dissertation. Indiana University: Indiana, 1967.

Ryan, Patrick J. *Imale: Yoruba Participation in the Muslim Tradition: A Study of Clerical Piety*. Scholars Press: Missoula, Montana, 1978.

The Drama of Devotion

Bleeker, Claas Jouco. *Egyptian Festivals*. E J Brill: Leiden, 1968.

Gaudeul, J M. 'From One Year to Another: Muslim Festivals.' *Encounter*. No 35 (1977): pp 1–14.

Jong, F de. 'Cairene Ziyarah Days.' *Die Welt des Islams*. Vol 17, nos 1–4 (1977): pp 26–43.

Lazarus, Yafeh H. 'Muslim Festivals.' *Numen*. Vol 25 (1978): pp 52–64.

Von Grunebaum, G E. *Muhammadan Festivals*. Schuman: New York, 1951.

A Healing Touch

Crapanzano, Vincent. *The Ḥamadsha: A Study in Moroccan Ethnopsychiatry*. University of California Press: Berkeley, 1973.

Ewing, J Franklin. 'Illness, Death and Burial in the Southern Philippines with Special Reference to the Tausug: I and II.' *Anthropology Quarterly*. Vol 40, nos 1–2 (1967): pp 13–25, 45–64.

Kasman, Edward Salkiya. 'Folk Medicine and Health Practices Among the Sulu Samals.' *Solidarity*. Vol 4, no 4 (1969): pp 44–51.

Kennedy, John G. 'Nubian Zâr Ceremonies as Psychotherapy.' *Human Organization*. Vol 26, no 4 (1967): pp 185–194.

Safi, Ahmed El-. *Native Medicine in the Sudan. Sources, Concepts and Methods*. Salamah: Prizes Series no 1. Sudan Research Unit: University of Khartoum, Faculty of Arts, 1971.

The Leadership in Question

Centlivres, Micheline and Pierre, and Slobin, Mark. 'A Muslim Shaman of Afghan Turkestan.' *Ethnology*. Vol 10, no 2 (1971): pp 160–173.

Lewis, I M. *Ecstatic Religion: An Anthropological Study of Spirit Possession and Shamanism*. Penguin Books: Harmondsworth, 1971.

Monteil, Vincent. 'Marabouts.' In Kritzeck, James and Lewis, William H (eds). *Islam in Africa*. Van Nostrand-Reinhold Co: New York, 1969: pp 87–109.

Pastner, Stephen L. 'Power and Pirs Among the Pakistani Baluch.' *Journal of Asian and African Studies*. Vol 13, nos 3–4 (1978): pp 231–243.

From Cradle to Grave

Bainbridge, Margaret. 'Life-Cycle Rituals of the Turks in Turkey: An Outline.' *Research Papers*. No 16 (1982): pp 1–11.

Barclay, U V. 'The Burial Rites of the Turks.' *Central Asiatic Journal*. Vol 14, nos 1–3 (1970): pp 195–227.

Casiño, Eric S. 'Folk Islam in the Life Cycle of the Jama Mapun.' *Philippine Sociological Review*. Vol 15, nos 1 and 2 (1967): pp 34–48.

Ewing, J Franklin. 'Some Rites of Passage Among the Tausug of the Philippines.' *Anthropological Quarterly*. Vol 31, no 2 (1958): pp 33–41.

Gaudeul, J M. 'Life Cycle of a Muslim.' *Encounter*. No 32 (1977): pp 1–13.

Granqvist, Hilma Natalia. *Birth and Childhood Among the Arabs: Studies in a Mudammadan Village in Palestine*. AMS Press: New York, 1975 (reprint of 1947 edition).

Hanifi, M Jamil. 'Child-Bearing Patterns Among Pushtuns of Afghanistan.' *International Journal of Sociology of the Family*. Vol 1, no 1 (1971): pp 53–57.

Lutfiyya, Abdulla M. 'The Family.' In Lutfiyya, Abdulla M and Churchill, Charles W (eds). *Readings in Arabic Middle Eastern Societies and Cultures*. Mouton and Co: The Hague, 1970, pp 500–525.

Times and Seasons

Blandell, Robert A. 'Safar Ablutions in Malacca.' *Moslem World*. Vol 33 (1943): pp 140–142.

Kennedy, John G (ed). *Nubian Ceremonial Life: Studies in Islamic Syncretism and Cultural Change*. University of California Press: Berkeley, 1978.

Robertson, Edward. 'The Days of the Week and of the Month in Arab Folklore.' *Journal of the Manchester Egyptian and Oriental Society*. Vol 20 (1936): pp 19–24.

Wulff, Inger. 'Bulun Sapal—A Month of Misfortune.' *Folk*. Vol 16–17 (1974/75): pp 381–400.

Knowing One's Place

Cammann, Schyler. 'Islamic and Indian Magic Squares.' *History of Religion*. Vol 8, no 3 (1968): pp 181–209.

Guellouz, Ezzedine. *Mecca: The Muslim Pilgrimage*. Paddington Press: London, 1977.

Jeffery, Arthur (ed). *A Reader on Islam: Passages from Standard Arabic Writings Illustrative of the Beliefs and Practices of Muslims*. Mouton and Co: 'S-Gravenhage, 1962.

Pingree, D. 'Astronomy and Astrology in India and Iran.' *Isis*. Vol 54 (1963): pp 229–246.

The World of the Ordinary Muslim

Bailey, Clinton. 'Bedouin Religious Practices in Sinai and the Negev.' *Anthropos*. Vol 77, nos 1–2 (1982): pp 65–88.

Thackston, Wheeler McIntosh. *The Tales of the Prophets of al-Kisa'i*. Twayne Pubs: Boston, 1978.

Powers, Patterns and Processes

Donaldson, Bess Allen. *The Wild Rue: A Study of Muhammadan Magic and Folklore in Iran*. Luzac and Co: London, 1938.

Haas, W S. 'The Zikr of the Rahmaniya Order in Algeria.' *Moslem World*. Vol 33 (1943): pp 16–28.

Zein, Abdul Hamid M el-. *The Sacred Meadows. A Structural Analysis of Religious Symbolism in an East African Town*. Northwestern University Press: Evanston, 1974.

Official and Popular Islam

Barclay, Harold B. 'Study of an Egyptian Village Community.' *Studies in Islam.* Vol 3, no 3 (1966): pp 143–166, 201–226.

Gibb, W H R. 'The Structure of Religious Thought in Islam.' *Moslem World.* Vol 38 (1948): pp 17–28.

Gulick, John. *The Middle East: An Anthropological Perspective.* Goodyear Publishers: Pacific Palisades, 1976.

Levy, Reuben. *The Social Structure of Islam.* Cambridge University Press: London, 1957.

Memon, Muhammad Umar. *Ibn Taimîya's Struggle Against Popular Religion.* With an Annotated Translation of his *kitâb iqtiḍâᶜ aṣ-ṣirât al-mustaqîm mukhâlafât aṣḥâb al-jahîm.* Mouton and Co: 'S-Gravenhage, 1976.

Belief and Practice: Which Interpretation?

Amin, Abdel Rahman M and Atteya, Salah el-Din M (Omar, T, Shihab, M and Afifi S, trans). *Rites of Pilgrimage.* The Supreme Council for Islamic Affairs: Cairo, 1967.

Farah, Caesar E. *Islam: Beliefs and Observances.* Barron's Educational Series Inc. Woodbury: New York, 1968.

Fodor, A. 'The Role of "Fir'own" in Popular Islam.' *Journal of Egyptian Archeology.* Vol 61 (1975): pp 238–240.

Staples, W E. 'Muhammad, a Talismanic Force.' *American Journal of Semitic Languages.* Vol 57 (1940): pp 63–70.

Sulaiman, Qaḍhi Muḥammad. *The Beautiful Names of God.* Daftar Rahmatun-lil-'Alamin: Patiala, 1930.

Waugh, Earle. 'Jealous Angels: Aspects of Muslim Religious Language.' *Ohio Journal of Religious Studies.* Vol 1, no 2 (1973): pp 56–72.

'Worlds' in Conflict?

Ali, Maulana Muhammad (compiler). *A Manual of Hadith.* Curzon Press: London, 1977.

Anderson, J N D. 'Tropical Africa: Infiltration and Expanding Horizons.' In Von Grunebaum, G E (ed). *Unity and Variety in Muslim Civilisation*. University of Chicago Press: Chicago, 1955: pp 261–283.

al-Bukhârî, Muḥammad bin Ismâᶜîl bin al-Mughîrah (Khan, Muḥammad Muhsin, trans). *Ṣaḥîḥ*. Vols 1 to 9. Kazi Publications: Chicago, 1977–79.

Goldsack, William. *The Traditions in Islam*. Christian Literature Society: Madras, 1919.

Guillaume, A. *The Life of Muhammad*. A translation of Ibn Ishaq's *Sîrât Rasûl Allah*. Oxford University Press: Oxford, 1978 (first edition 1955).

Margoliouth, David S. 'The Relics of the Prophet Muhammad.' *Moslem World*. Vol 27 (1937): pp 20–27.

Muslim, Imam (Ṣiddîqî, ᶜAbdul Ḥamîd, trans). *Ṣaḥîḥ*. Vols 1 to 4. Sh Muhammad Ashraf: Lahore, 1976.

Rauf, Muhammad Abdul. *Al Ḥadîth: Introduction and Sample Texts*. The Islamic Center: Washington, DC, 1974.

Royster, James Edgar. *The Meaning of Muhammad for Muslims: A Phenomenological Study of Recurrent Images of the Prophet*. University Microfilms International: Ann Arbor, 1971.

Trimingham, J Spencer. *The Influence of Islam upon Africa*. Longmans: London, 1968.

Power Encounter

Beyerhaus, Peter and Lefever, H. *The Responsible Church and the Foreign Missions*. Eerdmans: Grand Rapids, 1964.

Glasser, Arthur F. 'Power Encounter in Conversion from Islam.' In McCurry, Don M (ed). *The Gospel and Islam: A 1978 Compendium*. MARC: Monrovia, 1979: pp 129–142.

Inniger, Merlin W. 'Getting to Know Their "Heart Hunger" Is a Key to Reaching Muslims.' *Evangelical Missions Quarterly*. Vol 15, no 1 (1979): pp 35–40.

Scheunemann, Detmar. 'Evangelization among Occultists and Spiritists.' In Douglas, J D (ed). *Let the Earth Hear His Voice*. Worldwide Publications: Minneapolis, 1975.

Sheikh, Bilquis (with Schneider, Richard). *I Dared to Call Him Father*. Kingsway Publications: Eastbourne, 1978.

Stacey, Vivienne. *Practical Lessons for Evangelism Among Muslims*. Oriendienst: Wiesbaden.

The Gospel and the Ordinary Muslim

Behman, Francine. 'The Zar in Egypt.' Master's thesis. American University in Cairo: Cairo, 1953.

Denffer, Dietrich von. 'Baraka as Basic Concept of Muslim Popular Belief.' *Islamic Studies*. Vol 15, no 3 (1976): pp 167–186.

Dretke, James P. *A Christian Approach to Muslims: Reflections from West Africa*. William Carey Library: Pasadena, 1979.

Fakhouri, Hani. 'The Zar Cult in an Egyptian Village.' *Anthropology Quarterly*. Vol 41, no 2 (1968): pp 49–56.

Foster, George M. 'Peasant Society and the Image of Limited Good.' *American Anthropologist*. Vol 67 (1965): pp 293–315.

Goforth, Christian (pseudonym). 'The Entree of Media through Stress Factors in Muslim Culture.' In Shumaker, C Richard (ed). *Media in Islamic Culture*. ICB/ELO: Marseille, 1974: pp 107–112.

Jennings, George J. 'God is Not Dead in Islam: the Religious Dimension in Contemporary Arab Culture.' Paper given at the Second Annual Third World Conference and Returned Peace Corps Volunteers Convention: Omaha, Nebraska, 1978.

Lecerf, J. 'The Dream in Popular Culture: Arabic and Islamic.' In Von Grunebaum, G E and Caillois, R (eds). *The*

Dream and Human Societies. University of California Press: Berkeley, 1966: pp 365–379.

Lenning, Larry Gene. 'The Concept of Blessing and its Application to Mission in Islamic West Africa.' PhD dissertation. Fuller Theological Seminary: Pasadena, 1979.

Nimmo, Harry A. 'Themes in Badjaw Dreams.' *Philippine Sociological Review*. Vol 14, no 1 (1966): pp 49–56.

Padwick, C E. 'Dream and Vision. Some Notes from a Diary.' *International Review of Missions*. Vol 28 (1939): pp 205–216.

Parshall, Philip L. *Bridges to Islam. A Christian Perspective on Folk Islam*. Baker Book House: Grand Rapids, 1983.

Redfield, Robert. *Peasant Society and Culture*. University of Chicago Press: Chicago, 1956.

4

GLOSSARY

Some significant terms used in the text

Abû: 'father'; 'father of so-and-so'.

adhân: 'announcement'; call to public prayer.

ᶜafrît: species of jinn; from root meaning 'to roll in the dust'.

ᶜajûza: 'old woman'; medicine woman, herbalist.

alamat: 'sign'; often in a dream, Malaysia.

Allah al-Ḥayy!: 'God the Living!'; exclamation used in *dhikr* rituals.

aᶜmâl: 'supplication'; often special prayer by which to see a loved one in a dream.

ᶜamalîya: magic; supposedly of spiritual, not evil, nature.

ambal: offering boats, Siasi Tao Sug of the Philippines.

ᶜaqîqa: naming sacrifice and ceremony.

arkân al-'islâm: 'the pillars of Islam', five religious duties.

ᶜarrâf: diviner, fortune-teller (*ᶜarrâfa*, female).

ᶜÂshûrâ': 'the Tenth'; 10th of Muḥarram.

ᶜazîma: 'incantation'; used in exorcism.

bahasa: curer using divination, Yakan of Philippines.

bakhshi: shaman, Afghan Turkestan.

baraka: 'blessing'; often thought of in terms of some kind of positive, magic force available from holy people, places or objects.

bismillâh': 'in the name of God'; frequent exclamation used at the
beginning of an undertaking.

bôkâ: magical herbalist, exorcist and charm-maker among Hausa,
Nigeria.

bomor: indigenous healer; Malaya.

bororo: itinerant medicine-man, West Africa.

bulan sapal: 'month of Safar', Yakan of Philippines.

canis: 'dog', Latin.

chronos: 'time'; chronological time in the New Testament, Greek.

dâyat al-habîl: 'robe midwife'; female practitioner, Sudan.

dhikr: 'remembering'; rite of devotion especially associated with
Sufi orders.

dîn: 'religion'; religious practice in Islam.

duᶜâ': 'prayer'; in popular Islam denotes special prayer consisting
of a magical prescription of occult words or symbols. A *duᶜâ'*-
writer is a specialist in composing this kind of written prescription.

faqîh: 'theologian'; in popular Islam a mendicant dealing in folk
remedies, Sudan.

faqîr: 'poor'; mendicant belonging to a Sufi order, Sri Lanka.

Fâtiha, al-: 'the Opening One'; the opening sura of the Qur'ân.

fuqahâ': 'jurists'; early writers of dogmatic theology.

ghashi: 'one who faints'; effect of attack by jinn, Iran.

ghûl: species of jinn; from root meaning 'to destroy'.

hadîth: 'prophetic tradition'; a short account of some word or act of
Muhammad's. In its classic form it is passed on by one authority
who has received it from another. The chain reaches back to an
eye-witness.

hadr: from *hadara* 'to bring down'; in popular Islam it refers to the
bringing down of God to his worshippers as they remember him.
Becomes a trance-dance performed by devotees of possessing
spirits.

hâfiz: 'a guardian'; a person who has memorised the whole of the
Qur'ân.

hagîoi: 'saints'; reference always in plural in the New Testament,
Greek.

hajaru'l-aswad, al-: 'the black stone'; the stone which forms part of
the sharp angle of the *kaᶜba* in Mecca.

ḥajj: 'setting out'; pilgrimage to Mecca and surrounding holy places.

ḥakîm: 'a wise person'; local practitioner, Afghanistan.

Ḥamadsha: Sufi order of Morocco.

hamzad: twin *jinnî* to human, Iran.

hand of Fâtima: Fâtima was a daughter of Muḥammad by his first wife, Khadîjah. Protective talisman made of imprint or shape of hand, often with eye in middle of palm. It is painted or smeared on door lintels, cars, etc.

ḥasad: 'envy'; in malevolent sense.

ḥijâb: from 'curtain'; indicates any protective amulet.

hijra: 'migration', hejira; date of Muḥammad's flight from Mecca on the fourth day of the first month of AD 622. The Islamic calendar commences from the beginning of this year.

ḥirz: from 'to guard against evil'; protective amulet.

hoca: Muslim cleric, Turkey.

homo: 'man'; member of the human race, Latin.

ḥubb al-rashîd: tiny black seed used to combat jinn, Morocco.

ᶜibâdât, al-: devotional acts in Islam.

Iblîs: 'devil'; one of the names of the Devil.

ᶜîd al-Aḍha: 'Feast of the Sacrifice'; 10th of Dhû'l-Ḥijja.

ᶜîd al-Fiṭr: 'Feast of the Breaking'; 1st of Shawwâl, end of Ramaḍân.

ᶜîd al-Ḥajj: 'Feast of the Pilgrimage'; same as *ᶜîd al-Aḍha.*

ᶜîd al-Kabîr, al-: 'The Big Feast'; same as *ᶜîd al-Aḍha.*

ᶜîd al-Ṣadaqa: 'Feast of Alms'; same as *ᶜîd al-Fiṭr.*

ᶜîd al-Ṣaghîr, al-: 'The Minor Feast'; same as *ᶜid al-Fiṭr.*

Illiyun: related to *ilan*, 'blessing'; the seventh stage of celestial bliss.

ᶜilm al-taᶜbîr: 'science of interpretation'; of dreams.

imâmzad: special mausoleum, Iran.

îmân: 'faith'; in the sense of a formal declaration of belief in the six articles of the Muslim creed.

inikadowa: familiar spirit, Philippines.

Injîl: 'gospel'; the revelations made by God to and through Jesus.

iskoki: possession cult of Hausa people, northern Nigeria.

'ismâ' al-husnâ, al-: 'the Beautiful Names'; of God.

istikhâra: 'asking favours'; a divinatory practice of opening the Qur'ân at random, or counting out prayer beads.

jadoogar: village magician, Iran.

jâdu: black magician, Afghan Turkestan.

jallâbîya: long dress worn by men and women in Middle East.

jihâd: 'a striving'; religious war of Muslims against unbelievers.

jinnî: singular, male; *jinnîya,* female; of the species of spirits called jinn.

ka^cba: 'a cube'; the cube-like building in the centre of the Sacred Mosque at Mecca. It contains the black stone.

kairos: 'time'; a fixed time or season in the New Testament, Greek.

kalima: 'the word'; the creed of the Muslim.

kalimât al-shahâda: 'the word of testimony'; the confession: 'I bear witness that there is no deity but God, and that Muḥammad is his apostle.'

karâma: 'miracle'; authenticating sign of a saint.

Karbalâ': city in Iraq, celebrated as the site of the martyrdom of al-Ḥusayn.

al-Karisi: 'the Red'; named *jinnîya* of Turkey.

khâfi: from 'concealed'; type of jinn.

khamsa: 'five'; referring to five fingers of the human hand as used in a protective or aggressive gesture.

khaṭṭâṭ: 'calligrapher'; drawer of figures for purposes of exorcism by making an incantation.

khitân: 'circumcision'; rite of passage.

kismet: see *qisma;* 'fate'; Turkey.

koinonîa: 'fellowship'; New Testament, Greek.

kudîya: female practitioner, interpreter of dreams.

kutub, al-: plural *al-kitâb;* 'the book'; books special in a religious sense.

langgal: prayer-house or mosque, Yakan of Philippines.

langsuyar: ghost of a woman who has died in childbirth, Malaya.

Laylat al-Barâ'a: 'Night of Liberation'; 15th of Sha^cbân, Iran.

Laylat al-Mi^crâj: 'Night of Ascension'; 27th of Rajab.

Laylat al-Qadr: 'Night of Power'; 27th of Ramaḍân.

Mâddar-e: 'mother of so-and-so'; Iran.

madhrab: school of law, there being four in Islam.

madrûb: a state of being severely struck by jinn.

magpandi-pandi: ceremonial washing ceremony, Yakan in Philippines.

magtammat: ceremony to mark the end of a child's Qur'ânic studies, rite of passage, Yakan in Philippines.

magtimbang: weighing ceremony for persons born in month of Safar, Yakan.

Mahdî: the 'directed one'; a ruler to appear on earth in the last days.

Majmaᶜ al-Daᶜawât: 'Collection of Invocations' by Muḥammad Ibn Kiyâs al-Dîn; book dealing with the meaning and interpretation of dreams.

majnûn: 'possessed by jinn'; generic term for state of being harmed by jinn.

maklûᶜ: form of temporary possession by jinn.

maktûb: 'written'; what is fated for a person.

al-malâ'ik: 'the ones in authority'; the angels.

manâyâ: 'snared with rope'; expression for certain conception of fate.

mangubat: trance curer, Tausug of the Philippines.

maqyûs: form of being struck quite severely by jinn.

mârid: very strong and aggressive sort of jinn, try to kill their victims.

marturîa: 'witness'; with sense of martyrdom also, Greek.

mâ shâ'allah: 'what God wills'; expression used to ward off the evil eye.

mashhad: martyrium, Iran.

maskûn: state of permanent possession by jinn.

masqût: state of light, temporary possession by jinn.

matîyalûn: popular curers, Morocco.

matrûsh: state of being slapped by jinn.

mawlânâ: from 'protector'; official versed in Islamic theology, Pakistan.

mawlid: 'birthday'; birthday of a prophet or saint.

Mawlid al-Nabî: 'Birthday of the Prophet'; 12th of Rabîᶜ'l-Awwal.

mazâr: 'place of pilgrimage'; site of religious visits, usually a shrine.

momo: midwife, Uzbekistan.

muadhdhin: 'caller of the *adhân*'; caller to prayer.

Muḥarram: 'that which is forbidden', hence sacred; New Year's festival.

multazam: 'that to which one is attached'; part of wall of the *ka^cba*
  to which pilgrims seek to 'attach' themselves in an embrace.

murâbiṭ: 'one who has joined himself' to God; a living saint.

murshid: 'guide'; spiritual director, especially in Pakistan and
  India.

mushâhara: derived from *shahr*, 'a month'; evil force, akin to evil
  eye.

mushâr: state of being lightly struck by jinn.

muta'awwaqa: 'cutting of the flower'; process to free woman from
  history of problems in childbirth.

nafra: from 'to flee'; protective amulet.

naṣîb: 'set up'; descriptive word for fate.

nikâh: 'conjunction'; marriage contract.

Niṣfu Sha^cbân: 'Middle of Sha^cbân'; 15th of Sha^cbân.

No Ruz: 'New Day'; a joyous New Year's festival of Zoroastrian
  origin which is celebrated as an annual feast by Shî^cahs, Iran.

pamumutika: a diviner of sicknesses among the Tausug, Philippines.

pandai: a midwife and healer, Sulu Samals.

pangu-ngubat: medicine-man, Philippines.

pawang: practitioner employing familiar spirits in divination, Malaya.

phthonos: 'zeal'; New Testament, Greek.

pîr: 'elder'; used in Indo-Pakistan subcontinent of a popular religious leader.

qâbila: 'midwife'; popular female soothsayer, especially Morocco.

qadr: 'measuring'; fate.

qanna: 'jealous'; Old Testament, Hebrew.

qarîna: (*qarin*, male), 'the one united'; the spirit counterpart born
  into the supernatural world at the same time as the birth of the
  human baby.

qaṣîda: traditional Arabic poem, usually having a rigid, tripartite
  structure.

qibla: 'anything opposite'; direction of Mecca towards which all
  Muslims turn in significant official, and popular, religious rites.

qisma: 'dividing'; lot, destiny, fate.

qubba: a domed mausoleum.

rak^ca: from *rukû^c*, 'to prostrate oneself'; a section of daily prayers.

raksi: compilation of the numerical values of peoples' names, as spelled in Arabic alphabet, used for divination, Malaya.

ramal: diviner, Afghan Turkestan.

rawḍah-khânî: festival including passion play of martyrdoms at Karbalâ', Iran.

rîḥ: 'a spirit'; in popular Islam a spirit of a bathroom or a toilet.

rusul, al-: plural of *al-rasûl*, 'apostles'; prophets sent as messengers.

saḥḥâra: 'sorceress'; popular practitioner.

Ṣakhra, al-: 'the Rock'; the sacred rock at Jerusalem on which the Mosque of ᶜUmar, or Dome of the Rock, is built.

ṣalât: ritual or liturgical prayer, performed five times a day.

ṣalât al-istikhâra: 'prayer for conciliating favour'; special prayer for divining favourable future.

ṣandûq al-nudhûr: 'box for vows'; box at saints' shrines into which are placed the written vows of supplicants.

saum: 'fasting'; religious act performed during Ramaḍân and at other times.

sayyid: 'master'; refers to a possessing *zâr* spirit.

şeyh: professional healer, Turkey.

shâfiᶜ: 'intercessor'; saints in the sense of mediators with God for ordinary Muslims.

sharîf: Muslim in direct line of descent from the Prophet.

shawwâfa: fortune-teller.

shayâṭîn: plural of *shayṭân*; devils or demons.

shaykh: 'sheikh'; Muslim religious leader, sometimes head of an order.

shaykha: female practitioner at *zâr* ceremonies.

shaykh muᶜâshir: 'a sheikh who is on intimate terms with someone'; saint honoured by shrines named after him but where his body is not buried.

Shayṭân, al-: 'the one who opposes'; the Devil.

Shîᶜah: 'followers'; followers of ᶜAlî, first cousin of Muhammad and the husband of his daughter Fâṭima.

Sijjin: related to *sijn*, 'prison'; a deep pit in which is kept the book recording the actions of the wicked.

subḥa: prayer beads.

suḥûr: 'sorcery'.

sunna: 'a path, manner of life'; the custom, especially of Muḥammad, transmitted via the *ḥadîth* literature.

sura: from *sura*, 'a row or series'; chapter of the Qur'ân.

sutra: 'that by which something is concealed'; an article placed in front of a person who is engaged in prayer towards Mecca.

taᶜâwîdh: amulet, Afghanistan.

tabib: medicine man, Yakan in Philippines.

tafsîr: 'explaining'; term used for commentary, especially on the Qur'ân.

ṭa'ir: 'a bird'; used in Qur'ân to refer to fate.

Tâj al-Mulûk: 'The Crown of the Kings'; a book of magic revered as a *kutub* by Malay Muslims.

talajabîn: diviner, Afghan Turkestan.

ṭalla: diviner of jinn, Morocco.

tamîma: from 'to be complete'; kind of amulet.

tampot: shrine, Yakan and Tausug of the Philippines.

ṭarîqa: 'a path'; Sufi term for the religious life. Often describes the division of mystics into different lodges.

tashahhud, al-: 'the testimony'; a declaration of the Muslim faith, the first of the five pillars of Islam.

tashkîr: magic, supposedly of spiritual variety.

taṣlîya: descriptive word for *ṣallâ Allâh ᶜalayhi wa sallam* giving sense of 'God bless him and grant him peace'; used when reference is made to a prophet.

tasmîya: 'giving a name'; naming ceremony.

tawrât: 'Torah': the revelations made by Yahweh to and through Moses.

taᶜzîya: 'a consolation'; a model of the tomb of al-Ḥusayn at Karbalâ', carried in procession at the festival of *Muḥarram* by *Shîᶜah* Muslims.

tikkhâna: house of curing, after the death of a saint living at that site, Pakistan.

turba: mausoleum.

ᶜûdha: from 'to protect'; protective amulet.

Umm: 'mother'; 'mother of so-and-so'.

waḍḥ: from 'to make distinct'; protective amulet.

walî: plural *awliyâ'*, 'a near one'; saint or holy man.

waswasa: 'devilish insinuation, temptation'; a person *muwaswas* is 'obsessed with delusions'. It is a state precipitated by a death in the family or some other shock.

yâ sâtir: from *satara*, 'to cover'; the expression used when a visitor is requesting his host's permission to use a toilet.

yaşmak günü: 'day of the veil'; female rite of passage in Turkey.

yawm al-âkhira: 'the Last Day'; the Day of Judgement.

yawm al-dîn: 'Day of Judgement'; same as *yawm al-âkhira.*

yawm al-jumᶜa: 'day of assembly'; Friday.

Yahweh: 'the Lord'; the covenant name of God, Old Testament, Hebrew.

zakât: 'purification'; alms-giving, one of the five pillars.

Zamzam: the sacred well within the precincts of the mosque at Mecca.

zâr: possessing spirit, not normally exorcised.

zêlos: 'zeal'; New Testament, Greek.

ziyâra: 'visitation'; visit to tomb of Muhammad or grave of any saint.

Some significant names mentioned in the text

al-Ashᶜarî: Abû'l-Ḥasan ᶜAlî Ibn Ismâᶜîl al-Ashᶜarî was born AD 873. He was the founder of a sect with a strong view of the sovereignty of God. Essentially, he insisted on the otherness of God, and the requirement of absolute submission by man to God. His viewpoint provides inspiration for some of the reactionary, fundamentalist movements of today. Interestingly, in a historical sense, al-Ashᶜarî's view helped to popularise the concept of *qadr* (*taqdîr*), or fate.

al-Bûnî: Imâm Aḥmad bin ᶜAlî al-Bûnî died AD 1225. Author of the magic handbook *Shams al-Maᶜârif al-Kubrâ*, The Sun of the Greater Knowledge.

al-Bûṣîrî: Imâm Sharf al-Din Abî Abd Allah Muḥammad al-Bûṣîrî wrote *al-Burda*, The Mantle, a poem in honour of the Prophet.

al-Ghazâlî: Abû Ḥamîd Muḥammad Ibn Muḥammad Ibn Aḥmad al-Ghazâlî was a Sunnî theologian, often called 'the Proof of Islam'. He lived AD 1058–1111 and was the main catalyst in a synthesis of orthodox theology and mystic teachings. His major book was entitled *The Revivification of the Religious Sciences*.

Ibn Ḥanbal: Abû ᶜAbdi'llâh Aḥmad Ibn Ḥanbal (born AD 780) founded the fourth school of Islamic law. The modern Wahhâbîs base some of their teaching upon his views.

Ibn Isḥâq: Muḥammad Ibn Isḥâq was a Muslim historian who died about AD 768. He left a classic biography of the Prophet which was published by his disciple Ibn Hishâm.

Ibn Taimîya: Taqî al-Dîn Ibn Taimîya (AD 1263–1328) emerged as spokesman for the traditionalists (*Ahl al-Ḥadîth*) with a programme of renewed emphasis on the *sharîᶜa* (Islamic law) and a vindication of religious values. He spoke out strongly against the many forms of popular practices prevalent among his peers. Ibn Taimîya's thoughts influenced the late eighteenth-century Wahhâbî movement.

Ikhwân: Ikhwân al-Muslimûn, or the Muslim Brotherhood (mainly in Egypt) was founded by Ḥasan al-Banna' (died AD 1949), a watchmaker from Ismailia. It is a movement of conservative action calling for a purer expression of Islam, grounded in the simple virtues of the first believers.

al-Jazûlî: Imâm Sîdî Muḥammad al-Jazûlî. A Berber Muslim of the fifteenth century famed especially for his collection of formulas for praise of the Prophet. This is known as *Dalâ'il al-Khayrât*, or Signs of Blessing.

al-Mirghanni: Muḥammad ᶜUthmân al-Mirghanni (AD 1763–1853) founded the Sufi *ṭarîqa al-Mirghannîyya*. He also wrote a famous *qaṣîda* as the result of a dream. He called it *Mawlid al-Nabî*.

Mûsâ Ibn ᶜUqba: A contemporary of Ibn Isḥâq. Composed miraculous picture of the Prophet.

Sufism: Mystic tradition in Islamic faith. Jalâl al-Dîn Rûmî (died AD 1273) was one of the greatest Sufi poets in Persia.

Ummayad: Ummayad caliphate AD 661–750 with capital at Damascus.

Wahhâb: Muḥammad Ibn ᶜAbdu'l-Wahhâb (AD 1703–1792) was a native of Najd in Arabia, and founded the unitarian, conservative movement named after him. The Wahhâbî position (minus military and political power) has been reproduced in the Muslim Brotherhood in Egypt, and in the Jamaᶜat-i-Islami or Islamic Society in Pakistan.

5

NOTES

¹ Written up in Bill A Musk, *Popular Islam: An Investigation into the Phenomenology and Ethnotheological Bases of Popular Islamic Belief and Practice* (UNISA: Pretoria, 1984).

² I am especially indebted to Dr Paul G Hiebert whose seminars on the phenomenology of animism provided the seminal thoughts issuing in Chapters Eleven and Twelve of this book.

³ A common form of standardised transliteration is used. Some of the Arabic words in the text are not fully transliterated for ease of reading (eg final '*h*'s and some diphthongs).

⁴ Anecdote entitled 'Out with the Light' from *The World of the Sufi. An Anthology of Writings about Sufis and their Work* (The Octagon Press: Tonbridge 1979), pp 78f.

⁵ Arthur Jeffery (ed), *A Reader on Islam: Passages from Standard Arabic Writings Illustrative of the Beliefs and Practices of Muslims* (Mouton and Co: 'S-Gravenhage, 1962), pp 610f.

⁶ Adapted from J M Gaudeul 'From One Year to Another: Muslim Festivals', *Encounter* no 35 (1977): p 14. Used with thanks.

⁷ Muhammad ibn ᶜAbd Allâh, *Mishcàt-ul-Maśábih. A Collection of the Most Authentic Traditions Regarding the Actions and Sayings of the Muhammed*, trans A N Matthews, Vol 1 Books 1–11 (Hindoostanee Press: Calcutta 1809), Book 4, chapter 49, section 2:321.

[8] Süleyman Chelebi, *The Mevlidi Sherif*, trans F Lyman Mac-Callum (John Murray: London, 1943), p 22.

[9] Muhammad *op cit*, Book 5, chapter 3, section 1:360.

[10] Hani Fakhouri, *Kafr El-Elow: An Egyptian Village in Transition* (Holt, Rinehart and Winston: New York, 1972), p 93.

[11] Al-Ghazâlî's argument can be found in Al-Ghazzali, *The Alchemy of Happiness*, trans Claud Field (The Octagon Press: London, 1980), pp 64f.

[12] *The Quran. Arabic text with a new translation by Muhammad Zafrulla Khan* (Curzon Press Ltd: London, 1971), pp 438f.

[13] Tawfik Canaan, 'The Decipherment of Arabic Talismans', *Berytus*, vol 4 (1937): p 101.

[14] Imâm Ahmad bin ᶜAlî al-Bûnî, *Shams al-Maᶜârif al-Kubrâ* (Maktab al-Thaqâfîya: Beirut), p 41.

[15] Shems Friedlander (ed), *The Ninety-Nine Names of Allah* (Islamic Publications Bureau: Lagos, 1978), p 11.

[16] Schyler Cammann, 'Islamic and Indian Magic Squares', *History of Religion*, vol 8, no 3 (1968): p 200. Used with permission of the University of Chicago Press.

[17] Photos reproduced as Figures 18 and 19 kindly supplied by Middle East Media.

[18] Ezzedine Guelloz, *Mecca: The Muslim Pilgrimage* (Paddington Press Ltd: London, 1977), p 39. Used with thanks.

[19] Imâm Sîdî Muḥammad al-Jazûlî, *Dalâ'il al-Khayrât* (Dar al-Qur'ân: Cairo), p 32.

[20] Muḥammad *op cit*, Book 1, chapter 6, section 3:52.

[21] Summarised from Muḥammad bin Ismâᶜil bin al-Mughîrah al-Bukhârî, *Ṣaḥîḥ*, trans Muḥammad Muhsin Khan (Kazi Publications: Chicago, 1976–1979), vols 1–9.

[22] 'Collect for Pentecost 12', *The Alternative Service Book 1980* (SPCK: London, 1980), p 693. Used with thanks.

INDEX